William and Nancie: A Celebration of Marriage

Front cover: Golden Wedding photo of Nancie and William, taken by the pond in the garden of 'Windrush', Strensall York, on June 14th, 1968. *(Reproduced by kind permission of the Yorkshire Evening Press)*

Frontispiece: the house where Nancie was born

Back Cover: Nancie, as bridesmaid, aged about sixteen

Avon Mill House

AVON MILL HOUSE, EVESHAM: *home of* NANCIE *(1890-99)*

WILLIAM and NANCIE:
A Celebration of Marriage

The Story of
William Wallace (1891-1976) and Nancie Hancox (1890-1978),
their families, ancestors and descendants, and the times
in which they lived

by their daughter

Hilary Forrester (née Wallace)

MA St. Andrews
MA Cantab

Hilary M. Forrester

William Sessions Limited
The Ebor Press
York, England

© Hilary M. Forrester 1990

ISBN 1 85072 076 2

Text produced by CLAN SYSTEMS LTD; and typed by Susan Gebbie & Kathrin Humphry; printed and bound by William Sessions Ltd., The Ebor Press, York, England.

DEDICATION

This book is dedicated to the memory of my mother, Nancie, with gratitude for her unwavering support throughout our lives, fulfilling her role with commonsense and loving kindness. She dealt with any difficulties with dignity and humour; and showed us the way. I remember her with pride and much affection.

'William & Nancie' is my tribute to her

NANCIE among her roses (1963)

My first thanks are to my husband, who has helped so much on the home front that I have been able to concentrate on the research and writing necessary for this book. My special thanks go to all those cousins and friends who have welcomed me to their homes, driven me to many places which feature in the family history, and been generous with their encouragement and help in my quest. Re-discovering them has doubled the joy I have had in piecing together my mother's story. I am grateful to my elder daughter who rescued the "Archives", without which the book could not have been undertaken; to my son and his wife for again giving me hospitality in London; to my brother and his wife for providing special extra photographs; and very particularly to the (Wallace) cousin who read the completed text and made most useful suggestions, and to my son who did likewise.

CONTENTS

	Page
Illustrations	vii
Abbreviations	viii
Foreword	ix
Introduction	x
My Mother's Story	xii

Part 1 Nancie (to 1918) — 1

1	Hans the Cook	3
2	Birthplace of the Bard	19
3	The Quaker Connection	35
4	April 7th, 1897: the Birthday Treat	48
5	The Miller and His Daughter	53
6	The Little Blue Letter	70

Part 2 William (1891-1918) — 80

| 7 | William Wallace: Background and Youth (to 1911) | 81 |
| 8 | The Law: London Beckons (1911-1918) | 89 |

Part 3 William and Nancie (1918 onwards) — 96

9	William and Nancie Together (1917-1920)	97
10	William at Work (1919-1931)	103
11	Nancie at Home (1920-1935)	107
12	The Prince of Wales and Mr. Lloyd George (1917-1931)	121
13	Changes in the 1930's (1929-1940)	127
14	William and Nancie in Wales (1940-1944) and Home Again (1944-1949)	135
15	Spreading their Wings (1949-1963)	142
16	Folding their Wings (1963-)	154

Index of Persons	158
Acknowledgements	159
Bibliography and W.W.'s Publications	160

ILLUSTRATIONS

	Page
Nancie among her roses	v
Extract from 'Meditation on Marriage'	xi
Windrush: the house built by William & Nancie	xiii
1889 Nancie's family at Avon Mill House, Evesham	xiv
Nancie aged 6, 18, 21 and 26	1
John Hancox's Will (1824)	8
Hancox Family Tree	10
Lists of Hancox children; Whatcote Church; Village Stocks in Loxley Church; Hancox Signature	12
George & William Hancox (farmers)	16
Indenture between James Hancox and apprentice	21
Mrs Harriett Hancox	23
Jeremiah & Louisa Bebb; Cook's Alley; 17 College St.	27
Family Tree of Mrs J Hancox & Louisa Bebb: Stratford-on-Avon Grammar School; (Edmund) Owen Hancox	29
Manor Farm, Great Washbourne	32
James Hancox; Great Alne Mill	33
Letter sent to Elizabeth Ann Hawkes (1822)	34
Bretforton; Family Tree of Elizabeth Ann Hawkes	36
Inclosure Map of Buckland, Glos. (1779)	38
Family Tree of Thomas Hawkes; Evesham Friends' Meeting House; The Terrace, Ackworth School	41
Henry & Elizabeth Ann Fowler	46
Ackworth School (1840's)	47
Pictures from the Evesham Journal, 1897	48
Nancie in the garden	52
Evesham: The Avon Mills (1989); Owen's sketch of the Mills	54
Anne Fowler, aged 12, 21, and later	56
Bill-heads; Nancie and Dorothy in 1899	58
Nancie at Emwell House School; the Mill and the Millhouse Garden	60
Nancie aged 12 and 15; Anne & Owen Hancox	62
Owen with his umbrella; Ted; Rifle-practice	65
p.c. from Winnipeg; Avery as P.O.W.; Avery with mother; Hospital Lab	67
Top Farm, Weston Subedge; a family gathering there	69
Nancie's School photos, Bristol	71
St. George School, Bristol; Nancie's Attendance Sheet	72
Ridgeway Park House, Bristol; Boating & Swimming	74
Nancie & Uncle Joe; Jack Hancox at Great Alne; Nancie & Mary driving	76
Nancie: the favourite photograph; the King George Hospital	79
The Auld Hoose, 1867; William as a young man	80
Bible Class Certificate of Merit	85
William's little letter to his Father	88
William's pre-War Passport	94-5
Extract from 'Law Notes': September 1912	95
'Passing By' (song); honeymoon photos	96
Wedding-card; Ullswater (1952)	102
Pyrmont in flood	106
Pyrmont & Broad Campden: Nancie, the children & both Grannies	109
Summer Holidays (1926-9); Hilary & Jean at home; Dr. Gaynor	113
Sandsend; Party dresses; picnic outing and more holiday snaps	114
Pyrmont (1985); Sorensons; the level crossing; the dancing class	119

Windrush a-building	120
Lloyd George & family; Royal Garden Party, 1931	126
Windrush and the pond, tennis-court, etc.; pea-picking	131
Anglesey holidays: 1940 & 1958-9	134
Tan-yr-allt, N. Wales; Silver Wedding; air-raid shelter; Victory	138
Home Again: We have come through	141
Avery's & Ted's houses on Vancouver Island; the Rockefellers	143
Meeting in Victoria; the first grandchild; Princess Alexandra	145
William & Nancie in London (1958); Windrush in the Snow	148
The grandchildren; the Ruby Wedding	150
'On holiday' c.1962; Nancie and her Lilies	153

MAPS

1.	Greenwood (1822): part of Warwickshire	2
2.	Stratford-on-Avon (O.S. 1885)	31
3.	Evesham, Worcestershire (O.S. 1886)	47
4.	Henfords Marsh, Warminster (O.S. 1890)	58

ABBREVIATIONS USED

B.S.R.	(Benjamin) Seebohm Rowntree
I.C.A.	Industrial Co-partnership Association
I.G.I.	International Genealogical Index
J.B.M.	Dr John Bowes Morrell
J.J.H.	John James (Jack) Hancox (author of 'Family Notes')
J.R.V.T.	Joseph Rowntree Village Trust
J.R.M.T.	Joseph Rowntree Memorial Trust
N.E.W.	Nancie Etheldene Wallace
N.L.S.	National Library of Scotland
U.G.C.	University Grants Committee
V.A.D.	Voluntary Aid Detachment
W.W.	William Wallace

Currency: Until February, 1971, we counted our money in £'s, shillings and pence. Since the currency was re-devised, there are 100 pence to the pound, instead of 240 pennies.

d. signified the old penny

s. signified the old shilling (=12d.)

/. signified the old shilling also

FOREWORD

'A happy marriage is the crown of life: may you live long to wear it in your United Kingdom'. This was one lovely message received by the author's mother, Nancie, when she announced her engagement.

She did indeed 'live long to wear it', and so with William her husband gave to many a fine example of what marriage should mean.

I am glad to be able to write these words of introduction to the book by my sister-in-law, Hilary Forrester, about her parents, and the history of her mother's family. As we look back over the years seen through the story of one family with roots in various parts of our country, we can see the vital part played by marriage. These were men and women whom 'God had brought together', and their example meant much to their children.

There have always been threats to marriage relationships and the stability of family life. But perhaps these are more insidious and destructive today than they have been for many years. We may disagree about the best way to support and strengthen family life. But all of us should recognise its vital importance for human well-being.

This piece of family history will be an encouragement to all who read it. It will also open their eyes to how Hilary Forrester's ancestors faced up to the many changes shaping British society in their time.

August, 1990

Stanley Booth-Clibborn (Rt Revd)

Bishop of Manchester

Introduction

William Wallace (1891 - 1976), grandson of the William and Christina Wallace featured in my first book, "William & Christina: One Woman's Search for her Ancestors", was born to James Wallace, a shipping lawyer, and his wife, Alice, in Sunderland, at that time a thriving ship-building town. He was the eldest of five children.

Nancie Hancox (1890 - 1978) was born in Evesham, Worcestershire, close beside the River Avon, as her father owned the Avon Mills and had built for his family, many years before, Avon Mill House. She was the youngest of the eleven children born to Edmund Owen Hancox; by his second wife, Anne Fowler.

In this book, I present the lives of these two people, my parents, showing their different backgrounds and ways of life before their marriage in 1918; and their joint life afterwards. I shall detail the lives of Nancie's forebears particularly, as these have so far not been recorded. Starting with the handicap of their fathers dying before they had been trained and launched in life, they each found useful work to do; soon after their marriage William went to work in a Quaker firm and they lived in its garden village. Three children were born to them who each had the privilege of a Quaker education to the age of eighteen, followed by University.

Sometimes I have repeated details of the people in the story, and their relationships. This is deliberate, as most of it is unfamiliar to most of the readers. My aim has been to take all the hard-won strands of information and plait them together as seamlessly as possible to make an interesting story. I have had, necessarily, to be selective; but I have tried to show the interweaving of personal fulfilment at work and at home within the marriage.

In time, William and Nancie built for themselves and their family a spacious house in another nearby Yorkshire village, where they lived for most of the next forty years and more, until they died. War again cast its shadow, and the precious newly-built house had to be abandoned to others, for four years; the newly-planned garden was regretfully left behind when 'War Service' took them to Wales.

Before my sister died in March, 1989, she asked me if there was anything in her keeping which I would like. I asked for the family "archives" which she had offered to store when our parents' house was sold. These had been untouched not only since my mother's death, but most of them since her girlhood. I found, to my delight, hundreds of photos: many of Nancie's family back at least to 1861 (when her mother was twelve years old); and several bundles of letters. There was also a book of 'Family Notes', written in the late 1940's by her much older half-brother, Jack Hancox. These have enabled me to unravel threads that I never knew existed; by writing to and visiting, Record Offices, schools, libraries, houses, cemeteries, and places and people connected with her, I have discovered the story of my mother's early life. She came of a settled people: settled since the Saxon invasions: constant in family life, caring in relationships, close in family ties. They were creative craftsmen, skilled with their hands. They took part fully in the life of their community: James Hancox in mid-nineteenth century Stratford-on-Avon; Edmund Owen Hancox in late nineteenth-century Evesham; and the Fowler family in Evesham for several generations.

In those days, when the pattern of life was so very different, and survival often vitally attached to the family unit, there was less promotion of self and insistence on independence; more of the inherited pattern of staying together. The history of their forebears is of an unbroken chain of unbroken marriages, dependent not only on the economic necessity of remaining together, but perhaps also on a more determined effort to make the marriage work, and an abiding affection.

I found the quest exciting as I followed my mother, and her family before her, for several generations, and unravelled the tapestry of their lives: especially in the delightful places to which it took me, and the renewing and strengthening of friendships with cousins on my mother's side. In particular, it was most satisfying to discover so much more of her history, and to slot into context the remembered stories, comments and people of whom she spoke down the years.

William and Nancie both suffered from ill-health at times, and William's work combined with all he did beyond it for various causes - never content with less than the best he could do - was enough for two full-time lives. W.W. chose to work ceaselessly, but he managed to do this without ever forgetting the importance of his family life. So many, nowadays, seem to get so caught up in the demands of their careers and the social side involved, and often the need to travel far afield, that it erodes their home-based lives. I think that, provided the balance is kept between commitment to work and the claims of the family, a full and satisfying career can sustain and enrich a marriage. It did so in their case. He managed to do all he did because of the marvellous support he had from Nancie, whom he loved above all else. Their story might be seen as the story of many born at the end of last century who lived through more than three-quarters of this. And it is. Their changing conditions reflect the changes which were nationwide, of increased affluence, betterment of housing and employment, improvement in health, and enrichment of life: all these things William worked to help bring about for as many as possible.

But this is more than the story of one couple. My theme is the institution of Marriage, and how standards of behaviour are handed down so that they permeate the lives of future generations. Each successful lasting relationship strengthens the lives of those who are to follow. The best kind of marriage has value for the individual within each circle of love and security, as well as for Society as a whole. As an illustration of this theme, I offer the story of my parents in a marriage of true and lasting affection, which triumphed where others have failed. For almost sixty years they loved each other and gave love and encouragement to all with whom they came in contact. Looked at in the light of the current predicament of scattered and divided families; of children denied the care and support of two parents for whatever reason; and of the havoc wrought in adult relationships by stress, separation and temptation; I see the long life together of William and Nancie as a cause for Celebration.

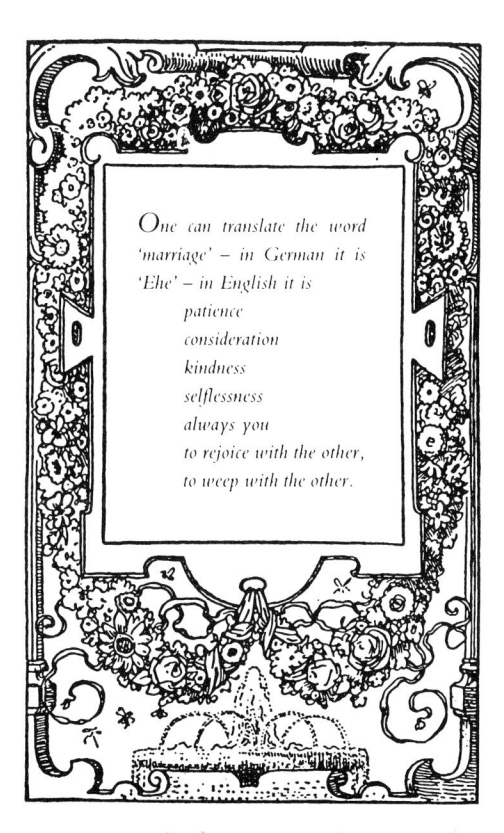

> One can translate the word
> 'marriage' – in German it is
> 'Ehe' – in English it is
> patience
> consideration
> kindness
> selflessness
> always you
> to rejoice with the other,
> to weep with the other.

Meditation on Marriage (extract) from a free translation by Elsa Noak
(of New Earswick) from the original by Hermann Oeser (published 1578 in
Strasburg, Alsace)

My Mother's Story

The specific bequests from my mother to me, when she died on March 8th, 1978, included a picture and two pairs of gloves. The picture is a water-colour painting of Avon Mill House, Evesham, (see Frontispiece) where my mother was born in 1890. Her father had built the house for his first wife and family, after he came to the Mill in 1870. They had created a beautiful garden beside the River Avon, and this also features in the picture, as does the pool with its fountain. We know that it was painted by one of the two gifted daughters of my grandfather's sister, but there is no record of which it was: Minnie or Lillian Bebb? Nor is there a date; but from the height and hugeness of the trees the painting must have been done towards the end of the 1890's.

Today, the garden has gone; there is a large concrete yard where delivery lorries turn. The mills are now used by the firm of Stocks Lovell; the house contains their offices; and, sweeping along behind the house, almost like the coaches of a train moving towards the mill, is a series of buildings, new and converted, to serve the purposes of the business. In the house, only the old staircase with its curving banister and the ghost of the upstairs drawing-room now used as the boardroom remain the same; but outside the Reception area built on instead of the front porch, there is a newly-created ornamental pool with goldfish; and a huge and beautiful magnolia. (See photos p.54).

The present owners - there have been several in the years since my grandfather sold the mill - are caring for the property well, and when we visited we received a most courteous welcome and a conducted tour of the premises.

And the pair of gloves? They are elbow-length, made of grey doeskin with tiny hand stitching and they belonged to my mother's mother's mother: Elizabeth Ann Hawkes. I did not understand at the time why my mother left the gloves to me. Now I think, from that and similar threads which bind us, she recognised my interest in my forebears long before I was aware of it myself. She must have seen that I was a 'continuity' person to whom the past, with its people and places and even material objects, was very important. The world is full of an infinite number of dichotomies; those in it can be divided in innumerable different ways. One dichotomy is between the people who take a 'narrative' view of life, aware that all that has happened to them throughout their lives adds up to what they are at any given moment; and in this narrative they include those who have gone before. The non-narrative thinkers choose to ignore or discard the past, and prefer to use contemporary guide-lines.

My mother's family, especially on the Fowler side, were keepers: conserving, for instance, the samplers worked by the young girls in each generation; having them framed (even to my own) and hung on the wall. They handed down items of family furniture, some beautifully crafted in the family workshops, as both sides included cabinet-makers. Some of the families built rather good, roomy family houses, still being fully used although no longer by private families as they are rather large for modern requirements.

At the same time as my grandfather, Edmund Owen Hancox, was building Avon Mill House, his father, James, was building 'The Limes' at Stratford-on-Avon, similar in size and form. This house, now extended and altered, is the Short Stay Home and Day Care Centre for the Elderly, under the Warwickshire County Council. 'The Limes' now has a staff of 5 officers, 20 care workers, 3 cooks, and extra support from Community Psychiatrist, Psychologist, Physiotherapist and Occupational Therapist, as well as other services. Little did James Hancox think that one day his newly-built house would have so many 'guests'.

In their turn, my parents built a house for their family on the edge of a village, six miles north of York. They lived in their house in Strensall (Old English: Streon's Hall), situated in 'Lord's Moor Lane', a name from feudal times, for over forty years. They created a garden out of what had been a field of sandy soil growing carrots or sugar-beet. The garden had a formal pool on the west side of the house below the sitting-room window; an informal one, with bog garden and a scree for alpine plants on the east side; and an extensive lawn which included a grass tennis-court. I understand better now why my mother designed and laboured on these pools, since I have visited one of her childhood homes near Warminster. Beyond the bottom hedge and the line of poplar trees, they developed a vegetable garden (and kept hens for a time to help the war effort).

Inside, the house is light and airy. Large windows, ivory-painted walls throughout as background for pictures, ornaments and flower-arrangements, and the light oak used for doors, staircases and window-sills, give a wonderful feeling of space. Everyone who has lived or visited there has been able to enjoy the peace, the harmony and the simplicity of the life-style created by William and Nancie throughout their marriage. In particular, now that I have studied Nancie's forebears and her legacy from them of grace and continuity in living, I see her achievement as a just inheritance from the earlier generations of her family.

Fortunately, William and Nancie were able to stay there together in the house and home they had created until they died in the late 1970's.

Part I of this book, 'Nancie', tells of the people, and the places they came from, in my mother's family, for at least nine generations. This is where I began.

To see her life as a whole, I added Part II, 'William', for the benefit of those who have not yet read my first book on William's forebears, and to give details of his life from 1911-1918.

Part III, 'William and Nancie', tells of the rest of their lives together.

Windrush, home of Nancie and William, 1935-1978. Taken prior to the addition (at the bottom left-hand corner) in 1961-2. Bars on the top windows because it was a playroom. Later, William wrote his Autobiography up there. Pool hidden by the roses

Avon Mill House: the Hancox family, 1889, the year before Nancie was born

Mary	OWEN	Helen
Fred	ANNE	
	Dorothy (on knee)	
	Ted	Avery

Part I Nancie

Taken by her cousin, Arthur Fowler, in the garden at Port Street, aged six (1897)
Bridesmaid (left) at the wedding of her cousin Florrie, in Bristol, aged eighteen (1909)
A twenty-first birthday portrait (December 1911)
In V.A.D. Uniform (as first seen by William in 1917) aged twenty-six

Chapter 1. Hans the Cook

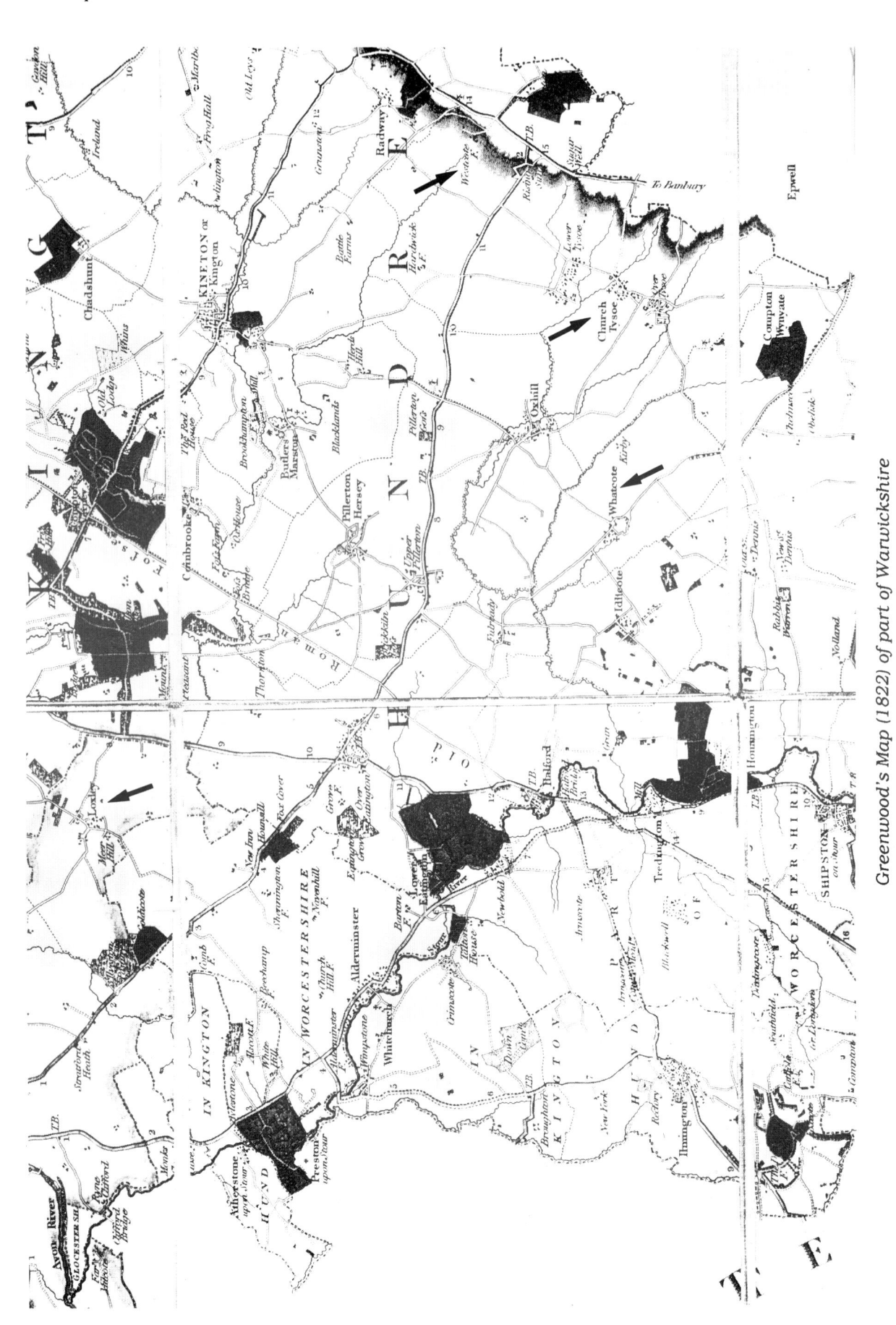

Greenwood's Map (1822) of part of Warwickshire

Chapter 1

Hans the Cook

'Hans the Cook' is the suggested origin of the surname Hancox. This is what my mother believed; and that her Hancox ancestors came from Denmark. She and others in her family had the facial bone structure and fair colouring common among Scandinavians. The spelling of the name varies: Handcoks, Hancuk, Hancoke, Hancoks, depending I suppose on the way it was pronounced as someone gave the name to the Vicar at a wedding or a christening, or to the enumerator for a Census Return. The speaker might have a heavy cold, missing teeth, or a bad gumboil which distorted the jaw, and the various individuals who wrote names down probably had their own individual ideas about spelling anyway.

Since my great-great-grandfather, **Joseph Hancox** (b. 1753), at least, our family has always spelt it HANCOX. There were hundreds of families in Warwickshire in the nineteenth century with that name in various spellings; in the village from which we come, variations of the name go back to the sixteenth century: 'Hanckes' in the earliest pages of the Parish Registers. In the main story, I have included only those whom I know to be related to us, and usually I have spelt it 'Hancox' unless there was a legal or other document with a variation.

My search began with a totally false trail. Family lore, carefully recorded, said that for five generations our Hancoxes had farmed at Steeple Barton in North Oxfordshire, not far from Banbury. Discovering in the National Library of Scotland (N.L.S.) that the parish church Registers for Steeple Barton were available at the Oxfordshire County Record Office, I went to Oxford post-haste. The Registers were there, but the Hancoxes were not: absolutely no trace at all. After that, information came piecemeal, slowly and often in the wrong order; but gradually, helped by Census Returns and the International Genealogical Index (I.G.I.), and visits to other Record Offices, and information from other cousins, I found that Joseph had farmed at **Whatcote**, a village in Warwickshire fifteen miles over the hill and across the county boundary from Steeple Barton. Much later, I confirmed that Joseph and at least five earlier generations of farming Hancoxes, had lived at another nearby village, **Tysoe**.

Now, after a year of delving, a story is still emerging which begins in the village of Tysoe, where Joseph Hancox and his fourteen siblings were born, and takes us on a tour of Warwickshire villages, clustered together in a small area to the east and south-east of Stratford-on-Avon. You will have to come with me to Tysoe, to learn about its past and to understand its traditions. Two miles from Tysoe itself are Westcote Manor, whose historical records date from 1242, and whose present building is a dream of old-world charm in its secluded hollow, and Westcote Farm, dating from Saxon times.

Close by Steeple Barton, in Oxfordshire, is the village of Westcote Barton. I guessed that someone confused Westcote near Tysoe with Westcote near Steeple Barton. Also, one family, the Seagraves, provided Rectors for the churches of Westcote Barton and Whatcote, and a vicar and a curate for Tysoe: all in the eighteenth-century. This could have suggested a link where none existed. One of the Seagraves from Westcote Barton was buried at Whatcote because his father was Rector there at the time. (One of my sources has pointed out that the link with Steeple Barton was that the grandfather of Joseph's wife, Elizabeth, married a girl, Elizabeth Freebury, who originated from there!) The early Parish Registers provide a lot of information, but sometimes they only tantalise because they suggest links which you may not be able to prove.

In wishing to find out more about the village of Tysoe, I was exceptionally lucky, as Tysoe - because of a particular baby born there in 1859 - is probably better documented than any of the other local villages which are not the home of a noble, land-owning family.

Elizabeth Ashby, whose immediate forebears had been prosperous farming folk and respected members of the Quaker Meeting at Sibford Ferris for about one hundred and fifty years, suffered from the misfortunes of her family when the foreclosure of a farm

Chapter 1. Hans the Cook

mortgage left them all but destitute. She went into service at Idlicote House, five miles from her home. Eighteen months later, she returned to her father in the village of Tysoe, where her baby, Joseph, was born. The baby's father was a man of very high rank, a member of a great land-owning family. Joseph Ashby grew up thoughtful and aware. Even though he left school at ten, he carved out for himself an informed and dedicated life, superior to that of the labouring folk who were his neighbours. He lived all his life except for the last few years in Tysoe, brought up on the stories, the cadences and the mysteries of the Bible. His mother used the huge family Bible for her daily reading especially during the days of her lying-in. In spite of her Quaker heritage she had Joseph baptised at church. Joseph had what the Quakers call a 'concern' to foster the community spirit and to improve the lot of his fellow villagers. He earned money first as a child by scaring crows; and after he left school by helping on the farms. Later, he carted stone from a huge quarry. All through his adult life he wrote articles, spoke frequently, chaired meetings, and, having joined the Methodist Church, was untiring as a lay preacher.

One of Joseph's daughters wrote a full and fascinating account of his life, 'Joseph Ashby of Tysoe'. One of his sons became a Professor and later the Director of the Agricultural Economics Research Institute at Oxford. Among the writings of Professor A.W. Ashby is the work entitled, 'One Hundred Years of the Poor Law Administration in a Warwickshire Village'. The village, of course, is Tysoe (1727-1827). These books have illuminated for me the long and interesting history of Tysoe village.

TYSOE

Tysoe, the only place so named in the British Isles, anyway, is said to have been called after the heathen God, TIW. It is known to have flourished under the Saxons because parts of the church date from then. Probably the name 'Hancox' really did have Saxon origins. In the early Saxon times, Tysoe grew corn in great abundance and was famous for it. In 1086 (Domesday Survey), when the village was called Tihesoche, it was recorded as containing: 23 hides (units of land of variable size in Old English law, each enough to support a household); land for 32 ploughs; 16 acres of meadow; and in 'Warwic' 3 houses paying 18 pence rent. It was then worth thirty pounds and had been held freely by Waga before the Normans came. The overall landlords from Norman times were the barons of Stafford (originally Robert de Stadford), but many of its plots were held by religious bodies. One of the three hamlets which together make up Tysoe was known as Temple or Templar (now Lower) Tysoe, because the knights Templar held land there. The other hamlets were Church (Middle) Tysoe, and Over (Upper) Tysoe.

This elongated parish, at least a mile from North to South, lies along the valley immediately below Edgehill: famous for the Battle in 1642, at the start of the Cromwellian Wars. Tysoe's eastern boundary is the road running along the ridge of Edge Hill, 700 feet high. The present County boundary with Oxfordshire follows the same course along the top of these hills. Tysoe's windmill has its own hill, south of the village towards Compton Wynyates. The three hamlets of Tysoe originated beside the three brooks which run down from the hills, curving in an amphitheatre above each water-course, which provide a water-supply, as well as high-quality, loamy soil. (see Greenwood's Map p.2). From the situation of these hamlets, Professor Ashby reckons they were made in time of peace - probably early Saxon. There are still traces of the village green which runs in narrow strips beside the main street. Once it sported the village stocks, for all to see who sat in them; it was also the place where the villagers gathered to conduct community business, or hear a visiting speaker. Up to the time of the Black Death, royal licences were obtained for fairs and markets in most of the bigger villages in the County as in the towns, and these took place in Tysoe - on and around the village green. Tysoe grew in size and development until 1870, when the population peaked at over a thousand. Until 1939, the villages on the northern slopes of the Cotswolds and Edge Hills had altered little since the Middle Ages. Above them was the steep escarpment from which Iron Age men looked out over the plain; below them lay the fertile lands of South Warwickshire and the Vale of the Red Horse.

Chapter 1. Hans the Cook

The Vale of the Red Horse took its name from the figure of a horse originally cut out in the soil of the locality, and conspicuous on the hillside. The huge 300 ft horse has been variously attributed to Hengist, a Saxon chief, whose armorial sign was the martial horse; or as a memorial to Richard Neville, Earl of Warwick, who slew his horse before the Battle of Towton (on Palm Sunday 1461) in order to "share the fate of the meanest soldier" by fighting on foot. Red Horse Farm (still nearby) was then leased to someone who, as payment, held an annual scouring on Palm Sunday to keep the figure of the horse prominent in the red earth. Locals assisting him received cakes and ale. The Red Horse has now vanished, probably at the time of the Inclosures (1798). Inclosure occurred when land-owners applied for an Act of Parliament to give them permission to fence in their land, thus reducing greatly the common land available to the villagers for grazing, fuel-gathering and growing small crops for their own use.

References to members of the Hancox family, though I cannot prove their close relationship, occur down the years. My mother's sister left a note of some of these:

1608 Thomas Hancox, master smith, aged 50-60 Cavalryman
       (In a list of men suitable to bear arms)

August 30th 1629 Edmond Hancox signed in a list of parishioners

1635 Edmond Hancox in a list of leaseholders

1685 John Hancox: will proved

1688 Richard Hancox: will proved

July 11th 1718 lease to Stephen Hancox chapman

and September 25th 1718 lease to Stephen Hancox grazier

In 1332, John Hanecok of Honynham was liable for tax for 1s.6d.,p.a. Another John Hanecok of Uptone liable for tax for 3.0d. There were only five other Hanecok and Hanecoks men listed in the Lay Subsidy Roll for Warwickshire of 6 Edward III, in that year, and no other spellings. In the Rolls of Warwickshire and Coventry Sessions of the Peace, 1377-97, I found that Iohannes Hancokes, Smyth of Luttel Alne (Little Alne: close to Great Alne, which features later) was said to have assaulted Thomas Mulward and taken fish from him, on October 27th, 1382. The following April, John Hancokes was tried at Warwick "for felony, the theft of fish and eels valued at 10/-", but he was acquitted. There were no Hancoxes mentioned yet at Tysoe in 1332, although **Westcote Manor** is named.

Lockersleye (Loxley, where Joseph Hancox lived later on) had twenty-two tax payers who included William Le Forester, Richard le Smyth, William le Gardiner, Robert atte Weller, etc. Whatcote had thirteen tax payers including The Lady of Whatcote, Robert the Chaplain and Thomas de Barton. By the Hearth Tax Returns of the later seventeenth-century, a number of Hancox, Hancocks and Hanwcke names occur.

The earliest 'Hanckes' recorded in Tysoe is the baptism of "Robart, son George, December 6, 1579". There is also a Marriage, in 1600, of Thomas Hanckes (with Elizabeth Somerton); and Burials from 1598 to 1691, using the same spelling. In 1693, we find "Thomas Handcocke, son Richard and Alice"; and from then on the more recent spellings are used.

The Hearth-tax lists (1665), show many houses in Tysoe with more than the one essential hearth which was excused tax; some even had five or six extra hearths. These were spacious homes, well-appointed for the times. Tysoe was then a pleasant and prosperous place to live and the sense of Community was strong. The Act of 1601, entitled 'An Act for Relief of the Poor', actually ordered the parish officials to raise enough money to enable those without the means of maintaining themselves to be employed and self-supporting. M.K. Ashby writes of the "comeliest houses, with mullioned and hooded windows and handsome doorways". Among the more recently built in Tysoe, there remain one or two houses which echo the old style. During the first half of the eighteenth-century, the small-holders began to lose out; by 1801, houses stood empty, while two or more families shared a single household, to save money. Inclosure had come in 1798, after the Act of Parliment in 1796, considerably later than in many places

Chapter 1. Hans the Cook

because so much of the land in Tysoe was *occupied by its owners*. Elsewhere, with absentee landlords, Inclosure was applied for and granted much earlier. In 1752, one year before our Joseph Hancox was born, only one "workless man" out of the large village applied to the Overseers for help. By 1774, five men were out of work throughout the winter. The law then said that able-bodied men must be given work, not money or free goods. Various schemes were introduced to try to implement this, but Joseph Ashby's daughter thought the villagers could not carry out satisfactorily the instructions from far away, though they might have contrived something themselves.

At that time (1775), lists of freeholders which include Thomas Hancox our Joseph's father paying 6s.5d. Land Tax, show that of 147 "townships", as villages were called, within the district only two had more freeholders than Tysoe, where thirty-six had voted in the Parliamentary Elections. These were local people used to looking after their community. Joseph Hancox would be brought up in an atmosphere of mutual help. But the problems were getting out of hand and the Inclosure exacerbated the position. The planting of the hedges, and the changes that were introduced, took away the freedom and pride of the local people in their own place. Fences shut them out; local landmarks were obliterated; and favourite spots could be reached only after a long detour. Furze which had grown on open hillsides, freely gathered for fuel, was eradicated. Common land available for grazing was eliminated. The change from intensive farming, often on a family basis, to large farms concentrating on pasture, meant less work to be had. For those who lived near centres of industry it was relatively easy to move off the land, but Tysoe's corner of Warwickshire was too remote. There was no highway tax until after the Inclosure Award, as there was no highway. For a time, Tysoe had remained a large, prosperous, old-world agricultural village.

When the difficult times came, the disadvantages of the "on the round" system of work which involved continuous rotation of casual labour fell most heavily on the women. They did better at home, being paid to mind a sick relative; or they could become pregnant in which case the authorities either compelled some one to marry the mother-to-be; or they paid her Poor Relief. It was the economic and social conditions, far beyond the control of the country folk, which led to greater illegitimacy. It became commonplace to be pregnant on marriage; and profitable to bring up your bastard on Poor Relief. Curiously, the only recognised "sin", according to Professor Ashby, was to produce a *pauper* bastard, chargeable to the parish! Efforts were always made to find the father, who was made to agree to provide for the child, or he was imprisoned. (Money was sent to Elizabeth Ashby from the birth of Joseph until he was earning).

In 1779 (a date which recurs in this story), Tysoe was visited by the press-gang. One repeated seducer was 'sent for a soldier', to save the parish the cost of his bastards. Parishes were naturally reluctant to pay more in poor relief than they could avoid. The Settlement Act of 1662 had decreed that all should get relief only from their own parish; and any other parish to which they had moved could refuse it. Vagabonds were branded with a 'V' on the shoulder; those receiving parish pay in 1662 were made to wear a Roman 'P' signifying pauper on a badge on their sleeves. Tysoe still has an Overseers' record of expenditure for cloth, thread and making such badges as late as 1749.

The combined effect of the changes in the pattern of agriculture, the famine years in the 1790's, the Napoleonic Wars and the consequent violent fluctuations in corn (and other) prices, pushed the least-favoured families in the villages below subsistence level. During the years 1727-1827, the growth of pauperism was horrifying. On July 9th, 1727, five poor people were paid 10s.6d. between them. One hundred years later, £27 10s.4d. was paid to well over one hundred cases of need, and half as many again in the Winter. The total annual amounts were: 1727 - under £59; 1827 - over £1,170. (And inflation was unknown). These were normal years for their times; in 1800, an abnormal year, nearly £3,000 was needed. The poor were relieved in their own homes for as long as possible. Tysoe rented out cottages to the homeless; the dreaded Workhouses were not built near rural villages. The Parish Overseers recorded that "Thomas Hancox's little house under the hill" had been let by them "to Widow Collins and anybody the Overseers think proper at one pound, eight shillings per year" (1770). The owner of the little house, Thomas Hancox, was our Joseph's father. Back in 1752, the Overseers had paid Thomas £2

Chapter 1. Hans the Cook

6s.6d. for mending the village pound, where stray animals were rounded up. No doubt they paid him for a succession of jobs, down the years. Houses were built, gravestones were carved, walls were repaired; there was plenty of work for a stone-mason.

Tysoe, as a self-respecting community of very long standing, organised itself to help its needy parishioners, especially after the small-pox epidemic of 1741, and the recurrences of the disease later. When there was famine in the village in 1795, the Overseers built a bake house, paid a baker, and supplied bread as needed at less than cost-price. They also subsidised coal, and maintained a brewhouse. Tysoe already had a malthouse, probably since the Middle Ages. This was a village community in which they all knew one another. They cared for the weaker members, and ran their own affairs. The village had a very long history of solidarity and enterprise, and a tradition of church-going. Joseph Hancox (1753) was born into this community, of which his family had been part for generations, participating in its tradition of caring.

Before the Inclosure Acts, almost every family had a little land round or near their cottage, even if they also had another occupation, such as stonemason. Thomas Hancox (bapt. 1723), as well as the little house leased to the Overseers, owned land. Perhaps he had inherited property from his father, Joseph, as he was the eldest son. Thomas himself died at the end of 1779 and was buried on December 7th in Tysoe. He had not made a Will. He was only fifty-six, and I think must have died suddenly and without illness sufficient to make him think his time was short. His youngest child was only nine. Thomas's wife, Mary, signed a document on August 25th, 1780, in which she said that she, "Mary, Relict of Thomas Hancox, Mason, Renounced, Relinquished and Disclaimed" all rights in her late husband's estate, wishing them to be committed and granted to her eldest son, John, of Lower Tysoe, Mason. It was her "free and Voluntary Proxy of Renunciation".

On September 13th, 1780, her eldest son, John, applied for Letters of Administration and swore that the Personal Estate at the time of Thomas's death did not exceed £300. The following day, John and another John Hancox from Gloucestershire, both of them designated "Yeomen", signed a fearsome-looking document promising to pay the Bishop of Worcester £600, if they failed to carry out the administrative work stipulated, within the required period. They had to gather the information, and "cause to be exhibited" a list of the Goods, Chattels and Credits owned by Thomas at the time of his death. These two John Hancocks (as the Document spells their name) were appointed by the Bishop of Worcester's Consistory Court as Administrators of the Estate. Once they had done their work satisfactorily, John, Thomas's eldest son, would inherit the whole estate, as "Death Duties" were not introduced until 1796. The threatened punishment of a fine more than double the value of the personal estate of the deceased was presumably to avoid idle claims or misrepresentations.

My cousin, Henry Hancox, and I found Hancox graves including this Thomas, and his wife, son and daughter-in-law in the South Plot in Tysoe churchyard: Thomas died December 4th, 1779, aged fifty-six; and Mary, his wife, died October 6th, 1792, aged sixty-six. They were our great-great-great-grand-parents. Beside them lie Richard, their son (died March 3rd, 1791, aged forty), and his wife, Elizabeth (died November 16th, 1795, aged thirty-six). Also in the Burial Register are:

Edward	(85)	22.2.1815 (brother of our Joseph's father, bapt. 6.6.1729)
Mary	(76)	25.3.1820 (Edward's second wife)
Thomas	(79)	22.4.1831 (brother of our Joseph; his Will follows)
William	(65)	6.5.1829 (brother of our Joseph)

From Thomas's brother, Edward (bapt. 6 June, 1729), there descended a line of Hancoxes who became Stone Masons in Tysoe. From this branch, a Dinah Hancox married Daniel Harris (also of Tysoe); their descendants have been put in touch with me through Worcester Record Office, and have given me extra information about this side of the family. It is thought that they may be related to Elizabeth Ashby of Tysoe, mentioned earlier.

Chapter 1. Hans the Cook

This is the last Will and Testament of me John Hancox of Tysoe in the county of Warwick Master I give and bequeath to my eldest son Robert my wearing apparel and my feather bed And I give and devise all my messuages lands tenements hereditaments and real estate and also all my personal estate of what nature or kind soever not hereinbefore disposed of unto my three sons Robert John and Thomas their heirs executors and administrators equally to be divided between them share and share alike as tenants in common And I do hereby nominate constitute and appoint my said son Thomas executor of this my last will and Testament hereby revoking all former wills by me at any time heretofore made In Witness whereof I have to this my last will and testament set my hand and seal this fourth day of November in the year of our Lord one thousand eight hundred and twenty four

Signed sealed published and declared by the Testator as and for his last will and testament in the presence of us who in his presence at his request and in the presence of each other have subscribed our names as witnesses thereto

John Hancox

Chas. Tawney
Robt. B. Lydon
Thos. Pain

Will of John Hancox (1747-1831)

Chapter 1. Hans the Cook

I have also found the last Will and Testament (dated November 4th, 1824) of this same John Hancox (bapt. 2 February, 1747), Thomas's eldest son. He died in Tysoe and was buried there on February 22nd, 1831. His age is given as eighty-one, but he must have been eighty-four. His Will is so straightforward and legible, especially compared with the "Gothic" script of the 1780 documents, that I will include it here. (See opp.).

As you see, by 1824 he was a Malster by trade (Modern Spelling: maltster: one concerned with the brewing of ale, by steeping of barley or other grain in water; allowing it to sprout; and drying it in a kiln. We have seen already that Tysoe had had a Malster from the Middle Ages). John appointed his youngest son to be his Executor; and he left his property to be shared equally between his three sons. Also as a second document dated 19th May, 1831, tells us, he left personal estate worth less that £100. This may be a reflection of the deterioration in prosperity so very marked in the fifty years following 1780, which I discuss elsewhere. Or perhaps he had distributed equally his inheritance from his father, claimed by him as eldest son in the Letters of Administration. John's wife, Elizabeth, is not mentioned in the Will, as she had pre-deceased him. (Buried on October 1st, 1826).

John's brother, Thomas, (bapt. 1751) died only a few weeks after he did. He was buried in Tysoe in April 1831, as already noted in the Burial list. In his Will, he styles himself "Thomas Hancox the elder of Tysoe...mason". He had made his Will on November 21st, 1830, leaving the bulk of his estate to the two daughters of his sister, Lydia: Decima and Mary Beck (bapt. 1799 and 1801). They got £25 between them and his "two pieces of ground in the Middle Tysoe Field. To hold to their heirs and assigns for ever as tenants in common subject to the payment of the mortgage due thereon". They also received his messuage or tenement in which Rebecca Hancox, widow, and Joseph Wilkes were residing; and his household goods, furniture etc. and £60 each. He left a long list of bequests of £5 to relatives, and £10 to his brother, John, although it seems these monies were to come from debts owed to him by John. Another list of bequests to the Marshall family and others were to come out of money owed him by his nephew, William Marshall, who himself got £30, perhaps a sum he had borrowed. John and George, sons of Thomas's late brother, (our) Joseph, got £5 each. Mary Beck, and Thomas's nephew, Thomas Hancox, son of his brother John, were to be his Executors. His signature is very shaky; either he could not see, or he could not control the pen. Mary Beck, spinster, on October 3rd, 1831, was sworn in as Executrix; Thomas's personal estate was not above £100, although his bequests totalled £275, most to be paid by other members of the family out of money owing to him, apparently.

Only thirty-five years later, in August, 1866, when Joseph's son, George (born 1800) died, his farm, between Stratford-on-Avon and Snitterfield, was valued at nearly £1,000. He left it to his wife.

I find that these documents - recently come to hand - give me an extra dimension of understanding of the lives of the people of Tysoe.

At the time of the Inclosure Awards in each village in England, two Maps were drawn: one to show ownership and division of land as it was; the second, about two years later, to show ownership and division agreed after the appointed Commissioners had visited and surveyed the land, and the Award had been made. On the first Map in Tysoe in 1796, John Hancox is shown as having two rods, twelve perches in the 'Area of Ancient Inclosures'. In 1798, on the second Map, almost all the land in the Parish was owned by Charles, Earl of Northampton, or the Hon. Mrs Mary Leigh. But at the northernmost boundary, close to the site of the 1642 battlefield, are two small adjacent plots in private ownership: I°n Hancox and Thomas Hancox. (These are our Joseph's two older surviving brothers - Richard having died. Joseph was farming elsewhere). John's place is designated 'Little Houses'; Thomas's, 'North of Andridge Hill'. Close by is the "public watercourse" of Andridge Ditch, which the Inclosure Award of January 17th, 1798, said must remain a public watercourse. John's land was larger than Thomas's, their respective payments being £1. 4s.10½d. and 15s 6½d.. Studying these old Maps, I also discovered, long after my earlier guess about the Westcote area of Tysoe being connected with the Hancoxes, that the lands owned by John and Thomas Hancox were indeed part of Westcote Manor. Because the Hancoxes had bought the land long before, they were

Chapter 1. Hans the Cook

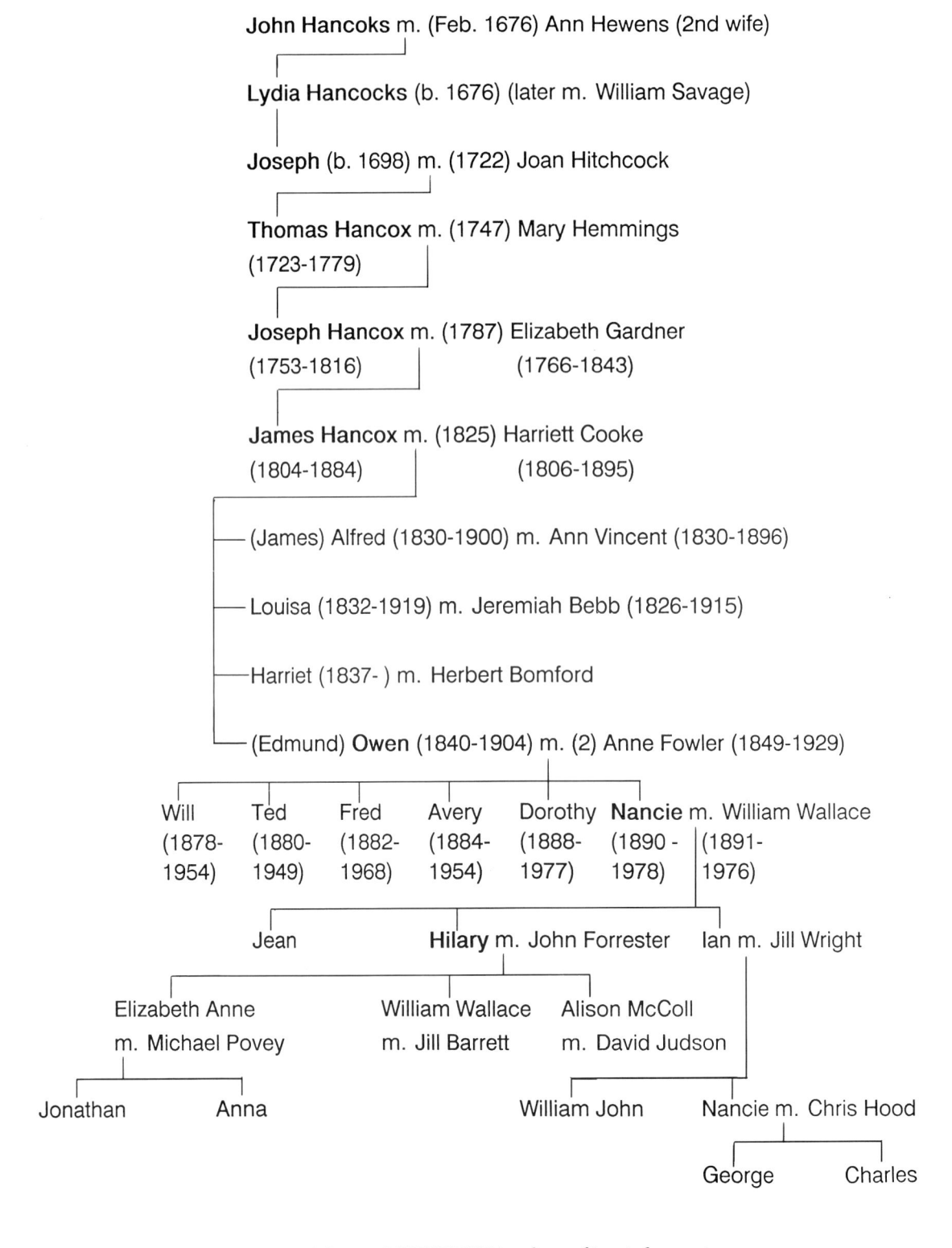

HANCOX FAMILY TREE
to show direct descent

John Hancoks m. (Feb. 1676) Ann Hewens (2nd wife)

Lydia Hancocks (b. 1676) (later m. William Savage)

Joseph (b. 1698) m. (1722) Joan Hitchcock

Thomas Hancox m. (1747) Mary Hemmings
(1723-1779)

Joseph Hancox m. (1787) Elizabeth Gardner
(1753-1816)   (1766-1843)

James Hancox m. (1825) Harriett Cooke
(1804-1884)   (1806-1895)

— (James) Alfred (1830-1900) m. Ann Vincent (1830-1896)

— Louisa (1832-1919) m. Jeremiah Bebb (1826-1915)

— Harriet (1837-) m. Herbert Bomford

— (Edmund) **Owen** (1840-1904) m. (2) Anne Fowler (1849-1929)

Will	Ted	Fred	Avery	Dorothy	**Nancie** m. William Wallace
(1878-	(1880-	(1882-	(1884-	(1888-	(1890 -	(1891-
1954)	1949)	1968)	1954)	1977)	1978)	1976)

Jean   **Hilary** m. John Forrester   Ian m. Jill Wright

Elizabeth Anne   William Wallace   Alison McColl
m. Michael Povey   m. Jill Barrett   m. David Judson

Jonathan   Anna   William John   Nancie m. Chris Hood

George   Charles

HANCOX FAMILY TREE to show direct descent

10

Chapter 1. Hans the Cook

able to keep it after much of the area around the village was enclosed. William Hancox bought land at this time; there was readiness to sell following the 'hard seasons' of 1794-5.

It was said that many farmers in the district made small fortunes in the opening years of the nineteenth century because wages were low, and corn-prices high. As farmers, the Hancoxes survived where the agricultural labourer faced starvation. They were not well enough off to indulge in the excesses of the rich; but they were not trapped in the prison of pauperism. Balanced between the two, they worked hard and prospered sufficiently to provide for their family. The lot of the village labourer was dire. One writer speaks of the "new hedges and deserted villages... the passive and unrecorded misery of the many, evicted or maimed by the community" as it marched towards a new life "through the wreckage of the old". He also wrote, "The agricultural labourer had one duty alone - to suffer in silence and breed sons for the Army and militia, daughters for the service of the gentry, hands of both sexes for factory and workshop. In the villages, they were at the mercy of the squire, parson and farmer, aided by the Surveyor of the Poor". Joseph Ashby's daughter wrote of the Seagrave family that they "registered themselves as 'Reverend Misters' and shut themselves behind high walls" while the parishioners were in dire need of help. Joseph Hancox's children were certainly marching towards a new life; they all grew up to adulthood and were sufficiently well-nourished to use their skills and brains in entrepreneurial fashion. All whom I know about reached at least their fifties and sixties. James, my great-grandfather, lived to be eighty.

OUR HANCOX FAMILY

Now let us look specifically at our Joseph, his forebears, and his own story. Joseph Hancox's parents, Thomas (bapt. 1723) and Mary (neé Hemmings), were married in 1747 at the village of Compton Wynyates, famous for its Tudor mansion, and home of the Earls of Northampton. It lies between Tysoe Windmill and Whatcote. Thomas and Mary had fifteen children, two more than Joseph himself was to sire. The list on p.12 shows the names and christening dates of Joseph and his brothers and sisters, from the Tysoe Parish Registers. Dates of death are added, where known. The births of the children span almost a quarter of a century. Eleven sons is quite an achievement. Compare it with what happens nowadays in a small Protestant village! Two or three of the children died young, but most lived to a good age: John (the eldest) to eighty-four, and Thomas (bapt. 1751) to his eightieth year.

Thomas Hancox (bapt. 1723), Joseph's father, was the son of another Joseph (of Oxhill bapt., 1698), and his wife, Joan (née Hitchcock) whom he married in 1722. Joan's parents were Edward Hitchcock and Joane (née Wickens) of Tysoe, married on April 25th, 1693; the Hemmings and the Hewens (see below) also came from there. This Joseph (bapt. 1698) was the illegitimate son of Lydia Hancocks (born 1676, bapt. November 1677 at Oxhill). She was daughter to John Hancoks and his second wife, Ann (née Hewens), whom he married at Tysoe on February 21st, 1676. In a deed dated about 1650 in Stratford-on-Avon Record Office, John Hancoks is referred to as a Carrier, a vitally important role in these early scattered communities. Here are our five generations of Hancoxes in Tysoe. (See Family Tree, opp.). In each generation, they would farm the equivalent of a small croft, even while pursuing a trade or other employment; it was the Inclosure Acts that put a stop to that. Our Joseph was a full-time farmer. Other members of the Hancox families held land in nearby Pillerton, of the Earl of Warwick estate (1480's); at one time in the fifteenth-century, they had Pillerton Manor; and a James Hancock and his descendants remained recently in the Pillerton area. (see Map p.2). One of the Hancock women married the brother of Ann Hathaway, wife of William Shakespeare.

For much of the information in this last paragraph and more, I am indebted to fellow-searchers into the Hancox family. One, I met by chance in the Stratford-on-Avon Record Office when he heard me mention the name 'Hancox'. It is with such chance encounters and co-incidental meetings that my search has been best rewarded.

Chapter 1. Hans the Cook

**Thomas Hancox &
Mary Hemmings' Children:**

	Baptised
John	(1747-1831)
Richard	(1750-1791)
Thomas	(1751-1831)
Mary	(1752)
Joseph	(1753-1816)
Edward	(1755)
Emma	(1756)
Elizabeth	(1758)
Nehemiah	(1760)
Lydia	(1761)
James	(1762)
William	(1764)
Samuel	(1767)
Robert	(1768)
Job	(1770)

**Joseph Hancox &
Elizabeth Gardner's Children:**

	Baptised
Mary (Cooper)	(1787)
Joseph	(1789)
William	(1790-1855)
John	(1792-1862)
Thomas	(1793)
Ann (Hancox)	(1795)
Robert	(1797)
George	(1800-1866)
Elizabeth (Bolton)	(1802)
James	(1804-1884)
Sarah (Williamson)	(1806)
Martha (Newbold)	(1809)
Job	(1812)

(1) Siblings and children of Joseph Hancox (b. 1753)
(2) Whatcote Church
(3) The Village Stocks in Loxley Church
(4) Hancox signature

12

Chapter 1. Hans the Cook

Joseph (born 1753) left Tysoe to farm at **Whatcote**, the next village to the West, close to Idlicote (see Map p.2). On New Year's Day, 1787, he married Elizabeth Gardner of Fullready in the parish of Eatington, her home church. He was thirty-three; she, twenty-one. Elizabeth, who had been baptised at Eatington, was the daughter of Thomas Gardner and Mary (née Powell), who both came originally from Honington, where Thomas Gardner was buried when he died (rather well-off) in 1808. Elizabeth received £20 on her father's death; and a share of her father's estate when her mother died. (Thomas Gardner's Will dated 15th February, 1808). Between 1770-1800, rising prices and low wages meant that many men in Tysoe and elsewhere could not earn enough to marry - and it was accepted that a man could not marry unless he could support a wife. Joseph waited till he was thirty-three, by which time he had land to farm. He and his wife were able to sustain a much better standard of living than the ordinary agricultural labourer and so give all their large family a good start in life.

During the fifteen years that Joseph and Elizabeth lived at Whatcote, she bore him nine children, who were taken to the old Norman church to be baptised. As you can see from the list of children and their christening dates (opp.), Mary the eldest was born ten months after the wedding; the others followed with varied intervals between: not at exact two-year intervals, as happened in many families then. All their names were recorded in Joseph Hancox's Family Bible.

Quartercote, as it was called in 1086 (Domesday Book), belonged at that time to Hugh de Grentesmaismil. It consisted of five hides - much less than Tysoe's twenty-three. It slumbered on for centuries, scarcely changing its ways. The little stone church of St. Peter at Whatcote (see drawing opp.), set aside in a corner of the village, stood undisturbed throughout seven centuries until the Second World War, when a German bomber, intent on blitzing Birmingham a few miles north, jettisoned a stick of bombs in the area. One bomb destroyed the Norman font, the six-hundred-year-old porch, and the nave, which have since been skilfully repaired. The Royal Oak Inn nearby is said to have originated for the lodging and thirst-quenching of the masons who built the church. Much later, Cromwell and his men came there for food and drink after the Battle of Edgehill in 1642.

'Whatcott Buryinges' (1572-1812) include this entry:

'Henrye Stanforde, a wounded soldier, a Hertfordshire man, October 26th, 1644.

What a long time he was a-dying: two years after the Battle of Edgehill, and so very far from home.

On October 23rd, 1801, Joseph Hancox signed a document swearing allegiance to the Lord of the Manor of Whatcote. A group of men: Matthew Batsford, Richard Fisher, Joseph Hancox, Thomas Marshall and Joseph Hawton: promised to perform their duties, and to pay four pence each. Joseph Hancox and Matthew Batsford were to be continued as Tythingmen and Fieldsmen (if I deciphered the old document correctly). Some of the men could only 'make their mark' with a X; but Joseph signed his name with a flourish. He formed the letters of his surname, as did all the Hancoxes at this time, in a particular way (see illustration opp.); and they spelt their name our way, though the earlier lawyers wrote it 'Hancock'.

Three years later, the others at Whatcote Manor signed again, but Joseph had gone. Along the winding country lanes, through the village of Eatington where they had married and across the Fosse-way (the old Roman road which cuts straight across the county) they had moved to Loxley, within less than four miles of Stratford-on-Avon. Joseph is listed as paying Land Tax at Loxley in 1803; he had been in Whatcote until at least April, 1802, when his daughter Elizabeth was baptised. At Loxley, the family were much better placed for the markets in the town, and for launching their children into work or apprenticeships. It must have suited them, as they both remained there until they died. Four more children were born at Loxley: James (1804), about whom I know the most, as he left many documents now in Stratford-on-Avon Record Office; and he was my great-grandfather, so much has been remembered and noted down about him; Sarah (1806); Martha (1809); and Job (1812). Joseph died at Loxley in 1816. Their daughter Anne, (born 1795), married her cousin, John Hancox, in 1817, and I believe that he continued to

Chapter 1. Hans the Cook

farm at Loxley. Elizabeth, Joseph's widow, remained in Loxley, although when she died in 1843, after a stroke, she was at Snitterfield, presumably at Spring Farm, where her son George lived. She was seventy-eight. Her son, John, was with her and reported the death. On her Death Certificate, Joseph is designated 'Farmer'. This was my first firm evidence that the Hancoxes were more than agricultural labourers, although it had seemed increasingly unlikely, the more I found out about them, especially knowing the sort of life led by their son, James, and other members of the family, in and around Stratford-on-Avon.

Loxley encircles the top of a small hill. The parish church of St. Nicholas, rebuilt in the mid-eighteenth century, lies lower down the hill, close to Loxley Hall. The day I visited the Hall, there was no one about except a workman in the outbuildings. The garden hedges were trim and beautifully cut. Just down the road are old gnarled laburnum trees, overgrown bushes, crab apple trees and other old fruit trees in a neglected orchard. Electric cables now cut through the orchard; light aeroplanes from the nearby flying club drone overhead; cars speed down the road. In the intervals of silence, wood pigeons coo, and I can then imagine what it was like in Loxley in the early 1800's.

Inside the church is a set of stocks (see photo p.12), and an amusing pulpit fall showing St. Nicholas (Father Christmas) in his pyjamas and bedroom slippers. The interior is almost unspoilt Georgian, with box pews and a pulpit entered by a door from the vestry, just as it would have been in Joseph's time. The pews now sport colourfully-embroidered hassocks; the whole church is beautifully maintained. During the Hancoxes' early years at Loxley, the vicar was George Huddesford, satirist and painter, who was a pupil of the painter Reynolds. He is the figure on the left in Reynolds' famous painting, "Portrait of Two Gentlemen", which hangs in the National Gallery. Loxley was not without evidence of people who could appreciate fine possessions and workmanship. James Hancox as a very young man learnt to make fine furniture.

"Next week", said the St. Nicholas current parish newsletter, "on St. Swithin's Day, (1989) there will be the Strawberry Fayre in the gardens of Loxley Hall, by kind invitation of Colonel Alex Gregory-Hood. Tickets 75 pence, to include a strawberry tea and admission to the garden". Listeners to the BBC serial 'The Archers' will be reminded how Nigel Pargetter at the Hall in "Lower Loxley" tries to support and entertain the village as generations of his family had done before him.

The name Pargitor turns up not far away from the lower part of the real Loxley. It features in the Tysoe Registers from 1756, in five different spellings. When I was checking the 323 Hancox entries for Tysoe in the I.G.I., I found Hannah Hancox, who had an illegitimate son in summer 1858. The name of the father is not given, but I think that Hannah wished to make sure that everyone knew who he was. She gave the baby's Christian names as "John Pargitor". Only two persons of that name are recorded in the I.G.I., as having been born in Tysoe earlier last century. One was John Pargitor, son of William and Harriet, christened 25th March, 1842, who, if he was the father, was either very precocious or had been christened long after his birth, a not uncommon occurrence. The other was John Pargitor, son of Thomas and Jane, christened 30th March, 1823. He would have been a man of at least thirty-five, not too young to marry and indeed perhaps already married at the time; or an enlisted soldier, home on leave, the autumn before?

John Pargitor Hancox was one of very few babies at this time in this place to be given a middle name. Throughout the nineteenth century, in villages like Tysoe anyway, it was rare to find more than one Christian name. This was almost invariably a name from another close member of the family, often from a parent or grandparent, or sometimes a name already given to a baby who had died - especially confusing.

The range of Christian names was limited, and was originally drawn from two main sources: Royalty, and the Bible. Among the Warwickshire Hancox daughters, for instance, Mary and Elizabeth are the most popular names; Ann and Sarah come next. The sons are frequently George, James, John, Thomas or William. The same names are found in family documents for hundreds of years. All these girls' names were built into the Wallace family in the Borders, from at least the eighteenth century onwards, except for Mary. Joseph also was not popular among the Presbyterians in the north; but Mary and Joseph were very popular in the Church of England. They were the first two names

Chapter 1. Hans the Cook

chosen by the Hancox family in the late eighteenth century at Whatcote. Some unfortunates were saddled with names we might consider rather heavy to-day: Nehemiah, Ezekiel, Job, Emmanuel, Keziah, Caleb and Malachi.

As I stood below the church tower of Saint Nicholas at Loxley and gazed up at the sundial with its message, "I die to-day and live to-morrow", I thought of the bones of my great-great-grandparents lying under my feet, no headstone visible. Their names are in the Burial list: Joseph, May 2nd 1816, and Elizabeth, December 14th 1843.

No one else comes during the hour I spend in and by the church. The Vicar has to divide himself nowadays between three parishes; and on "Sea Sunday" this month of July, these three parishes, as far from our coast as anywhere in Britain, will pray particularly and give an offering for the Missions to Seamen. How many from this Parish have gone away to sea or out to work somewhere else, and never come back? All of the Hancox family except Ann, so far as I know: to Stratford-on-Avon, to Snitterfield, to Ettington, and in the next generation much further afield.

This is what I have gleaned so far about Joseph and Elizabeth's twelve other children, siblings of my great-grandfather, James:

Mary, their firstborn, (1787) married William Cooper on New Year's Day, 1811, the twenty-fourth anniversary of her parents' marriage. The wedding was in Loxley, where Joseph and Elizabeth were still living.

Joseph (1789) married Ann (born c. 1797), and farmed at Honington. They had at least seven children, of whom John the eldest (born 1819) married his cousin Mary Hancox, daughter of his father's brother, William. (See next para.)

William (1790) was a butcher and provision merchant in Eatington, and lived there for many years. "Upper Eatington", as it was known in medieval times, was originally a Saxon village. The road from Eatington to Stratford, originally Roman, had been a salt way in the Middle Ages. The Society of Friends (Quakers) were established in the village since 1664 at least; and George Fox, their famous founder, preached nearby in 1678. There is still a little Quaker Meeting House, which was built in 1684. Fields in the area were enclosed by Act of Parliament in 1758 during the reign of George III. The nearby rivers were the Stour and the Dene; one of the minor waterways in the district was called Wagtail Brook.

Before the changes made at Eatington by the owner of Eatington Park, Evelyn Shirley, the reigning squire, there had been a large village green with a set of stocks and a village cross. There was a Vicarage, a Mill and a Cottage: all cleared away to increase the parkland near the big house. For at least 150 years afterwards, the stump of a very large tree still remained by the site of the village green. In 1873, when the Railway came to Eatington, the squire changed the spelling to Ettington to avoid confusion about the pronunciation.

William the butcher, also designated "farmer" in 1822, went up the hill along the Stratford road on Sundays to his church, Saint Thomas à Becket, built in 1794, with the reputation at that time of being the ugliest church in the county. It was built because the older one in Lower Eatington had fallen into ruin. In time this second church had to be replaced by the present one, built in 1902. All that remains of the church on the Stratford road is the tower, and a long-disused graveyard, cared for by an enthusiastic voluntary custodian. I went to Ettington and was directed to the old church tower. Behind it, in an overgrown plot, we were shown a gravestone with William's name on it, and the date July 11th, 1855. Other names on it were deciphered with difficulty: Mary, 1848; Louisa, June 4th, 1841; Mary, November 27th, 1853, aged thirty-one years; and John.

What church records revealed was that William (born 1790), brother of my great-grandfather James, had married on 24th February 1817 his cousin Mary, daughter of John Powell Gardner, brother to his mother Elizabeth. William, who spelt his name Hancock, and his wife Mary, had John (named for Mary's father) (1817); Elizabeth (named for William's mother) (1818); William (named for himself) (1819); Ann (probably named for Mary's mother) (1821); Mary (for her mother) (1822); Louisa (1823) and Hannah (1827). This was a traditional way of selecting names for children, still prevalent in

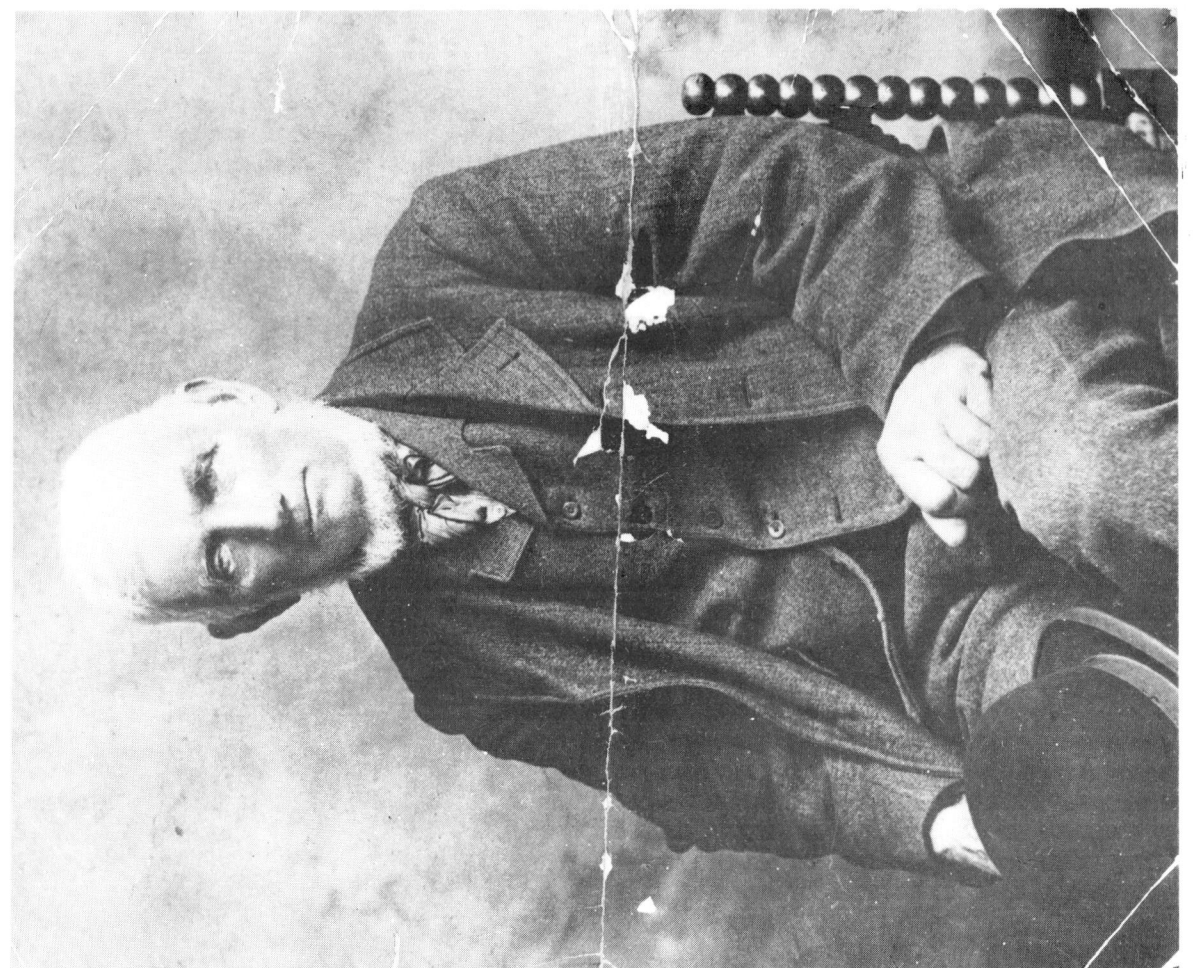

Chapter 1. Hans the Cook

(1) George Hancox, died 1924 at a great age: son of Thomas (b. 1793), and grandson of Joseph (b. 1753). He lived at Whatcote

(2) William, eldest son of this George

Chapter 1. Hans the Cook

Scotland and the north of England in the twentieth century. Three of these children died in infancy: Ann (eleven days); Hannah (seven weeks); and Elizabeth (three months); two more when they were seventeen. I do not know the cause of death of their son, John, 1834, as that was before Civil registration began. Louisa, seventeen in 1841 "poisoned herself while she was deranged". In the light of this tragic tale you will see why descendants of Joseph and Elizabeth, grandparents of these children, say with pride that "Joseph and Elizabeth reared all their thirteen children".

Of William's family, only Mary remained. On January 24th, 1853, at the age of thirty-one, she married her cousin John Hancox, son of her father's brother, Joseph of Honington. Mary died in late November of the same year. When I heard this, I thought she might have died in childbirth, but the death certificate says "Emphysema", suggesting instead some lung trouble. William's wife, also Mary, had died in February 1849, of paralysis which lasted three years. Now he was alone. His thoughts turned to his own latter end. He made a Will dated January 12th, 1854. His brothers, James and George, were his executors. They were the two who had best established themselves. This document is both useful and revealing, as it lists all William's surviving siblings in January 1854 and gives the married names of his sisters. His first named legatee is his son-in-law, John Hancox, son of his brother Joseph (Joseph is not listed, so either his son took his share or he was already dead). There follow all William's siblings, brothers first in age order: John, Thomas, Robert, George, James and Job; then his sisters (Mary not being named, so presumably dead without issue): Ann Hancox, Elizabeth Bolton, Sarah Williamson, and Martha Newbold. William instructs his executors to give each sibling's share, should they predecease him, to their issue; if they have none, the share reverts to the other siblings.

When William died eighteen months later, his property was put up for auction with the following notice:

"July 25th, 1855. At 6 o' clock in the Evening, at the Chequers Inn, Eatington, Warks, Dwelling House and Premises with the Garden in Front, Shop, Brewhouse, Piggeries, two Stall Stable and Cart Hovel with a Piece of Garden Ground near to the same, the whole being situate in Eatington...late in the occupation of Mr William Hancox, butcher and shopkeeper, deceased...Bidding by not less than £2; purchaser to give a 'place of abode' at the fall of the hammer and pay 10 per cent deposit and the remainder by September 29th next by which date property cleared; after which all rents to purchaser. If the purchaser does not comply with conditions, his or her deposit absolutely forfeited".

John (1792) married Sarah Ann Barnes. More than that I would not have known, if I had not noticed an entry in the 1851 Census for Stratford-on-Avon. The 1851 Census is the first to give the place of origin of each person recorded, and is invaluable for family searchers. For my father's family in the Scottish Borders, it enabled me to work backwards for nearly a century, and sideways across the country, once I found the parish where a particular generation had been born. Sometimes it can be misleading; for instance this John told the 1851 enumerator that he had come from Loxley. He had, but he went there from Whatcote only when he was fourteen. It was the entry for another brother that took me to the Whatcote register.

The 1851 entry for Shakespeare Street, Old Stratford, goes like this:

			Origin	County
Edwin George Hancox	head	25	Stratford-on-Avon	Warwickshire
Elizabeth	wife	26	Loxley	Warwickshire
Sarah Anne	dau.	4	Stratford-on-Avon	Warwickshire
Ellen	dau.	2	-do-	Warwickshire
Catherine	dau.	1	-do-	Warwickshire
John	father	59	Loxley	Warwickshire
	widower		Joiner	

John Hancox was a fairly common name in that district at that time, but "half a minute", I thought, "aged 59 in 1851? That means born in 1792. It is our John". So then

Chapter 1. Hans the Cook

I knew he had a son Edwin, born about 1826 in Stratford-on-Avon, and he had been a joiner by trade. Edwin's wife had come from Loxley, the Hancox family home since 1803. Sarah Ann, John's wife, was dead, but John was living with his son's family, and had three little granddaughters, the eldest named for her Hancox grandmother (Sarah Anne). This is how, through Parish Registers, Birth, Marriage and Death Certificates, and Census Returns, relationships can be gradually established, and interpreted through study of the social history of the period, and actual visits to the places. John died in the Workhouse at Stratford-on-Avon on May 10th, 1862, of Old Age. (His occupation is given as Cabinet-maker).

Thomas (1793) married Ann in about 1821. They had six children (one of whom George (see photo p.16) had at least eleven children between 1856 and 1881). James Hancox, the grandson of George's eldest child William (see other photo p.16) lived in Stratford-on-Avon until he died in 1989. (His widow supplied these two photos).

Ann (1795) married her cousin, John Hancox, at Loxley in 1817 (May 9th).

Robert (1797) married Elizabeth Summertown of Whatcote at Stratford-on-Avon; they had three sons: Thomas, John and William. Robert witnessed his younger brother George's wedding at Snitterfield.

George (1800) of Spring Farm, Snitterfield, married Harriet (née Marshall), whose Uncle Joseph was a grocer in Stratford-on-Avon. They had many children, including Caroline, who married George Garlick, a schoolmaster. Among George and Caroline's many children was one, Ralph, who became a Judge of the High Court in Calcutta and who was murdered there. George Hancox died in 1866 of chronic gastritis which had troubled him for years.

Elizabeth (1802), witness at the wedding of her brother, James, in 1825, married John Bolton three years later (August 18th, 1828). Edmund Cooke, James's new brother-in-law, was his other witness. (My grandfather, Edmund Owen Hancox, was named after him).

Of Sarah, Martha and Job, James's younger siblings, at present I know no more than their christening dates at Loxley, and that they were still alive in 1854, the girls having all married.

There is also a remarkable letter (just found) from Wanganui in New Zealand, dated 1851. Addressed to 'Dear Cousin' (Mr Alfred Hancox, Carver and c., Henley Street, Stratford-on-Avon), it is from Sarah Williamson's son. He had been in New Zealand just a year, after a sixteen-week voyage; most of the letter tells of the condition of the soil, and the agricultural scene. It encourages another relative to join him, and asks for an early reply.

I am greatly indebted to James, my great-grandfather, born 1804, tenth in the family. He seems to have been very well-organised and successful in his business. His family papers, now lodged at the Record Offices, tell us a great deal. He was a man of property, and much sought after by his own family and others for help with their affairs. All his working life was spent in Stratford-on-Avon, and though at first he retired elsewhere, he returned to Stratford for his last ten or twelve years.

All the members of this large family remained closely in touch, helping each other as and when they could, as did the Galbraiths and Wallaces from the Borders. Before the Welfare State, it was usually the family who provided a safety net when necessary. The families from which my generation comes were tremendously loyal to each other, as this story will unfold. They supported each other in times of illness and bereavement, as well as enjoying their company. Death came early to some, but many lived well beyond the allotted span; and the marriages lasted.

Chapter 2

Birthplace Of The Bard

Stratford-on-Avon was one of the Plantation towns of the Middle Ages: developed by landowners, merchants, Bishops, even the King, at strategic points on trade-routes, to encourage business and enrich those well-placed to reap the benefits. Most main roads radiating from London had one or more 'planted' towns at strategic points. By 1297, there were over one hundred and twenty 'planted' towns in England, although really they reached their peak on the eve of the Black Death (1348-9). Stratford-on-Avon, in its first year, was sufficiently important to be represented in Parliament.

Many old town-names have 'ford' in them, obviously because a place where the river could be crossed was important for transporting people and goods. But when at last a bridge was built such as at Stratford, the place chosen for the bridge was likely to be at a quite different part of the river. So the new town of Stratford-on-Avon has the fields of the Old Stratford village on three sides and the River Avon on the fourth. The very name "Old Stratford" suggests that the present main town is a plantation. So does the regular pattern of its streets, and the fact that its parish church - Holy Trinity, where Hancoxes were baptised, married and buried - is outside the borough. Only where there is no church already could a New Town have its own church without infringing rights. The Bishop of Worcester, in whose diocese the new town fell, agreed to it. He stood to benefit from a thriving town, which would swell his coffers.

The new boroughs were usually small and compact, both because everyone wanted to be as near the market-place as possible, and because small towns were easier to defend. Also, the local population needed their fields. Even in the mid-nineteenth century, when railways came to towns, the station was often placed quite a distance away. I'd naturally noticed this, but did not know that, as well as the lie of the land, its position was partly because there were ancient charters which gave the right to take toll from all goods loaded within the borough. On my visits to Stratford-on-Avon, last year, I used the original Ordnance Survey Map of 1885 for walking about the town. So precise and well-structured was the original grid that I had no difficulties in finding my way about.(See Map p.31) Sometimes the New towns were welcomed by the Old, sometimes not. Violence and litigation could erupt in rivalry between them. The relative sizes of the Old and New Stratford-on-Avon are shown in the 1801 Census: New Stratford-on-Avon 109 acres; Old Stratford-on-Avon 6,385 acres!

This lively activity of trade and travellers in Stratford would offer ideas and entertainment to an observant boy like William Shakespeare, poet and playwright. There are many well-known stories about his life as a young man. One which is not known is about a tree, in his day known locally as the "One Elm". It grew in the Birmingham Road at Stratford-on-Avon, and the local legend was that he and his schoolmates used to gather under it. As the tree grew bigger over the centuries, the roots pressed upwards through the road and became dangerous to passing coaches, even upsetting some. In 1845, the Stratford Corporation commissioned James Hancox (my great-grandfather), local cabinet maker and timber merchant, to cut down and remove the tree.

A telescopic dining-table was made from the tree in James Hancox's workshops; his older son, Alfred, did the actual work involved, while serving his apprenticeship at the time. The rest of the tree was sold to a Birmingham firm who had it made up into various objects which were sold principally to Americans, who even then were keen to have anything associated with Shakespeare. Alfred left the table to his daughter, Mrs. Clara Louisa Shakespeare (I can find no connection between her husband's family and William Shakespeare). She sold it forthwith to her aunt, Mrs. Louisa Bebb, Alfred's sister, about whom I shall tell more later. When Louisa's unmarried daughter, Minnie, died in 1945, the table came into the possession of Louisa's grandson, Reverend Douglas Bebb of the Methodist Church, whose letter to 'The Times' on 13 August, 1964, is my source of this information about the tree. I have just found the press-cutting of his letter, cut out and dated in my father's hand writing, among the family archives. I have quoted freely from

Chapter 2. Birthplace of the Bard

it. He says that the table has a small plaque on it which reads, "This table was made in 1845 by James Hancox of Stratford-on-Avon from the One Elm Tree under which Shakespeare played with other boys". Reverend Bebb, a great-grandson of James Hancox, was prompted to write the letter, twenty-five years ago, apparently by an article in 'The Times' on "Shakespeare's Tree Souvenirs". The table remains with Reverend Bebb's widow and daughter. I have seen it.

To this town came **James Hancox** (born 1804) as an apprentice cabinet-maker in about 1817. He may have walked in every day from Loxley or he may have lived with his older brother John (born 1792) who became a joiner in Stratford-on-Avon. He very soon established himself at the Henley Street end of Cooke's Alley, and quickly gained a reputation for fine furniture and upholstery work. His business prospered.

Next door to James's shop in Cooke's Alley, lived a burgess of Stratford-on-Avon, Henry Cooke (or Cook: documents have both), whose family business for generations had been coopering, the making of tubs and casks etc., an important trade then. In those days, an apprentice-cooper was rolled in a barrel at the end of his apprenticeship, before he could become a journeyman. This ceremony was re-enacted at Stratford-on-Avon, some years ago as a reminder of an old custom.

The Cooke family had been in business in the same place for so long that their street, which still connects Henley Street with Wood Street, is called 'Cook's Alley'. In the old days there was a sign painted on the wall of Cooke's Alley saying 'Cooke Cooper'. This was painted out in the early 1940's I am told. Could it have been part of the move to obliterate all place-names on signposts, etc. to baffle the Germans? Now there is an ordinary name-plate, or rather four name-plates, designating the pedestrian alley. (See photo p.27). (In 1851, Edmund Cooke (49) and his wife Helen (35) from Alcester were occupying the Cooke's Alley house. Alcester, a few miles north of Stratford-on-Avon, is an old Roman site on the River Alne. It too, was almost certainly a Plantation town and is important later in this story).

Henry Cooke, Edmund's father, and his wife, Charlotte, were married in December, 1798. She was born Charlotte Harris, her father William Harris having married Susannah Snedwell on 12 November, 1769. Henry and Charlotte Cooke had four sons and three daughters. (See Family Tree p.29). The eldest daughter was (Isabel) Harriett, two years younger than James Hancox. She fell in love with the boy next door, and as James reciprocated and was already in a position to support a wife by the age of twenty-one, they married on October 3rd, 1825, in the parish church of Holy Trinity, Stratford-on-Avon. All of their four children were christened in the same church; their baptismal dates in the Register are:

James Alfred (known always as Alfred)	5th November, 1830
Louisa Matilda (who much later styled herself Louise)	12th September, 1832
Harriet	15th August, 1837
Edmund Owen (known latterly as Owen)	16th December, 1840

Edmund Owen was the father of my mother Nancie. The only one of these names which came from the Hancox side was that of James. Louisa Matilda, Harriet and Edmund were names in the Cooke family. In the family records, and even on his gravestone, Edmund Owen's birthday is given as October 9th. As I know from his Birth Certificate, now obtained from London, he was really born on November 9th, a special day for us as he shares it with our daughter, Liz: eldest grandchild of William and Nancie.

James, of course, had apprentices in his cabinet-making and upholstery workshops, apart from his eldest son. Stratford-on-Avon Record Office have many Hancox papers, among them an original Indenture, drawn up between James Hancox and Thomas Wright with the consent of his mother, Mary, of Halford Bridge, Warwickshire, on 10th July, 1838, for the boy to serve for five years, nine months, and five days under James's tuition. (See opp.) It is an elaborate document which places stringent conditions of discipline on the apprentice. 1838 was the same year that James was commissioned to re-upholster the chairs in the State Room at Windsor Castle, preparatory to Queen Victoria's wedding. We still have in the family a piece of the old-gold-coloured fabric with

Chapter 2. Birthplace of the Bard

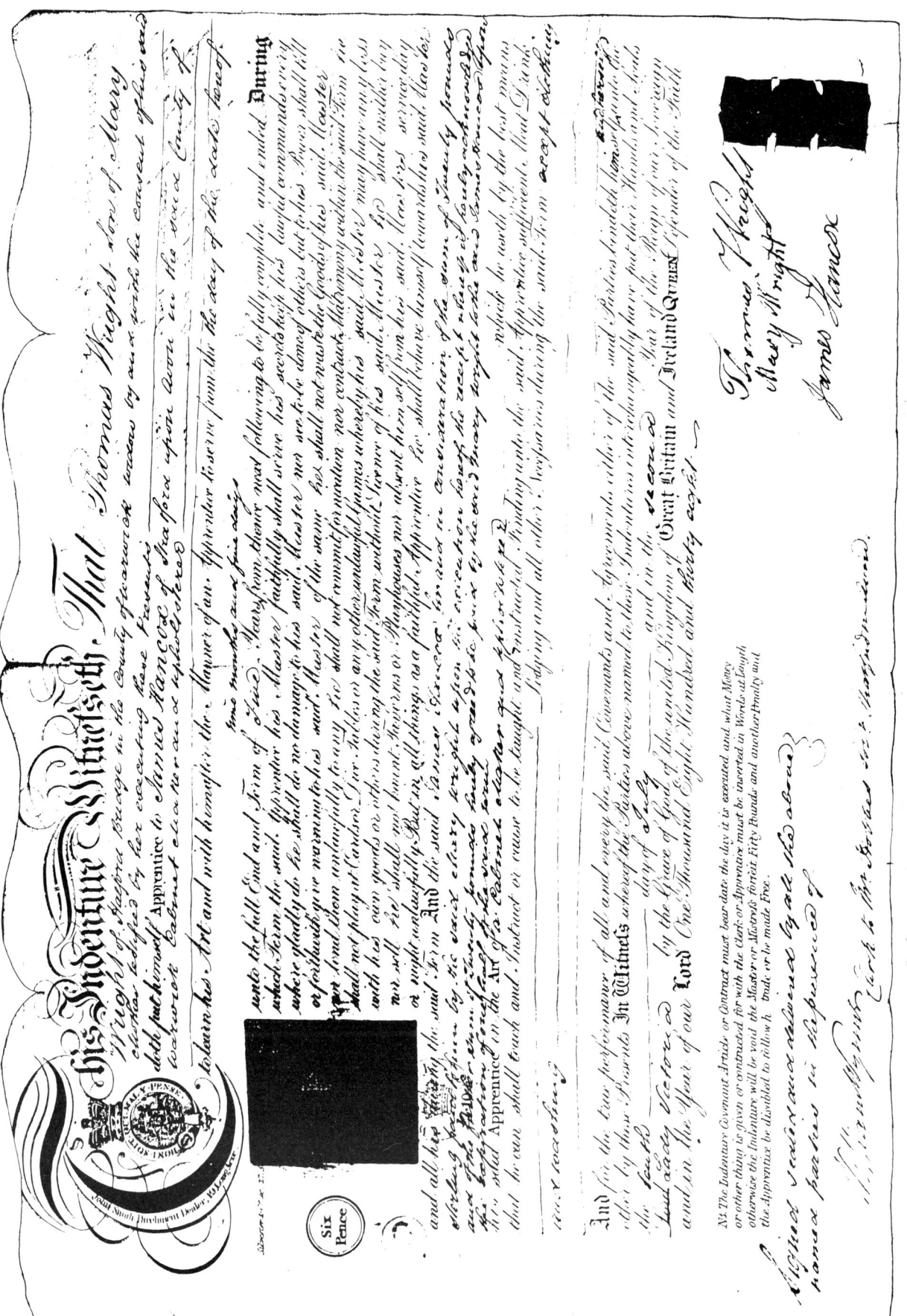

Indenture between James Hancox and Thomas Wright (and his mother, Mary) for Thomas's apprenticeship to James

Chapter 2. Birthplace of the Bard

a raised design that was used for the work at Windsor. In the following year, 1839, Mr. Henry Cooke agreed to let premises in Henley Street, Stratford-on-Avon, to Mr. James Hancox for seventy years at a stated rent of Ten pounds per annum! So little did money values change, nor were they expected to change, that this was reasonable then. Imagine it now!

In 1851, the Census Returns show that James employed eleven men in his workshops. His elder son, Alfred, who made the telescopic table, now aged twenty, is designated 'Carver'; and this skill was to recur in later generations, most notably in the hands of my mother's much-loved brother, Will. He carved as a hobby, being an engineer by profession, and created a different pattern of linen-fold for each member of the family. I have three chests made by him, the same linen-fold design on each: a blanket-sized oak chest, saying 'Hilary, her chest', in the Elizabethan style, with the date of my twenty-first birthday; this was my mother's present to me; a smaller model of the same thing complete with sliding tray, given by Uncle Will on my marriage, as a sewing box; and a very small one to hold handkerchiefs, made from apricot wood, from Uncle Will on my twenty-first birthday. Others in the family also received appropriate chests.

Alfred, helped by his father, went into the biscuit business, but this did not last. On March 20th, 1862, he put up the premises of the Steam Biscuit and Saw Mill, Mulberry Street, Stratford-on-Avon, for sale. His father subsequently bought the Corn Mill at Henley-in-Arden for him, where he remained until he retired and went to live at Wootton Wawen in a lovely, detached Georgian house, with an "Adam Porch", I am told. When his wife, Ann Vincent (1830-96), died there, he returned to one of his own houses in Stratford-on-Avon: No.13 Albany Place. James had bought property in Stratford-on-Avon over the years in Wood Street, Henley Street, Albany Place, Wellesbourne Grove, Waterside, etc, as well as a Mill for each of his two sons. He also helped his son-in-law, Jeremiah Bebb, to establish an ironmonger's shop in Stratford-on-Avon. He was punctilious about fair divisions and was obviously a wealthy man. After about 1860, he is referred to as 'Gent' being by then able to support himself without working. At one time he was offered "Shakespeare's House", as a dwelling-house, for £100; it is now owned by the nation and visited by millions of tourists. He inspected it, but considered that the uneven floor-levels, small rooms and awkward stairs, made it inconvenient for his wife. He built a modern house for her instead. As I tell later on, James and his wife lived in various places after he retired, usually to be near members of their family, returning finally to Stratford-on-Avon in the 1870's.

Alfred had a son, Frank, and a daughter, Clara Louisa, who became Mrs. Thomas Shakespeare and lived in Hoddesdon, Hertfordshire. Alfred fell out with both his children, and he adopted his son's daughter Florence, (one of Frank's four children) to whom he left his property. When he died, he was buried beside his wife at Wootton Wawen, to whom he had four years before inscribed the gravestone: 'In rememberance of a loving wife, Ann Vincent Hancox, died March 18, 1896 aged 66'. Considering the account left by my Uncle of the scene at Alfred's funeral: Florence, the granddaughter, in tears, and the son and daughter "in high dudgeon" at being left out of the property, it is interesting to know that the inscription on Alfred's tomb-stone reads: 'Erected by his daughter, Clara Louisa Shakespeare'. Perhaps what she got for the table he left her helped to pay for the stone; or perhaps her husband was comfortably off. Florence was made a Ward of her grandmother, Louisa Bebb, and lived with her at Ridgeway House, Fishponds, Bristol, during her holidays from boarding-school at Clevedon. You will meet her again in a later chapter.

James's wife, Harriett (Cooke), worked a sampler at the age of eleven. She signed it 'Harriott (sic) Cooke November 1817'. She used to tell how the news of the victory after the Battle of Waterloo came to Stratford. She remembered the coach from London thundering into Stratford and the coachman waving his whip and shouting, "We've beaten Boney! We've beaten Boney!" Harriett died in her ninetieth year; her maternal grandmother, Susannah (née Snedwell), had lived to her hundredth year. Susannah gave her granddaughter Harriett on her wedding in 1825 a linen table-cloth which she had embroidered for her. She must have had remarkable eyesight in her nineties, unless she had sewn it years before, and put it by. I had heard of this tablecloth given to Harriett by

Chapter 2. Birthplace of the Bard

her granny, and was intrigued to come across a letter to my mother describing how the cloth was found 130 years after Susannah's death, "got among some legal papers", and was handed over to Avery, son of Jack and grandson of Owen Hancox, in 1962: yellow with age.

Reverend Douglas Bebb, grandson of Louisa (neé Hancox), found and copied a press cutting about his great-grandmother's death and funeral, from the local paper in Stratford; as well as being of interest to the family, it shows how such occasions were reported in 1895.

Grandma Harriett Hancox (1806-1895)

DEATH OF MRS HANCOX. - We have this week to announce, with regret, the demise of Mrs Harriett Hancox, who passed away at her residence, 17, College Street, Stratford-on-Avon, on Friday morning last, at the advanced age of 89 years. The deceased lady was the widow of Mr. James Hancox, late of the Limes, who established and carried successfully for a number of years the business now in the hands of Messrs Fowler and Hawley, Henley Street. She was born at Stratford in the year 1806, being, therefore, one of the oldest inhabitants of the town, and was well-known and much respected by all who lived here for any length of time. Although generally refraining from any public act of charity, she had a kind and sympathetic nature, was very liberal in her gifts to the poor, and a regular subscriber to various philanthropic institutions. The funeral took place on Wednesday, deceased being interred in the family vault under the Avenue leading to the Holy Trinity Church. A number of beautiful wreaths were placed on the coffin, which was composed of polished oak, with heavy brass furniture, the breast-plate bearing the simple inscription "Harriett Hancox, died February 22nd, 1895, aged 89 years." The mourners included Mr. E. O. Hancox, Evesham and Mr. J.A. Hancox, Wootton Wawen (sons of deceased), Mr. H. Bomford, Oversley, and Mr. J. Bebb, Bristol (sons-in-law), Messrs. G.H. Bomford, J.J. Hancox, J.H. Bomford, and W. Hancox (grandsons). Mr. F. Winter, undertaker, High Street, carried out the funeral arrangements.

The reference to the "family vault under the avenue leading to the Holy Trinity Church" is because a number of these vaults were allotted to 'burgess' families. The Cookes had had one for a long time. When I was a child in the early 1930's my mother took me to see the paving-stone above the vault with 'Cook' carved upon it. My Uncle Jack (J.J. Hancox in the above list) has left an account of his recollection of Harriett's funeral in 1895: 'I went down into the Vault (under the Lime Tree Avenue which leads up to the parish church in Stratford-on-Avon) approached by stone steps from the side of the Avenue - and saw the last niche left for her coffin in the wall of the vault... you could probably still find her name on the paving on the right hand side of the Avenue, facing the church rather nearer the church than half-way'. J.J. Hancox wrote this in 1947. Sadly, on a recent visit I could find no trace of the carved name: 'Cook'. But I have since discovered that these same lime trees were planted by another relative on the other side of the family. John Butcher who married a niece of the Mrs Elizabeth Hawkes who will appear in the next chapter (on Nancie's mother's side) was a nurseryman, in Warwick Road, Stratford-on-Avon. John Butcher's father, born 1802, planted the lime tree avenue in Holy Trinity church-yard. He also grew Barbarossa grapes at two guineas per lb and pineapples at £5.00 each which he supplied to the French Court of the period. He won Royal Horticultural Society silver medals for grapes in 1852-3 which led to a request from Queen Victoria to take some vines and plant them at Windsor, which he did.

Louisa Matilda Hancox, James and Harriett's elder daughter, born August 15th, 1832, was a high-spirited and romantic girl who had a surprisingly unchaperoned freedom as a seventeen-year-old. This is shown by a Diary she wrote (from January 1st to October

Chapter 2. Birthplace of the Bard

15th, 1849) entitled "Memorandum of daily events for the year 1849". It was found among her papers after she died, seventy years later. In 1849, as well as celebrating her seventeenth birthday, she received at least three proposals of marriage and became engaged to Jeremiah Bebb.

Louisa had left school by Christmas 1848, when she was sixteen, and used to help in her father's shop. Sometimes she was left to manage alone, and on January 13th records that her parents had both gone to Warwick; the shop was very busy, and as she was speaking to a gentleman in a carriage, one of her admirers came by and bowed and waved. "I dared not return the salute", she wrote, "or the gentleman might have thought my over-politeness directed at himself!" Louisa often mentions sewing jobs she has done to help with the upholstering: making a mattress case, a bolster case, two blind tapes, etc. She tidied the show-room and work-room. She also helped at home, mending the coat of her young brother Owen (who was nine that year); making lard, pork pies, gooseberry jam and all kinds of pies and cakes. She was not so keen on all the household duties. She wrote: "Washing washing; I declare it seems nothing but washing at our house. How soon a month passes and each month has its washing day." What a lot there must have been, with a wash day only once a month!

Henley Street where the Hancoxes lived had insufficient garden, so James had acquired what Louisa called the 'New Town garden'. Here Louisa went with her sister Harriet, and young brother, Owen. One day they planted convolvolins (sic), another day some gilly-flowers; on yet another visit, a Holy Thistle! Sometimes they had a bonfire with shavings and "all old sticks and a quantity of bad hay". The garden had a summer-house, and on 17th June, they papered it with lining paper.

Much of Louisa's interest was centred in the Baptist Chapel in Payton Street, where the family now worshippped. On January 1st she opens the Diary by recording that she "Arose at six and went to a Prayer Meeting, thus commencing as I would wish to continue the year by praying and praising God." On January 7th she assisted the singers in the evening "at the request of Mr. Bebb" and returned with him to supper. She taught in the Baptist Sunday School and took her work seriously, attending a teachers' Quarterly Meeting on March 27th, after which she wrote: "A sweet spirit of unity and friendship seemed to pervade the heart of every teacher present." Mr. Bebb then accompanied her home. (There is frequent mention of young men who came to the home both invited and uninvited). The Sunday school was extended into a secular night school to give additional help in reading and writing to the Sunday School children. She and Mr. Bebb were two of the four teachers.

Louisa was a keen musician and the owner of a piano (its delivery on February 9th is recorded). She also played the organ regularly for the Chapel Services except for a few weeks early in the year when she was unwell. On her resuming the playing on February 11th for the evening service, she records that "John (one of her admirers) persisted in pulling the stops out for me. We did not break down in the singing" (as she half-expected). This John's attention became tiresome, and on June 26th we read, "though perhaps I appeared pleased with him, I was far from being gratified with his over polite conduct." She had also had to rebuff another admirer: "Mr. Sugden came to speak to me; I dare not hesitate to say no to his offer, he left after tea with very different feelings from what he had hoped or expected." Mr. Sugden, the young Chapel pastor, had been an almost daily visitor, sometimes contriving to spend the whole day with the Hancox family and calling, for instance, on the pretext of borrowing some gum for his postage stamps. He once "came in very unceremoniously while Mr. Bebb was here."

As the summer progressed Louisa fell ever more deeply in love with Jeremiah Bebb. On July 26th, she wrote: "Soon after twelve we started for Welcombe..The gentlemen played at cricket until teatime, then we went round the gardens and hothouses, after which we danced in the temple: Mr. Bebb came at eight and though it began raining... yet a feeling of content and happiness which all day I had sought in vain took possession of me. Can it be that the presence of him who has always seemed indifferent and reserved to me should create in me feelings that the kindness and attention of my friends had failed to awaken. During the day I appeared the gayest and merriest of the party but this was all assumed. Could anyone have seen my heart they would have found it mingled not in those gay

Chapter 2. Birthplace of the Bard

scenes of pleasure, but wandered on to the approaching hour which, I determined, should decide whether I might hope to gain the loved one or ever must despair to be loved by him, who only can gain my heart."

A few days later her doubts were resolved: "August 5th: An eventful day in my life, for I may no longer consider myself to be free, yet to be in bondage is sweet since he to whom my heart is bound, is what I always fondly hoped and wished my dearest earthly friend might be," and on August 7th her father gave his consent. Her birthday (August 15th) entry is brief: "Today I am seventeen.. Mr. Bebb arrived, spent a pleasant hour together, he gave me a nice book entitled 'The beauties of Modern Poetry', and also a lock of his hair."

The overall picture from the Diary is of a hard-working, sensible girl, who got a great deal of fun out of life. She attended Chapel assiduously, although for her the visits were sweetened by the presence of "Mr. Bebb". She was obviously totally trusted by her parents to behave well, a trust she did not abuse. She was out late frequently, often until eleven or twelve, sometimes with Mr. Bebb and at other times with her girl friends. She enjoyed telling jokes and making people laugh. She went on "sprecing excursions" with her friends, coming back late at night. On one such, "a party of us went to Tiddington to tea. A. and I amused ourselves with riding about (her father had just given her a pony) and breaking down branches of apple and pear trees to obtain the fruit." (presumably in her friend's orchard). Boating on the Avon was another form of entertainment, taking visiting friends "nearly to Tiddington and back home to dinner at two". Her reference to the famous Stratford Mop is only that her parents went to it that year and stayed till after ten. But she mentions briefly the May Fair (14th May) and the Cheese Fair (25th September). Cheese-making was an important country industry at that time. A great thrill, when visiting an uncle at Brandon (between Coventry and Rugby), was to go down to the station to see the trains, and actually to travel on one for a visit to Coventry and back.

On occasion, Louisa records that she was unwell: on 17th March, her doctor (Mr. Southam Burman MRCS of Wood Street) prescribed a mustard plaster on her side; but on 1st September she noted: "Not so well; took two or three sorts of medicine". She was then grieving greatly for her friend Bessy, who was mortally ill. She frequently visited Bessy, "my earliest friend and most loved companion", who died on September 4th. A few days before "Mr. Bebb came at eight, found me in the garden...relieving my heart of its weight of sadness by showers of tears." October 3rd was pronounced a "fast day" by order of the Bishop. Mr. Bebb spent the afternoon with her; at six she went to a friend's where several others, including her betrothed, had gathered. "We did have a spree. After tea Bebb and I went a walk up the Warwick road; we did not reach home till after twelve." She adds, "Patent way of keeping fasts."

Louisa went several times to Welcombe where the family obviously had friends. The gentlemen played cricket; they went round the gardens and hot houses and afterwards danced in the Temple. In mid-October, she had another outing which she records in full. A Mr. William Bennett, who had returned to Stratford-on-Avon on September 28th after a seven-year absence in America, invited her to go with him to see his sister at school at Barford. It is rather surprising that, engaged as Louisa already was, she consented, and was allowed to go about with men friends, quite unchaperoned. This is her account of the day's outing: "Mr. Bennett called directly after breakfast we started in our pony carriage and went straight to Leamington Spa instead of as I had expected to Barford. William ordered dinner at One and while it was preparing we went a walk. We returned to dine and afterwards he took me down the Parade. At five we started back and arrived at Barford just as they were beginning tea we stayed there about two hours then proceeded home. We talked on indifferent topics till we got to Caplows when he asked me if I was engaged. I knew his motive for asking me and endeavoured to evade the subject; but when he repeated the question I assured him that my engagement with Itala (which he was aware of) was an engagement of the heart, and that I did not, even if I could, break my vow to one I loved so well as Itala. He offered me many apparent inducements to become *his* wife he expressed his willingness to stay in England or to return to America, whichever I might think best, but I answered that any, and every, offer which he might

Chapter 2. Birthplace of the Bard

make would prove unavailing since they could never induce me to give him any but a negative answer. Finding it useless to urge his own suit further, he expressed his interest in my welfare and his wishes for my happiness, the same time entreating me to make sure that I really loved Itala Bebb and then to give him my entire affection and confidence, to be ever faithful and devoted to him." And she was. Jeremiah with his dark good looks; serious-minded; travelled, compared to her; was adored by her for seventy years. (See photos of both, taken 1905 opp.) We do not know how or why she came to call him 'Itala'.

At this point the Diary ends, except for another entry, seventeen years later: "September 26th, 1866: Seventeen years since this page was written by me in my Father's house. Tonight I am alone in my home in Wood Street, my dear husband is gone to the Mayor's Feast, my two little girls are at Great Alne and my darling boy is in bed. Where shall we be in another seventeen years. May God preserve and bless us all." Great Alne (Alcester) is where her brother Owen lived, and at that time also, James and Harriett Hancox. Her daughter, Minnie, wrote her first letter home to her 'Dear Mama', on bright blue note paper on this visit to her grandparents.

Louisa's "two little girls" were (Rosa) Minnie (b.3.1.1857, d.3.1.1945), and (Isabel) Lillian (b.19.2.1860, d.14.9.1944): both very gifted at Art. They both became Associates of The Royal Academy of The West, and The Royal College of Art in London, respectively. Lillian married a fellow Associate (Emil Scales Perkin whose name is said to come from Pierre de Quin, Lord of the Scilly Isles). Louisa's "darling boy" was her surviving son (Evelyn) Charles (Louis) Bebb (b. 1865). The first son had died in infancy. When Owen and his family moved to Bristol, Charles had the house next door in Fishponds Road (see Chap 6). Charles's son, Evelyn Douglas, became a well-known Methodist Minister; he it was who wrote the letter to 'The Times' about Shakespeare's Elm Tree. He compiled a book about the Bebb family, with many photographs and other memorabilia.

Louisa's only granddaughter, Isabel, used to go with her mother, Lillian Perkin, to spend every September until she was eight at Ridgeway Park House, near Bristol, where Louisa and Jeremiah lived for many years. I knew Isabel well, at the times we were both living in Oxford, and benefited from notes she left about her side of the family. Using these notes, and the I.G.I., and research of my own, I have learnt something of the history of the Bebbs. Louisa's husband came from Barton in Herefordshire, where his father, also Jeremiah, owned land. Jeremiah I married Mary Smith from nearby Staunton-on-Arrow on January 6th, 1823. On his marriage certificate, he is described as 'gentleman'. My cousin, Prue (Bebb), has miniature portraits of Jeremiah I and his wife Mary, painted at the time of their marriage, dressed in 'Jane Austen' costumes. He is wearing a bright blue cutaway coat, and she has a low-necked dress with a blue bodice with white lace at the neck and the ends of the short sleeves. (See Charles Brock's illustrations to the Macmillan edition of 'Pride and Prejudice').

Jeremiah I and Mary had two daughters: Mary Anne (1823) and Anna Maria (1825), before Jeremiah II (4.8.1826). He was followed by Catherine (Kate) (1828) and George (1831). It seems quite likely that the rather unusual name of Bebb came from the Flemish Huguenots named Baebe, fleeing to England after the Revocation of the Edict of Nantes (1685), when weavers are known to have gone to Welshpool. Perhaps Minnie and Lillian Bebb daughters of Jeremiah II inherited their artistic talent from their Huguenot forebears. Louisa did not meet any of her husband's sisters until two years after she was married when a lady was ushered into the drawing-room, who said, "I am your sister-in-law, Kate". Louisa had not even known that Jeremiah had any sisters. Kate outlived her husband, John Wall, who was fourteen years her junior. Isabel remembered her Great-aunt Kate as wearing "anglaises", those long curls which fell over the ears. Isabel also remembered her Grandma Louisa as a somewhat intimidating old lady, but kind and generous. Her Grandpa was "a dear, shaggy old man who called me Queenie and walked about with me on his shoulder while I clung to his thick curly hair". See photos opp.).

Ridgeway Park House was an enormous and ugly house. Isabel found the long corridors and high ceilings almost frightening, but the furniture was beautiful and the grounds attractive to a small child. A circular drive led past a Lodge dated 1704, lined for some yards on one side with Victoria plum-trees and a big mulberry tree. In September, the

Chapter 2. Birthplace of the Bard

(1) Jeremiah and Louisa Bebb at Ridgeway Park House in 1905
(2) Cook's Alley, Stratford-on-Avon; and 17 College street, Old Stratford.

Chapter 2. Birthplace of the Bard

fruit was ripe on them all. Under the great spreading cedar tree, cannon-balls that had fallen during a Cromwellian siege still lay around. (More details about Ridgeway in Chap 6).

Aunt Minnie (Bebb), Isabel wrote, was a painter of animals; she was asked to paint the head of a cat, postage-stamp size, for the Dolls' House presented to Queen Mary by the nation in 1924, and now in Windsor Castle. She lived with her parents at Ridgeway for many years and devoted herself to painting. She nearly had a very different kind of life. William Barton, a friend of her sister's husband, fell in love with her. Six of them, including Minnie and William Barton, arranged to meet in the Ante-Room to the Refreshment Room at the Royal Academy in London. Minnie arrived second to find her suitor on a couch, fast asleep. When the others came Minnie said she had refused him and sent him away. Over forty years later, Isabel heard her uncle ask Minnie what had happened? She replied that she had refused William Barton because she could never have married a man who drank. The others who were present exclaimed, "But he was a teetotaller!" William Barton had travelled all night, sitting up in the train to be there on time. He had then fallen asleep. Far from being a drunkard he was a thrifty man, as there were special cheap rates by night. About fifteen years later Minnie became engaged, but her fiancé died just before the wedding. In the late 1890's either Minnie or Lillian painted the delightful picture of Avon Mill House. (See Frontispiece.)

Louisa and Jeremiah had to wait nearly five years after their engagement (which took place on the day after Jeremiah's twenty-third birthday) until he was in a position to marry. In the 1851 Census, Jeremiah (24) was assistant to David Plumb (31) Ironmonger (born in Loxley) and his wife Sarah (39) from Birmingham. The Plumbs (including five children, aged between eight years and four months) all lived together (with Jeremiah) in Wood Street, Stratford-on-Avon. Jeremiah later had his own ironmonger's shop (helped by his father-in-law) at the corner of Wood Street and High Street. My mother's sister, Dorothy, left a note that they used to have a carving knife with 'J. Bebb Stratford-on-Avon' engraved on it. Louisa married Jeremiah in the Baptist Church, Payton Street, on March 25th, 1854: the same year that her Uncle William at Eatington was mourning the loss of his wife and all his children. (Chap 1).

As we know from Louisa's Diary entry, she and Jeremiah were living in Wood Street in 1866. By 1868 they had moved to Burton Street, Bath, from which they wrote to say they wished to continue their Baptist membership at Stratford-on-Avon as they had not yet been able to "unite with a church of our own denomination". In January, 1872, their names were removed from the Payton Street Church roll as non-attendants, as they had not sought fellowship with any Baptist Church in Bath "though repeatedly urged to do so". Perhaps it was at this time that Jeremiah became associated with the Salvation Army. He was never a full-time member, but he did preach at their Services over a considerable number of years, and when he was quite elderly the Salvation Army produced a post-card size photo of him with a tall top-hat, to be sold in aid of Salvation Army funds. He was then Treasurer for his branch of the Salvation Army, though not a full member. I cannot trace the church adherence of Jeremiah and Louisa in Bristol, but assume that by the turn of the century anyway they probably had connections with the Methodists. Louisa's younger brother, Owen, who moved to be near her in 1903, was buried by a Methodist minister; and as we have seen already, her grandson became one.

All branches of the family had their roots in the Church of England: in Tysoe (Warwickshire); Bretforton (Worcestershire); and Buckland (Gloucestershire). As the years went by, they were caught up in the wave of Non-conformism which swept the country. Various members of the family worshipped with Quakers, Baptists, Unitarians and Methodists. James and his son, Edmund Owen, were independent-minded men and free-thinking. In this, they closely resemble the Wallace forebears from North Northumberland on the other side of the family. James Hancox had joined the Baptist Church in Stratford-on-Avon in 1841, just a few months after he had taken his fourth and youngest child to be baptised at the parish church of Holy Trinity. His wife, Harriett, was also baptised into the Baptist Church in 1841.

Jeremiah Bebb was admitted to the church fellowship in Stratford-on-Avon on 1st October, 1848. He had been a member of the Independent church, Dudley, baptised by a

Chapter 2. Birthplace of the Bard

Family of **MRS JAMES HANCOX** of Stratford-on-Avon and her daughter **LOUISA BEBB**

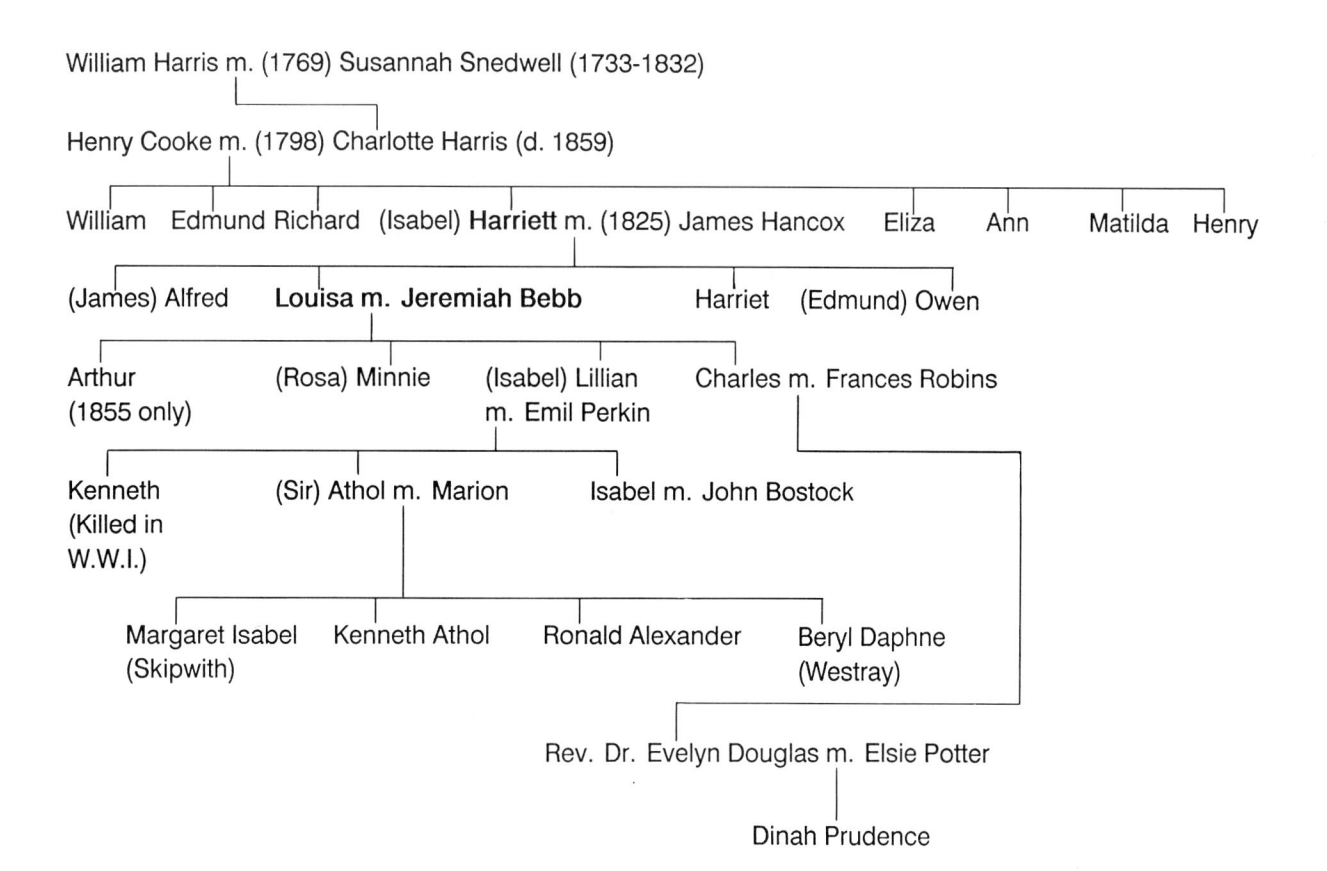

William Harris m. (1769) Susannah Snedwell (1733-1832)
└─ Henry Cooke m. (1798) Charlotte Harris (d. 1859)
   ├─ William
   ├─ Edmund
   ├─ Richard
   ├─ (Isabel) **Harriett** m. (1825) James Hancox
   │ ├─ (James) Alfred
   │ ├─ **Louisa** m. Jeremiah Bebb
   │ │ ├─ Arthur (1855 only)
   │ │ ├─ (Rosa) Minnie
   │ │ ├─ (Isabel) Lillian m. Emil Perkin
   │ │ │ ├─ Kenneth (Killed in W.W.I.)
   │ │ │ ├─ (Sir) Athol m. Marion
   │ │ │ │ ├─ Margaret Isabel (Skipwith)
   │ │ │ │ ├─ Kenneth Athol
   │ │ │ │ ├─ Ronald Alexander
   │ │ │ │ └─ Beryl Daphne (Westray)
   │ │ │ └─ Isabel m. John Bostock
   │ │ └─ Charles m. Frances Robins
   │ │   └─ Rev. Dr. Evelyn Douglas m. Elsie Potter
   │ │   └─ Dinah Prudence
   │ ├─ Harriet
   │ └─ (Edmund) Owen
   ├─ Eliza
   ├─ Ann
   ├─ Matilda
   └─ Henry

(1) Family Tree of Mrs James Hancox and Louisa Bebb
(2) Stratford-on-Avon Grammar School
(3) Silhouette of Owen Hancox as a boy, done by himself

29

Chapter 2. Birthplace of the Bard

Mr. Swan of Birmingham. The Baptist Minutes in Stratford-on-Avon record that Jeremiah's former Pastor sent a letter "highly satisfactory of his Christian Character". Louisa, Jeremiah's wife, was proposed for membership of the Baptist Church in Stratford-on-Avon in September 1854 (six months after her marriage) and was baptised on 5th November. Much later, when they all moved away from Stratford-on-Avon in different directions, their Membership lapsed, but not before 1857, when James Hancox gave land to the Trustees of the Baptist Church in Payton Street, presumably for them to erect a Sunday School (opened in 1861). Baptist Meetings began in Stratford-on-Avon in 1826; and the present Chapel was erected in 1835, though refurbished and re-opened in 1842. When James and Harriett returned to Stratford-on-Avon in about 1873, he was re-instated in the roll of Baptist Church members. They remained in the list of communicant members at Payton Street until their deaths in 1884 and 1895, respectively. Yet, as we know, Harriett, who had been unable to attend the chapel services from 1887 because of infirmity, was buried in her family vault in Holy Trinity.

James's going, as was his coming, was somewhat mysterious. There are two records of his baptism in 1804 (unique as far as I know): one at Loxley, the other by the Rector (Reverend James Davenport) of Stratford-on-Avon. I could not find any record of his burial at first. He died on April 8th, 1884 at his home, "The Limes", Alcester Road, Stratford-on-Avon, of pneumonia, brought on, my Aunt Dorothy said, after he was shutting a five-barred gate with difficulty, and he slipped and lay in the wet and mud some time before he was found. He was eighty years old, and outlived all his siblings, so far as I know. The notices in the paper were brief and cryptic. In two successive weekly issues of the 'Stratford-on-Avon Herald', it said: 'DEATHS: on 8th inst. at The Limes, Stratford-on-Avon, James Hancox aged eighty years (in his eighty-first year)'. After the first notice on April 11th, it added: 'Friends accept this the only intimation'. There were *no* details given about the funeral. I looked for the burial in the Baptist records. No luck. I tried the Loxley Burial Register in case he had returned to his birth place. No sign. The Record Office had told me James was buried in the 'new' non-denominational cemetery on Evesham Road on 12 April, 1884 as they know that no burials were carried out in the Parish *churchyard* after 1880. After an hour spent searching the gravestones in this cemetery on what was luckily a mild day for November, I helped the groundsman to search the records. No James Hancox buried there. Finally, almost by chance, I saw an entry in the Burial Register for the Parish Church, Holy Trinity: James Hancox buried April 12th, 1884, aged eighty - (signed) G. Arburthnot. I'm still wondering whether his widow arranged for him to go into her Family Vault under Lime Tree Avenue, and wished it kept quiet! I can see no other explanation. James left a Will, dated 17th February, 1869, in which he left his 'dear Wife Harriett' his sole executrix. She did not sell 'The Limes'; it reappears in Owen's Will, dated October 26th, 1894 (see Chap 6). James's Will was so simple, short and concise that probate was granted in less than seven weeks.

Harriet, James Hancox's younger daughter, married into the well-known and remarkable family of the "Worcestershire Bomfords". They have an ancestral tree, parts of which go back four hundred years, drawn up relatively recently by one of the present members of the family. Harriet's husband was Herbert Bomford of the Manor Farm, Great Washbourne, near Beckford, Gloucestershire. (See photo p.32). She was married in June, 1865, from the Old Mill House, Great Alne, where her parents went to keep house for their younger son, Edmund Owen. Harriet had four sons: Seymour, Henry, James Herbert and Nelson. The older two emigrated to Canada and the youngest to South Africa. Bert, the third son, became a journalist and then an Auctioneer and "quite a successful public man in Alcester". Harriet and Herbert moved from Great Washbourne to Oversley Lodge Farm, from which he was for a while in partnership in the milling business with my grandfather, his brother-in-law, Edmund Owen Hancox. When Herbert died, Harriet went to live at No. 19, College Street, Stratford-on-Avon, until she died in her nineties. As I was writing this chapter, my cousin Henry Hancox drove me for a day all round these Warwickshire villages to many of which my Bomford cousins had already taken me (though Tysoe was a first with Henry). He also took me to No. 19, College Street, Old Stratford, to show me where he had visited "Aunt Harriet" as a boy. She was a fearsome old lady, who all but terrified him. His abiding memory of her is her insistence that she used to drive her carriage horses herself and not depend on a coachman. It was at the

Chapter 2. Birthplace of the Bard

Ordnance Survey Map of Stratford-on-Avon, 1885
Arrows: 1. The Limes 2. Cook's Alley 3. Baptist Church 4. Grammar School

Chapter 2. Birthplace of the Bard

Great Washbourne Farm that Charles Hancox, one of Owen's sons, was to have his accident.

The Atch Lench branch of the Bomfords (the family owned farmland all over Worcestershire) were totally committed Baptists, building and maintaining the Baptist Chapel there, which is now a listed building. Later there was a second link with the Bomfords, when my mother's first cousin, Mary (Mollie) Fowler, married John (Jack) Bomford and lived thereafter at Sherrif's Lench, north of Evesham. Her children (now my age or more) have been for me a most lucky find. They have welcomed me, though we had barely or never met before; given me hospitality on a generous scale; driven me around the countryside; and supplied me with much information. Without them, my search would have been more difficult and much less fun.

Like Shakespeare, James's youngest child (Edmund) Owen, my grandfather, was born in Stratford and went to King Edward's Grammar School. (See photo p.29). Before he sat the Entrance exam in 1849 his older brother, Alfred, took him and had his curls cut off. The test consisted of reading a chapter out of the Bible, writing and sums (according to a note left by Nancie's sister Dorothy). Edmund Owen was so small when he started at about the age of nine, that the others called him 'Bantam'; "his pluck", wrote his eldest son, "being in inverse proportion to his size". He was very good at his lessons, especially Maths and languages, and soon learnt to write "a most perfect copper-plate hand". Once, when he reacted too quickly to a boy who by accident stuck the point of his steel pen in Owen's hand, Owen knocked the boy off his seat. The punishment for the display of temper was to write one thousand times, 'Nemo omnium mortalium semper satis est'. He never forgot the truth contained in it: 'No-one is always wise'. The two black marks from the pen nib remained on his hand all his life; his rather quick temper stayed too - though Nancie never spoke of it.

In Owen's seventeenth year, (1857), his father apprenticed him to be a corn miller, to John Elvins of Great Alne Mills, near Alcester. It is interesting to me that both James's sons became corn millers, though there had been none that we know about in the family before, except perhaps a long tradition from centuries in the corn-growing district of Tysoe. In time, Owen's eldest son, Jack, took over at Great Alne Mill, followed by his son all his working life. Perhaps the genes of 'Cook' and 'Hans the Cook' were responsible. When Owen finished his apprenticeship, his father sold his business in Stratford-on-Avon and bought Great Alne Mill for his son. James and Harriett moved to the Mill, to run the house for Owen until he married in 1867. They then moved to Beckford to be near their newly-married daughter Harriet at Great Washbourne (see Chap 5).

James and Harriett moved around, always to be near family; but in the early 1870's James bought land in Stratford-on-Avon, to build himself their very spacious dwelling in its own grounds with a paddock, called 'The Limes'. They lived there until James died in 1884, when Harriett went to a smaller house at No. 17, College Street (see photo p.27). until her death in 1895, as described earlier in this chapter. Alfred was the only member of our Hancox family to return to live in Stratford, so far as I know, by the following year, though Owen's widow was to come there about fifteen years later, with my mother. One of the Fowlers from Evesham had been in Stratford-on-Avon since soon after 1860, when her father had bought her James Hancox's business. She was Nancie's eldest Fowler aunt, Aunt Bessie. (See next Chap.)

Manor Farm, Great Washbourne, Gloucestershire: home of Harriet and Herbert Bomford

Chapter 2. Birthplace of the Bard

(1) James Hancox (1804-84), Stratford-on-Avon: Nancie's grandfather. On the back of this miniature, which has just come to hand, Nancie wrote his name and dates and "Buried in the family vault"! (See p.30)
(2) Great Alne Mill, near Alcester

Chapter 3. The Quaker Connection

A copy of the first and last pages of the letter sent to Elizabeth Ann Hawkes, by a member of the Society of Friends, 3 months before she left home for Ackworth Friends' School

Chapter 3

The Quaker Connection

The Hancox side of the family is fairly well-documented but it has not been so easy to unearth details about the forebears of **Anne Fowler**, my mother's mother. For Census Returns, her father, Henry, said simply that he came from Upton-on-Severn. I can find nothing in the Parish Registers to substantiate this. The I.G.I. offered only one Henry Fowler in the year he was born (1803): son of Humphrey and Ann, Chipping Norton, Oxon (Particular Baptists), and there is no known connection. There were several Fowlers in **Evesham**, settled in trade: some had been silk weavers. They may have been relatives, and the reason for Henry's coming there for his apprenticeship as a cabinet-maker, but it is all speculation.

Henry Fowler's wife, **Elizabeth Ann Hawkes**, although equally reticent about her early life until after her family had grown up, left some clues; and by gathering in all that was known about her and following up every lead, a good deal can be learnt. My mother knew that her grandmother E.A.Hawkes had gone to Ackworth School (a Quaker Boarding School in West Yorkshire, founded in 1779, where my sister and I also went in the 1930's). There was also the letter, written to Elizabeth Ann by a member of the Society of Friends to give her guidance, which my mother had framed. For years, it hung above my sister's bed. Now it has come to me. (see opp.). Beyond that, we knew of no other Quaker connection.

I heard that Elizabeth Ann Hawkes was born in **Bretforton**, a picturesque village, a few miles outside Evesham, Worcestershire, in 1811. Visiting Bretforton, I found many of the buildings unchanged since the days of Elizabeth Ann, indeed since centuries before: the sixteenth-century Fleece Inn; the remarkable old barn in the gardens of the old Manor House; the building that housed the blacksmith's forge, and the house beside it where Elizabeth Ann and her sisters were born, beside the Church. Elizabeth Ann's half-brothers and half-sister had been born there, too.

Elizabeth Ann's mother, also Elizabeth, was born Hadland; her mother was the daughter of John and Ann Ingles: all from Bretforton. Elizabeth's brother, Richard Hadland, had a daughter who married the John Butcher who planted the Lime Tree Avenue at Holy Trinity Church, Stratford-on-Avon, and the vines at Windsor Castle (Chap 2). John Butcher's son, John, had two daughters, well-known to me: Emily and Elsie. Elsie wrote down her recollections: 'Looking Back at Ninety One' and its 'Postscript' in 1971, where I learnt about the lime trees her grandfather planted. Perhaps he also supplied the trees for James Hancox's new house 'The Limes'. One of the Butcher ladies met by chance Nancie's mother in the train when she was travelling home from London after Nancie's wedding, in June, 1918, so she was thrilled to get a first-hand account of the occasion to take back to the family.

Bretforton (with fourteen different ways of spelling between A.D. 709-1546, they say) seems to mean simply 'a broad ford'. The Ford family had belonged there for generations - probably originally 'the people who lived by the ford'. Elizabeth Hadland (Elizabeth Ann's mother) was married first to **William Ford**, the blacksmith whose parents William and Ann (née Lawrence) had married in Bretforton (November 29th, 1764). Their son, William (bapt. December 14th, 1765), had brothers Thomas (bapt. October 1st, 1769) and Henry (bapt. March 27th, 1782); and sisters Ann (bapt. January 1st, 1772) who married Henry Byrd (August 15th, 1794), Sarah (bapt. September 29th, 1776) and Susannah (bapt. December 5th, 1779).

William and Elizabeth Ford (née Hadland) had three sons: James (bapt. 1794); William (1798) and Moses (1799); and a daughter Winifred (1797). Sadly, William, the father, features in the Burial List at Bretforton on February 9th, 1800; he was only thirty-four years old. Did he have some accident at the forge, or get knocked down in icy conditions? He must have been physically strong to be a blacksmith for twenty years. The son, William, had also died at six months old in 1798 and Henry, brother of William, the

Chapter 3. The Quaker Connection

Family of **ELIZABETH ANN HAWKES** of Bretforton, Worcestershire

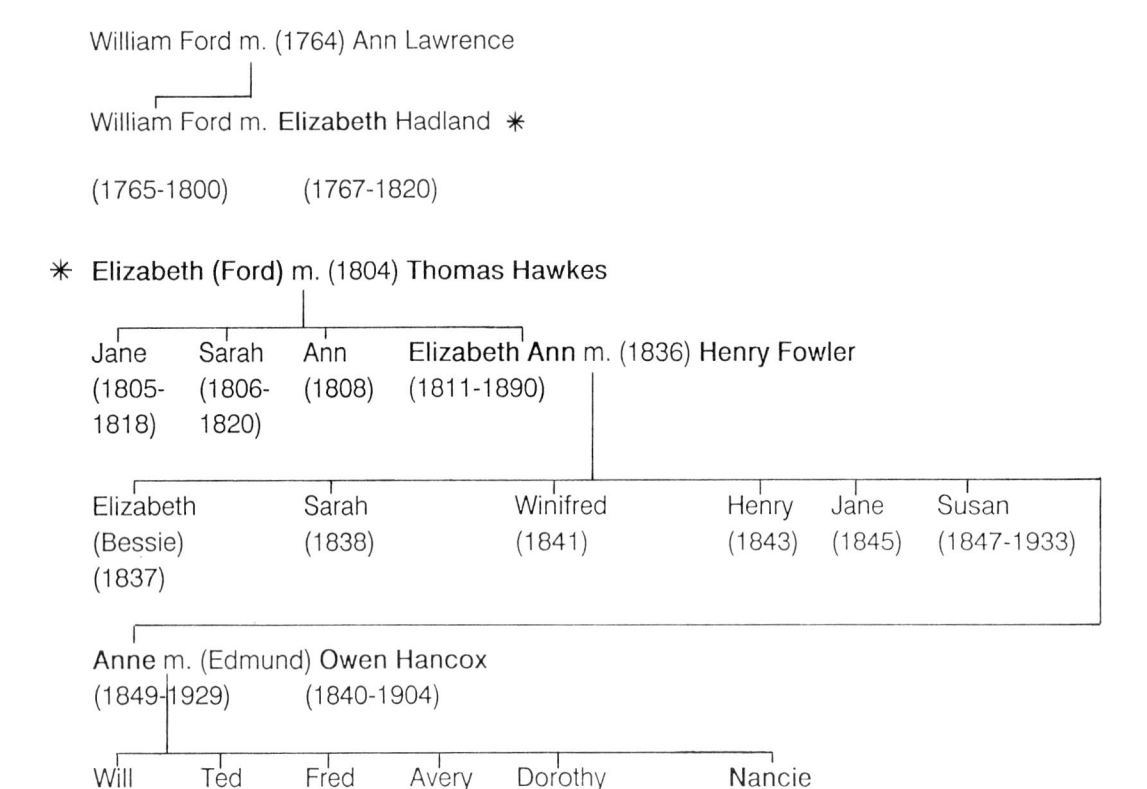

```
William Ford m. (1764) Ann Lawrence
        |
William Ford m. Elizabeth Hadland  *
(1765-1800)     (1767-1820)
```

* Elizabeth (Ford) m. (1804) Thomas Hawkes

```
Jane      Sarah    Ann      Elizabeth Ann m. (1836) Henry Fowler
(1805-    (1806-   (1808)   (1811-1890)
1818)     1820)

Elizabeth   Sarah     Winifred    Henry    Jane     Susan
(Bessie)    (1838)    (1841)      (1843)   (1845)   (1847-1933)
(1837)
```

Anne m. (Edmund) Owen Hancox
(1849-1929)   (1840-1904)

Will   Ted   Fred   Avery   Dorothy   Nancie

(1) Family Tree of Elizabeth Ann Hawkes
Bretforton: (2) the blacksmith's forge, used by William Ford, and
Thomas Hawkes (small door on right). Note the uneven roof
(3) the adjoining dwelling-house, lived in by the blacksmith and family

Chapter 3. The Quaker Connection

father, may have died six months before he did in 1799 at the age of sixteen. Another version has this Henry Ford emigrating to the U.S.A.; though not so far as we know related to the Henry Ford of motor-car fame! Elizabeth Ford was now on her own except for her mother-in-law and her family, with (probably) three small children. I'm told she had to sell the blacksmith's shop and the adjoining house (see photos opp.) "to pay outstanding debts".

John Ingles (ancestor of Elizabeth Ford née Hadland), had bought this Blacksmith's forge in Bretforton from John Ashwin in 1603, so I suppose it may have come to William Ford on his marriage to Elizabeth Hadland, through her mother. At some point Thomas Hawkes, Elizabeth Ford's second husband, must have bought it back, as it was inherited by his daughter Elizabeth Ann Hawkes, whose husband, Henry Fowler, eventually sold it after he backed a bill for a friend who was unable to pay and he needed the money to meet the bill.

The 1851 Census for Bretforton shows:

Elizabeth Ford (59) widow Blacksmith employing one man. (She came from Moreton-in-Marsh, Gloucestershire).

Anne Ford (31) Unmarried daughter Seamstress - born in Bretforton. Perhaps when Thomas Hawkes left, between 1811 and 1818, William Ford's son James became blacksmith. From the Census Returns, I knew Elizabeth Ford was widowed by 1851. Thomas Hawkes's Will which has just come to hand, tells me she had already lost her husband and was herself designated 'Blacksmith', by 1841. In the early 1860's I find that George Ford was the blacksmith in Bretforton. Let us suppose he was James's son, for whom his widowed mother was keeping the business going. By 1868 George is no longer listed there. Today, the premises are used for other purposes.

After William Ford's death in 1800, **Thomas Hawkes** from **Buckland**, beyond Broadway, Gloucestershire, came as Village Blacksmith. Nearly five years later, he married Elizabeth Ford, his predecessor's widow. He is recorded as twenty-eight years old, she thirty-eight years old. The ceremony took place in Bretforton Church on December 16th, 1804; one of the witnesses was Susanna Ford, younger sister of the late William (Her sampler, worked as a child, is still in the family). Over the next six years Thomas and Elizabeth Hawkes had four daughters, in contrast to the sons borne by Elizabeth to William Ford: Jane (born December 1st, 1805 and bapt. February 9th, 1806); Sarah (born November 28th, 1806, bapt. January 25th, 1807); Ann (born January 28th, 1808, bapt. May 29th, 1808) and **Elizabeth Ann** (born March 17th, 1811, bapt. June 30th, 1811). Bretforton Baptismal Register is very unusual in giving dates of birth as well as baptism, for some years. Although Elizabeth Ann's date of birth is given as 17th March in the Baptismal Register, it is recorded as 18th March on her gravestone and 19th in the Ackworth School entry!

Jane Hawkes died at the age of thirteen and was buried at Bengeworth, on the outskirts of Evesham, so the family must have moved there from Bretforton before 1818. Sarah (and her mother) both died at the beginning of 1820. Ann had lived only a few months, buried at Bretforton August 4th, 1808. That same year Elizabeth Hawkes also lost her first mother-in-law, Ann Ford (61), mother of William, buried at Bretforton. So, from the age of eight, Elizabeth Ann was an only, motherless child. Sarah had worked a sampler at the age of eleven. It consists of verses of a hymn, and hangs now in the house of a relative in Evesham.

As I was studying the Bretforton Registers on July 13th, 1989, I came across this entry in the middle of the Marriage Registers: July 13th, 1808 - hottest day ever remembered - people died in the fields, 14th and 15th, 1808 - very very hot until 2.00 am on 16th there was the most tremendous thunderstorm. Many stones, like quarter pound brass weights with a white transparent spot in the middle. It broke all the windows "that stood in a North East direction".

Thomas Hawkes, father of Elizabeth Ann, was known to us all simply as the man who came to be blacksmith when William Ford died in Bretforton. Luckily my cousins knew that he'd come from Buckland, a tiny village so close to the county border that I thought it was in Worcestershire and not Gloucestershire. Perhaps it was once. The county

Chapter 3. The Quaker Connection

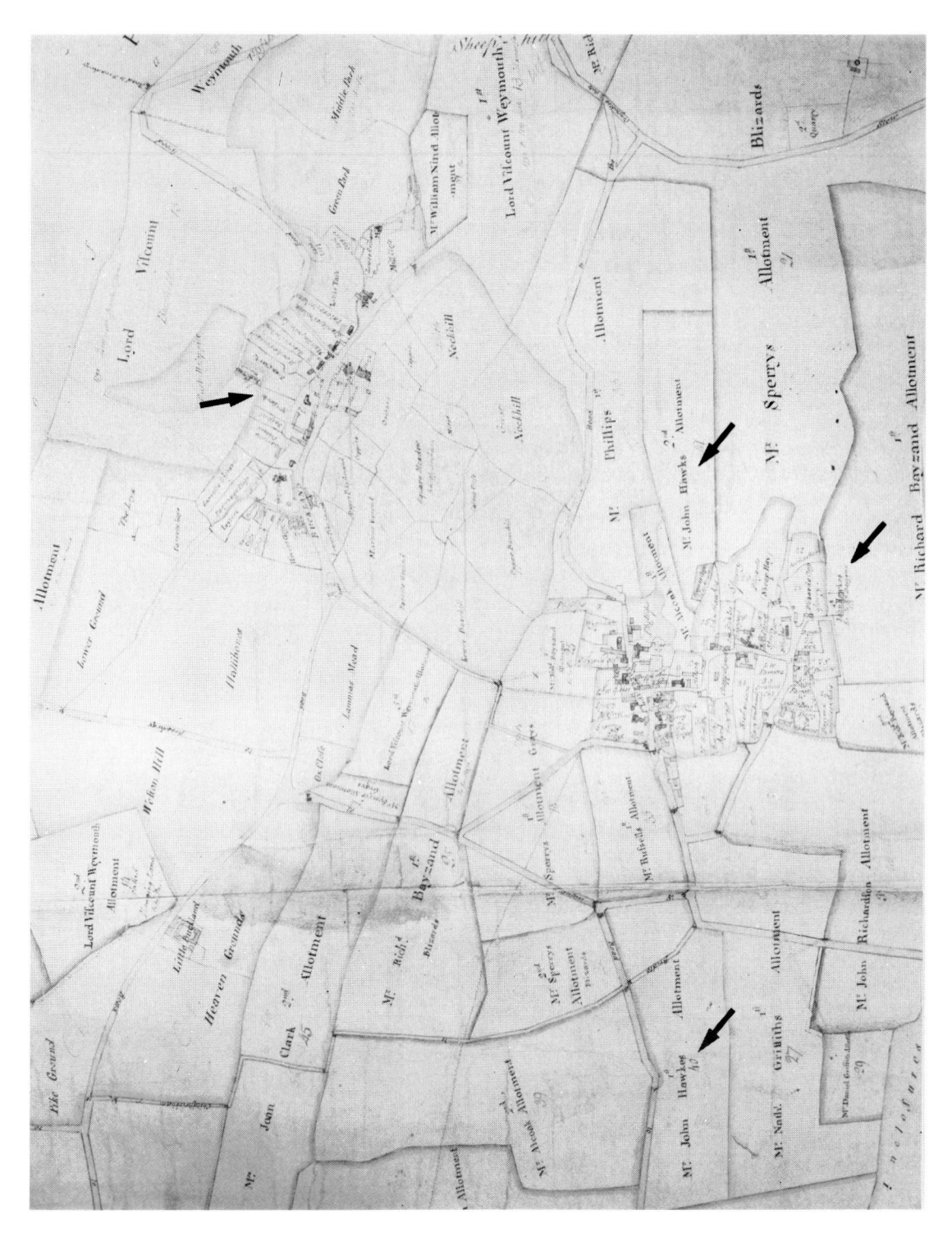

Inclosure Map of Buckland Village, 1779 (D 2001)

Chapter 3. The Quaker Connection

boundaries have fluctuated remarkably in that part of the country, over the years. A chance meeting in a little café in Evesham, and a few words exchanged with a stranger, told me that Buckland is in Gloucestershire. I pursued this, first by letter, and by the I. G. I. lists in Edinburgh, and then by a special visit to Gloucester Record Office.

Again, good fortune helped. A much earlier searcher, whose family had come from Buckland, had studied the parish registers and compiled them in a book, easy to read. In half-a-day, I found Thomas and his family (back several generations), his neighbours, and the probable links with Evesham and district. I also found a map of Buckland village and surrounding land, showing enclosures of 1779, and including fields, orchards, houses, etc. owned by members of the Hawkes family. (see Map opp.)

Among the curious sixteenth-century names in the Baptismal Register: Blissard, Warckman, Apparie, Izode, Gylks and Gloceter - and the homeless women designated 'a wandering woman' and 'Agnes, a goer aboute': there are records of 'Haucks', changing gradually to 'Hawkes'.

The earliest entry of a Hawkes in the Buckland parish register is when Katherine Hawkes married John Wormington (the name of a nearby village) in January, 1545; also, Anne Hawkes (married 1557) and Frances Hawkes (married 1614). They each must have had a father (or mother, anyway) of the same name when they were born (before records began in 1539) and their parents would be Hawkes of one generation earlier. So we are back at least to before 1500. There were a number of Hawkes in the surrounding villages in the mid-sixteenth century e.g. Anthony, church warden in Little Barrington (1551); Thomas, sidesman at the church in Lower Swell (1556 and '68); William, church warden in Stoke Orchard (1551); and many others.

The earliest Thomas Hawkes definitely related to ours had a son Thomas, baptised 1668. Thomas senior was blacksmith in the neighbouring village of Laverton (also on the 1779 Map). His son, Thomas, (bapt. 1668) and his wife, Mary, had at least seven children between 1698 and 1711 (see chart p.41). Their son, Thomas (bapt. 1706), married Martha Dyer on February 12th, 1731. They had at least eight children, one of whom, Joseph (bapt. 1747), and his wife, Jane, also had at least eight children. I have not yet traced Jane's family; the marriage is not recorded in the county of Gloucestershire, nor in any of the surrounding villages. Their eldest child **Thomas** (bapt. 1777) carried on the trade of the preceding generations of his family and became a blacksmith. In this capacity he moved to Bretforton by 1800, and married Elizabeth Ford in 1804.

In 1791, when Thomas-who-went-to-Bretforton was nearly fourteen, a girl from Buckland, Elizabeth Davis, married Thomas Stephens of Offenham, the next village to Bretforton. Perhaps that is how Thomas Hawkes heard of the vacancy there? Perhaps they, or other friends, coming to the wedding of Thomas's sister, Hannah, in 1800, told of William Ford's death. All travellers brought news; and those on horseback would go from one blacksmith to another. Ten years before Thomas was born, a Thomas Rose of Bretforton had married Ann Roberts of Buckland, most likely a relative of the Hawkes through a Hawkes - Roberts wedding in 1732; another possible link.

Hoping to learn more, somehow, about Elizabeth Ann Hawkes, I got in touch with Ackworth School. They sent me a copy of the booklet produced for their bi-centenary in 1979, from which I realised that Elizabeth Ann Hawkes's father anyway must have been a member of the Society of Friends, as only the children of such were allowed to go to Ackworth, during its first one hundred years. Mrs. Betty Limb, an archivist at the school, read out to me over the telephone all that was recorded about Elizabeth Ann:

'Elizabeth Ann Hawkes born March 19th, 1811; aged twelve in 1823 when admitted

Thomas and Elizabeth Hawkes - parents - of Evesham

Elizabeth Ann Hawkes sponsored by Worcestershire Monthly Meeting

Went home April 26th, 1825 with John Fricker'.

John Fricker was not known at the school, nor known to be connected with them. (He may have been a Friend, able to travel that way, or a member of Worcestershire Monthly Meeting, who agreed to fetch her home. There were Frickers in the Evesham district at

Chapter 3. The Quaker Connection

that time).

The realisation that Elizabeth Ann's parents were Quakers sent me to find any documents about the Society of Friends in Evesham, in the Worcestershire Record Office. I discovered a tantalising reference to her father, Thomas Hawkes, in a membership list dated 1837-59 inclusive: "Thomas Hawkes in the employ of Richard Burlingham, Evesham, *from preceding list*. Dissolved by Death 30 January, 1853 - registered 31 January at Evesham". But the preceding list was missing; and the only other list, 1899-1922, revealed no 'Hawkes' at all. I wrote to the Society of Friends in London asking for help. They sent me some details about Richard Burlingham (1779-1840), born the year that Ackworth School had been founded, and who died the year my maternal grandfather, Edmund Owen Hancox, was born in Stratford-on-Avon.

Richard Burlingham had an ironmongery business in High Street, Evesham, where he had gone to live in 1805. He was very active in the ministry for the Society of Friends from 1809 onwards, and especially from 1830-40. He travelled widely in Great Britain and Ireland, attending yearly Meeting in Dublin four times, as well as General Meeting in Aberdeen. He was a Birthright Member (viz. entered by his parents at birth) of the Society and obviously an important Friend. Needing some-one to run his business in his absence, he took Thomas Hawkes into his employment. Thomas would be increasingly involved as Burlingham was away so much. Thomas must have admired his employer and his beliefs, because he joined the Society of Friends himself and worshipped at Evesham Meeting in Cowl Street. The Meeting house, with a delightful sheltered garden-cum-graveyard at the back. is still there (see photo opp.). Cousins of mine - on my father's side - now worship there. When Thomas's wife (54) and daughter Sarah (13) died (on February 2nd and January 18th, 1820), they were buried in Quaker ground at Evesham, although "not in membership" as the record says. The local members of the Society of Friends developed a 'concern' for little Elizabeth Ann and, in 1822, the Worcestershire Monthly Meeting arranged to sponsor her, and send her to Ackworth School for two years for her education. It seems to me a hard thing and a brave thing for both Thomas and his daughter to have done.

This much my mother had often told us: Thomas went with Elizabeth Ann to Derby by coach, which took a whole day. The following morning he put her on a second conveyance bound for Ackworth, and he went home, not to see her again for two years. The fees and the travelling expenses had to be found either by the parents or by the Society of Friends. There was an arrangement by which a parent could ask for the expenses of the journey, if necessary, according to the distance between home and school. 2d. per mile was allowed if over fifty miles, and the same for the return journey, IF the child stayed two years. Some parents would not take the money; and one parent walked (leading his horse) seventy miles to bring his boy to school, without claiming any assistance.

I have found, in a handkerchief sachet which I once made for my mother, and which came back to me, a beautifully-embroidered white brush and comb bag with "E.H." large and bold on the cover. This must have belonged to Elizabeth Ann. It reminded me instantly of the pyjama cases and brush and comb bags which my mother made for us to take when we went to Ackworth School, with our initials similarly embroidered. Made of linen, mine are still in use after nearly fifty-seven years. Elizabeth Ann's was made at least one hundred and sixty-five years ago.

Ackworth School was founded by Dr. John Fothergill, a prominent and much-admired London physician connected with St. Thomas's Hospital, London. A man of deep Quaker roots, his grandfather had been one of George Fox's early followers, imprisoned at Richmond, Yorkshire in 1678. His brother, Samuel, was a well-known Quaker preacher. Dr. Fothergill, who took a medical degree at Edinburgh University, wore the traditional style of Quaker dress. As was the Quaker custom, he refused to remove his hat before "any save God alone" (including the King).

Dr. Fothergill was born at Carr End, North Yorkshire, beside Semerwater, the lake near Aysgarth. One day he was riding on horseback in the vicinity of Ackworth when he saw the future school building standing empty and deserted. It had been built in the late 1750's and early 1760's, by the London Foundling Hospital. For some years before, they

Chapter 3. The Quaker Connection

Family of **THOMAS HAWKES** of Buckland, Gloucestershire

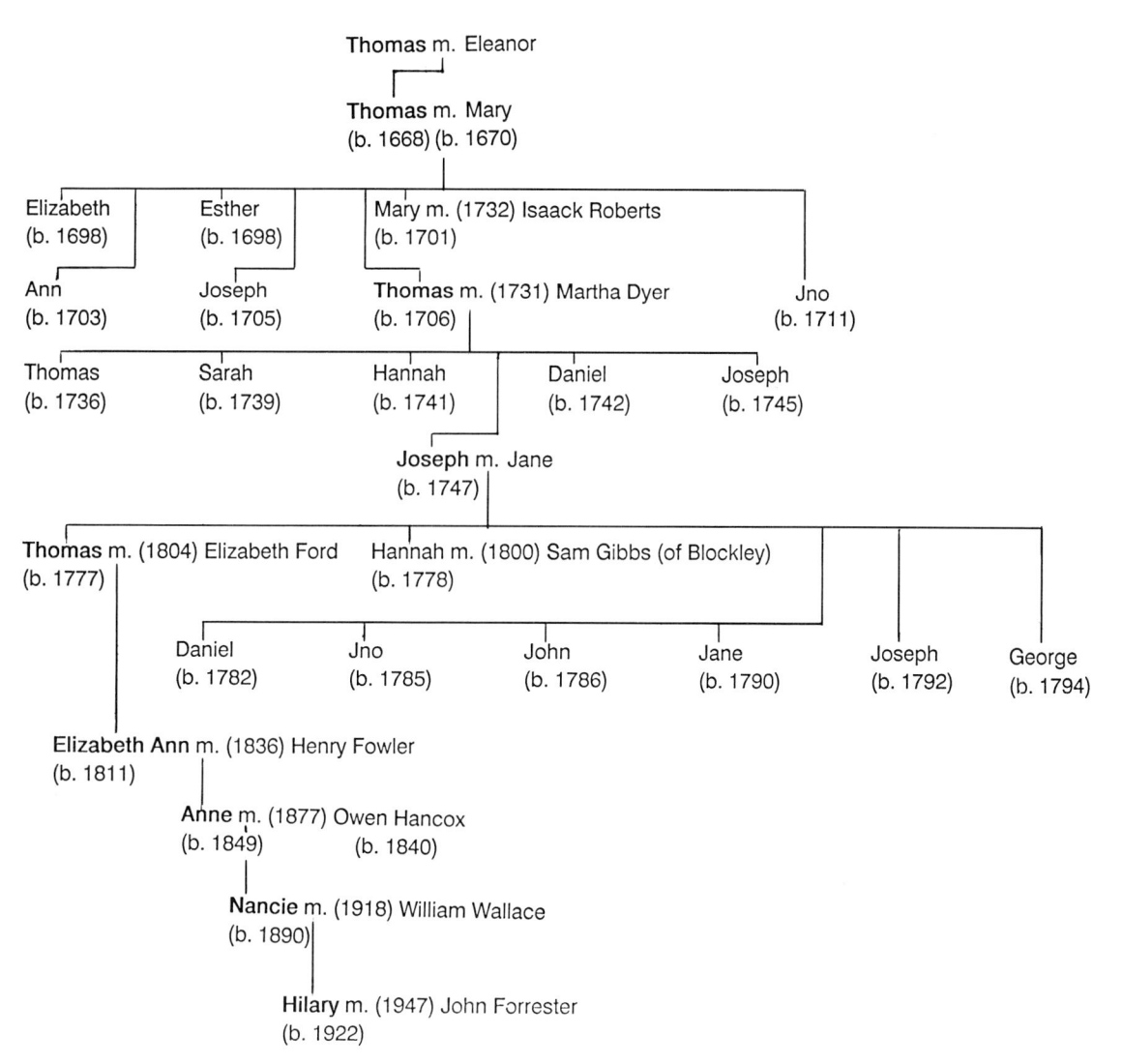

- Thomas m. Eleanor
  - Thomas m. Mary
    (b. 1668) (b. 1670)
    - Elizabeth (b. 1698)
    - Esther (b. 1698)
    - Mary m. (1732) Isaack Roberts (b. 1701)
    - Ann (b. 1703)
    - Joseph (b. 1705)
    - **Thomas** m. (1731) Martha Dyer (b. 1706)
      - Thomas (b. 1736)
      - Sarah (b. 1739)
      - Hannah (b. 1741)
      - Daniel (b. 1742)
      - **Joseph** m. Jane (b. 1745)
        - **Joseph** m. Jane (b. 1747)
          - **Thomas** m. (1804) Elizabeth Ford (b. 1777)
            - **Elizabeth Ann** m. (1836) Henry Fowler (b. 1811)
              - **Anne** m. (1877) Owen Hancox (b. 1849) (b. 1840)
                - **Nancie** m. (1918) William Wallace (b. 1890)
                  - **Hilary** m. (1947) John Forrester (b. 1922)
          - Hannah m. (1800) Sam Gibbs (of Blockley) (b. 1778)
          - Daniel (b. 1782)
          - Jno (b. 1785)
          - John (b. 1786)
          - Jane (b. 1790)
          - Joseph (b. 1792)
          - George (b. 1794)
    - Jno (b. 1711)

(1) Family Tree of Thomas Hawkes
(2) Evesham Friends' Meeting House
(3) The Terrace, Ackworth School

41

Chapter 3. The Quaker Connection

had sent infant foundlings to Ackworth to be reared by cottagers there and in the surrounding villages until they were about five years old. The aim was to rescue foundlings, nurture them in the country, employ them with spinning and weaving cloth, and place them as apprentices in nearby industrial areas. But there were so many children it was impossible to oversee them; out of a group of seventy-five girls aged seven who were apprenticed to Leeds manufacturers, only fifty-one survived - and in a very bad way - to be taken back to Ackworth.

In 1773, the Foundling Hospital at Ackworth, like other Branch Hospitals, had to close, as Government grants ceased to support them. The spacious and well-proportioned stone buildings, of two large wings linked by colonnades to the south-facing central "mansion house", were up for sale. When no buyers were interested, the London governors urged destruction of the buildings, hoping for a better price. Dr. Fothergill who was supported by the local Vicar persuaded the Society of Friends to open a boarding school for the children of Quaker parents "not in affluence". It was to be for boys and girls aged nine to fourteen. As such it offered a chance for Elizabeth Ann Hawkes to receive a wider education than she would have had at home, the companionship of other girls her own age, and the influence of older, caring women. The establishment of the school was a real pioneering act as the Quakers had been neglecting the intellectual training of the young while concentrating on the "significance of the inward revelation of the Truth".

On October 18th, 1779, a brother and sister, Barton and Ann Gates, arrived from Poole in Dorset as the first pupils. By the end of the year there were forty-nine pupils, and from then on the numbers rapidly increased. By 1780 there were one hundred and eighty boys and one hundred and twenty girls (about the same numbers as there were in our day in the 1930's).

Dr. Fothergill in his 'Letter to a Friend in the Country' (published 1778) stressed that an essential feature of Quaker education was the habituating of children "from their earliest infancy, at stated times, to silence and attention"; he saw it as of great advantage to them, both to advance in a religious life, and also as "the groundwork of the greatest human prudence". In the early days, the Meeting house was unheated and the benches they sat on were backless though both of these privations were corrected just before Elizabeth Ann Hawkes went. One writer described the girls entering the meeting house, "with gentle steps, all uniformly arranged in their white caps and tippets, which gave as they dropped successively, regularly and silently, into their places, the fanciful idea of a fall of snow".

In 1804, the year of Elizabeth Ann Hawkes's parents' marriage (and James Hancox's birth), two thousand oaks, ashes, elms and larches were planted at Ackworth. One of its features from early on was the Great Garden beyond the grass and the flagstones between the East and West Wings. (See p.47). Small individual gardens to give occupation in their leisure-time had been introduced for the boys.

By the time Elizabeth Ann joined the school in the fifth decade of its existence, many of the conditions had been ameliorated. Steam pipes had been introduced to heat the class-rooms; and hot air flues were placed under the floor in the Meeting house, where back rests for the benches were soon introduced and the flags boarded over. Discipline was strict, but after 1817, rewards for good behaviour were given as well as punishments for bad; and solitary confinement was substituted for excessive corporal punishment, which had never been the sadistic floggings sometimes found elsewhere. Indeed at times of rebellion among the pupils, these were often met with understanding and leniency.

The girls washed in a huge, rough trough; it was very cold and they got chilblains. Both boys and girls bathed in the BATH: cold water, fed by a Chalbeate spring with a yellow scum. It was about three-quarters of a mile from school, a forbidding-looking pool, surrounded by stone walls. The boys bathed naked with no towels, at six a.m., three days a week; on the other three days the girls had the use of the bath, wearing the worn-out "day dresses" of former scholars, often much too big, in place of bathing costumes. These dresses were of rough brown cotton, very simple and ankle length. They were worn with a large white pinafore and a little cap. The girls had two roller towels between the lot which was not much use. After the bathe, the children had to march back to school for their Spelling lesson before breakfast. Eventually the authorities allowed the pupils a piece of bread between swimming and spelling.

Chapter 3. The Quaker Connection

From 1821-1848, there was a voluntary society called the 'Association for the Improvement of the Mind', for essay-writing, the holding of meetings and the formation of a library and a museum. There was also a school periodical with articles, essays and verses (1821-7), called 'The Censor;' and during the exact time that Elizabeth Ann Hawkes was at school, the 'Ackworth Gazette', primarily for news items. Ackworth was well to the fore with such publications; Eton and Westminster already had periodicals, but Harrow (1828) and Rugby (1833) were later with their school newspapers, and debating society respectively.

Elizabeth Ann Hawkes would learn Reading, Spelling and English Grammar; Writing and Arithmetic, as did the boys. She would also learn sewing and knitting; (spinning had been abandoned in 1817). History and Geography were introduced as subjects of interest, in both lessons and leisure-hour pursuits. Poetry and Verse-speaking were also popular (as in my time). Latin was introduced for the most promising boys, the year Elizabeth Ann Hawkes left.

From 1816 onwards, every pupil was presented with a Bible - as I was when I went in 1933. Mine is an edition of the Authorised Version which states that the world began in 4004 B.C.. Elizabeth Ann would see Joseph John Gurney, the brilliant, scholarly, handsome younger brother of Elizabeth Fry, famous for her work among prisoners. It was he who introduced the presentation of Bibles to each newcomer, urged them to read it, and personally examined the children on it at the end of a year, awarding prizes for proficiency and good conduct. He encouraged Scripture teaching at Ackworth for thirty years. When he came for Committee Meetings he used to distribute sixpences and half-holidays liberally, and was much-loved. "Boys and girls alike would gather round him, 'like a swarm of bees'," writes Elfrida Vipont in her account of Ackworth School (1779-1946). (See p.47).

In 1824, Ackworth School, which had otherwise a good health record, had a disastrous epidemic described as an "inflammatory epidemic fever," in which several patients died, including one of the masters. The school nurse and a second master died in the second epidemic. Luckily, especially for all her descendants, Elizabeth Ann survived. After the epidemics, the ventilation was improved; more animal food was introduced into the diet; and the boys got warmer clothing in winter, including nightshirts! Some accommodation for the boys to wash themselves occasionally was also provided; prior to the epidemics, this had not been available. The drains were improved.

Ackworth School was a family, including baker, shoe-maker, gardener, tailor, husbandman and mantua-maker. The School Farm was part of the premises; the School Inn, across the road from the front of the school, was part of the extended community. For some pupils it was a very happy place to be - compare William Howitt (1802-6) who wrote home that in spite of the cold and the severe discipline, "I find myself very comfortable". But others - e.g. John Bright (1822-3) - wrote that he spent "a year of much discomfort". Provided she could keep warm, and was not too homesick, Elizabeth Ann probably found much to enjoy and interest her in her two years at Ackworth. The face in the photographs of her as an elderly lady does look rather severe, and as I look at it I think of the cold, the chilblains, the homesickness, the unpleasantly warm milk (fresh from being pasteurised) which we *had* to drink, and the unbuttered bread served out if the "meal" was a small rasher of bacon; of the punishment I got (even one hundred and ten years after Elizabeth Ann Hawkes was there) of being banished to bed in silence for Saturday afternoon, if I had forgotten not to speak at certain times during the day. Without doubt, though, Elizabeth Ann was a strong character and has been revered and much remembered by her seven children, her grandchildren, her great-grandchildren and other descendants. It was quite likely her influence which caused Nancie's older siblings to be sent to Sidcot Friends' School, so she cannot have hated her time at Ackworth; perhaps she loved it.

Elizabeth Ann Hawkes said little about her early days for many years - in fact, until her family had grown up. I have created the picture of her time at Ackworth from the histories of the school and my own knowledge of it. From other sources, we know what happened to her later. After she returned from Ackworth, we are told she went to a Quaker school in Bristol. The only possible school actually in Bristol then was the

Chapter 3. The Quaker Connection

Friends' First Day School which met only on Sundays, to teach under-privileged people in a poor district how to read and write. Quite likely, there were other schemes for alleviating poverty or providing some employment, run by the Quakers on other days in the week; but we know nothing more of what she did. I think she might have gone to Sidcot Friends' School near Bristol, where her grandchildren were to go sixty years later; but the school has no record of her as a pupil, and I don't know if she was there in some other capacity.

Elizabeth Ann married **Henry Fowler**, both of Bengeworth, Evesham, on August 25th, 1836, in St. Peter's Church, Bengeworth. She was twenty-five; Henry was eight years older, almost exactly the same age as James Hancox. Henry Fowler, also very reticent, I'm told, about his early life, gave his place of birth, as I have said, as Upton-on-Severn, Worcestershire. Those who knew him spoke of his alluding to a very unhappy childhood with an aunt or step-mother with whom he did not get on; but he looks cheerful enough as an old man in his photograph. (see p.46). He, too, had come into the town, in his case, Evesham, from the country to be apprenticed to a cabinet-maker; had set up his own business in Port Street, Bengeworth, just over the Bridge from the town itself; and founded a dynasty of Fowlers.

Bengeworth, in the early nineteenth century, was a miniature town in its own right, with roots that went back to long before the bridge over the River Avon to Evesham had been built. Even in the nineteenth century it had its National School: now a garage. Offenham is a nearby village across the fields. I've heard from more than one source that Thomas Hawkes and other bachelor brothers or nephews of his also lived at Offenham. My mother's half-brother, Jack, records being taken to see them once as a small boy in 'around' 1878, where they lived, at Old Parks Farm, Offenham, a big old family house, perched just above the River Avon (it has been extended and is now a hotel): "two elderly bachelor uncles Hawkes", Jack said. Jack particularly remembered a dense thicket of Filbert Nuts which grew in the sloping garden down to the River Avon "just ripe enough for a small boy to pick". In the 1851 Census Return there were no Hawkes at Old Parks Farm. Thomas was staying in Port Street, Bengeworth, near his daughter and her family. He was a visitor at the house of Ellen Downes (widow). Anne Fowler, my mother's mother and Elizabeth Ann Fowler's youngest child, was not yet two and lived a few doors away. In 1853, Thomas died of 'Natural Decay' and was buried in the Quaker graveyard in Evesham. In his Will, dated March 3rd, 1841, he had made his daughter, Elizabeth Ann Fowler, his sole Executrix. To her he left the premises at Bretforton, inhabited by Elizabeth Ford, blacksmith. Both his witnesses were ironmongers.

Thomas Hawkes was both thoughtful and literate, as is shown by one more "treasure" which I have: a book out of his library which my mother gave me so long ago that I don't remember when or why. Its cover is of tooled leather, with 'T. Hawkes' cut deep into the front; and inside it is inscribed 'S.H. Fowler The gift of her dear Granpapa Hawkes 1851' in what looks like Elizabeth Ann's handwriting. 'S.H.' was Sarah (Hawkes) (b. 1838) so she would be thirteen at the time. The book contains two long "Letters to a Lady" which run to nearly 300 pages: "Free Thoughts upon the Brute-Creation or, an Examination of Father Bougeant's Philosophical Amusement, & c." M.DCC.XLII.; and "The Contempt of the Clergy Considered" M.DCC.XXXIX.. The first is by John Hildrop, M.A., Rector of Wath, near Rippon in Yorkshire; the second, 'By an Impartial Hand'. The book still has its brown paper wrapper with the address and stamp, having come to my mother from Evesham by open-ended book post, while she lived at New Earswick.

In the Parish Registers of St. Peter's, Bengeworth, (the Fowler family's church) the section for Baptisms (1813-1843) has a column for the "Quality, Trade or Profession" of the father. White-smiths are conspicuous during the early years. An Attorney-at-Law jostles sack-weaver, Sawyer, Skinner, mason, bargeman, hatter, blacksmith, brick-maker, ostler, hostler and cabinet-maker; gate-keeper, water- man, surgeon and hired servant: all bring their babies to be baptised. Some wove bags or stockings, others dressed flax, made shoes, milled flour and baked bread. The 'tavern-keeper' of 1815 later became the 'publican'. Plaister, Nailor, Vintner, Laborer (sic), Farmer, Gardener and Post-boy: all had children. Cordwainer, Gloveress, Oil-cake Merchant, Fell-Monger, Ribbon-weaver came along with the Gentleman, the Registrar (from 1837 when compulsory registration was

Chapter 3. The Quaker Connection

introduced), the Auctioneer and the Policeman. In June 1840, when regular posts began, the local "Letter-carrier" registered his child. (No pun intended).

Henry and Elizabeth Ann Fowler had six daughters and one son (Henry) who carried on the furniture business in his turn.

Elizabeth Ann named her daughters for her mother **Elizabeth** (bapt. December 6th, 1837); her mother's sister-in-law by her first husband **Sarah** (bapt. November 7th, 1838); her mother's only daughter by her first marriage **Winifred** (bapt. August 6th, 1841); and her own dead sisters **Jane** (bapt. February 1st, 1845); **Susan** (bapt. August 7th, 1847), and **Ann** (bapt. March 22nd, 1849). **Henry** (bapt. May 14th, 1843) would be named for his father.

Elizabeth, the eldest, remembered as "Aunt Bessie", had a good head for business. Her father, Henry Fowler, bought for her James Hancox's shop in Stratford-on-Avon when James retired, soon after 1860. It was unusual then for a young woman to have her own business. In treating his eldest child as he would have done a son, Henry Fowler was well before his time. Elizabeth subsequently married James Hawley on January 29th, 1866; the shop was then known as Fowler and Hawley. It remained for so long that people still remember it. More recently it was Organ's - now being demolished. At first in Stratford-on-Avon, Elizabeth had attended the Baptist Chapel where the Hancoxes worshipped; but on her marriage she felt she should join her husband in his church: the Wesleyan Methodists. This is recorded in the Minutes of the Baptist Chapel. In her later years she was "a stately lady of ample proportions, noted good taste, and an excellent business woman", wrote my Uncle Jack. "She was a strict Plymouth 'Brother' and delighted in long Graces before and after meat, (which included tea). She did not hold with Theatres and Dances or other frivolities. But in spite of all this was most kind and good and cheerful to a degree". Uncle Jack was truly sorry when she died, though he found her funeral service long and tedious, as one "elder" after another rose to speak, emphasising again and again that although "our departed sister" was safe for ever, the rest of us, as outsiders, stood little chance hereafter.

Aunt Bessie had two daughters: Winifred, who did not marry; and Gertrude who married Thomas Meadows, fruiterer of Stratford-on-Avon. As with James and Harriett Hancox, Thomas lived "over the garden wall" from his bride. Meadows, Fruiterers, is still in Stratford-on-Avon; a son of Gertrude and Thomas is a doctor, not far away. Aunt Bessie sold the business about 1896. She was well enough off to live comfortably at No.4, Warwick Road (now superseded by the bus station), and to have a summer cottage called "La Quinta" at Broadway. Dorothy, my mother's sister, remembered the bead curtain in the hall of the cottage, and that Gertrude was married from Broadway on October 25th, 1893 (Dorothy's fifth birthday).

Sarah was crippled with arthritis and lived in a wheelchair (died 1903). Some said at the time that she had been "born too near Elizabeth". There were only eleven months between them. **Susan** "a typical Victorian lady", my cousin says, devoted all her life to looking after Sarah, refusing offers of marriage. She out-lived Sarah by thirty years, and latterly had a trim little house up the road towards Offenham and Bretforton called 'The Hollies'. **Winifred** married John Nash from a Farming family at Inkberrow (another link, I'm told, with the story of 'The Archers' and 'The Bull'). He made money as a Pork-Packer in Chicago, returned to live at Bevington Hall and later at Birkenhead Park where Uncle Jack visited while at Manchester University. They returned to U.S.A. and stayed in Cleveland, Ohio. There were fourteen children in the family including two sets of twins! One son joined the British Navy, commanding a destroyer in the 1914-18 War; one son, William, married a niece of John D. Rockefeller I, the famous American multi-millionaire philanthropist. When one of Winifred's daughters, Margaret Nash, (b. 15.9.1881 in Worcestershire, England) died in Tryon, North Carolina on January 26th., 1976, her niece, Betsy Nash, sent my mother a copy of the 'Tryon Daily Bulletin', headed 'The World's Smallest Daily Newspaper', which contained the obituary notice. The outside measurements of the paper are 8½" x 10¾": smaller than a page of this book!

Jane married a Belfast Irishman, Hugh Small, who was also a Chicago Pork Packer - presumably a friend of John Nash. Hugh Small died when still young, leaving his widow with two small children: Sarah and Henry John. Jane brought her children back to

Chapter 3. The Quaker Connection

Tettenhall while the son was a pupil at the Great Western Engineering Works; and finally in Beale - Cooper's Lane, Evesham. Their seventeenth-century "Cottage" features in the following chapter. It was said in the family that John Small (as he was always known) gave up his career to please his mother who wished to return to her native town. She developed eye trouble, and later became blind. John took up Market Gardening and Farming; Sarah devoted herself to looking after them both. Whenever my mother mentioned the name of her "Cousin John Small", her voice softened and her face lit up. Because of this, I perservered until I found his home, which introduced me to the delightful cousin now living there, as well as to the house, and memories of "Cousin John". He was, they say, "taken over by his women" (mother and sister) who did not wish him to marry; he is remembered with affection by all who knew him.

Ann, the youngest, was my mother's mother. A very sweet-natured lady. I tell of her elsewhere. She was always known as 'Nancy'.

Henry married Mary Hughes (known as Polly), a relation of the Bomfords of Atch Lench. Their eldest child, Henry, chief Locomotive Engineer of the London Midland and Scottish Railway, and Director of Productions, Ministry of Munitions, 1915-19, was knighted for his services. He once showed a cousin a fountain pen he lent to King George V to sign some documents during the War, when Henry knelt down for the King to use his back as a writing desk. In 1927, he designed the extra-powerful (Fowler) locomotives of the "Royal Scot" class, used to avoid the necessity of double-heading heavy trains. He was very much a family man and kept in touch with everyone, writing letters and calling when possible. He came to Oxford in 1932 to see my mother when we were staying there for a Balliol Conference (explained in a later chapter), so I remember meeting him there. Recently, I've spent a happy day with his son.

Arthur (an artist), Jane (Jen) (a nurse) and Elizabeth (Bess) worked away from home, but both girls (unmarried) returned to live with their father in Evesham. (Hugh) Alexander, at first a market gardener and then an estate manager for a Lady who bred scented rhododendrons; Charles who took over the family business; and Mary, the youngest, who married early Jack Bomford of Atch Lench, complete the family. Charles married Jack Bomford's sister, Isabel Lucy, known as "Riz", which doubled the relationship. Mary (known as Mollie), two of whose children have helped particularly with my search, was born on April 7th, 1887, a few weeks before Queen Victoria's Golden Jubilee. The following chapter finds Mollie on her tenth birthday.

Four of Nancie's siblings went to a Quaker School between 1880 and 1895, although the only link I know is through their grandmother's time at Ackworth, and other families in Evesham who also sent their children there. Nancie married a man who became a Quaker; she and her William brought up their children within the Society of Friends, and gave them all a Quaker education from the age of five, a link which still endures. One of Nancie and William's grandchildren has joined the Society of Friends and is a very active member. The Quaker connection continues.

Henry Fowler and his wife, Elizabeth Ann (née Hawkes), who lived in Bengeworth, Evesham: parents of Mrs Owen Hancox

Chapter 3. The Quaker Connection

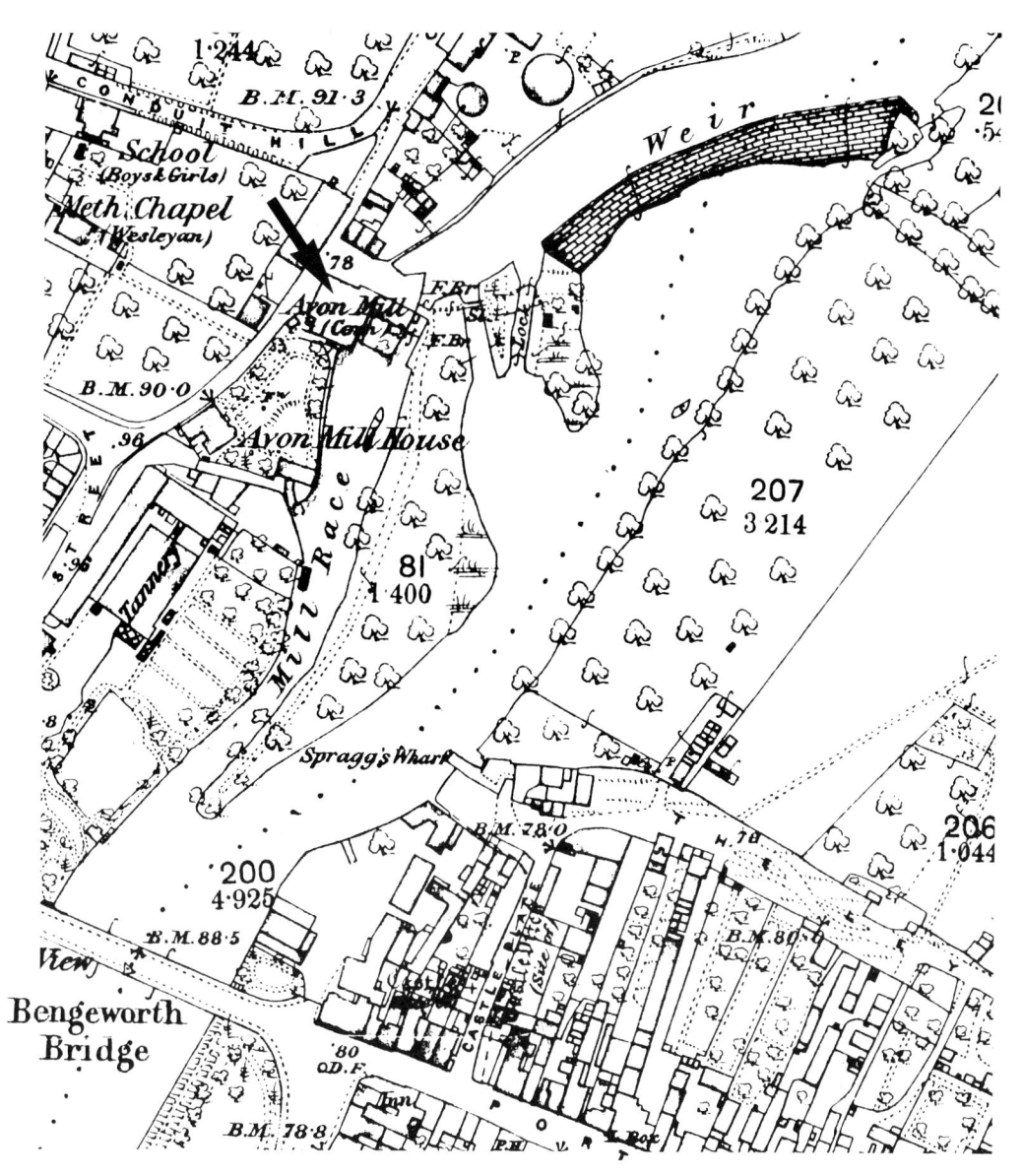

(1) Ordnance Survey Map of Evesham, 1886
(2) Ackworth School and its Gardens, early 1800's. Brothers and sisters were encouraged to walk and talk on the flagstones. Perhaps the distant group represents Joseph John Gurney with the pupils gathering round him 'like a swarm of bees' (p.43)

Chapter 4. April 7th, 1897: the Birthday Treat

MARKET GARDENERS in 1897 used carts like this one, parked in the Market Place. Note the Jubilee flags.

BRIDGE STREET beflagged, with all Evesham en fete— this glimpse of a bygone age dates from 1897 when the town turned out to celebrate the Diamond Jubilee.

(1) These two photos are taken from the Centenary copy of the 'Evesham Journal' (July 22nd, 1960): sent in by readers who cannot be traced
(2) An Evesham Crew in 1897. The crew consisted of Harry Fowler (bow), E.J. Bomford, John Small and J.J. Hancox (Stroke). They won both the maiden and junior events at the Evesham Regatta

Chapter 4

April 7th, 1897: the Birthday Treat

Mollie was roused from sleep by the distant sound below of clattering hooves on the cobbled street, as the horse-drawn carts came down the hill between the houses. They had left the fields and farms out in the countryside around Evesham before dawn, and now, laden with produce, they were on their way to the station to catch the early trains to the city markets. Growers in the Vale of Evesham had been famous for generations as far as their vegetables and fruit could travel. Before the railways came, they supplied Tewksbury, Cheltenham, Worcester and Birmingham; their asparagus was sent as far as Bath and Bristol. Since the railways, they supplied towns further away, even London, especially with asparagus. But first the cauliflowers and lettuces, and later in the summer the plums and the cherries which grew beyond the church of St. Peter, Bengeworth, at the top of the hill, had to pass below Mollie's bedroom window.

She thought, "It's rather like the people, too: like my great-grandfather Hawkes, who came in from Bretforton as a young man to work in the town." Of course, she had never known him, as he died ages before she was born, but they still talked about him quite a bit, and there were books and things that had belonged to him. She had known her Granny Fowler - just. Not very well, as Granny, who had been born a Hawkes and had also come in with her father from Bretforton, had died in 1890, soon after Mollie's third birthday. People seemed to stay a while, once they got to Bengeworth; both Granny and great-grandfather had stayed till they died. They must have liked it. She liked it very much and she couldn't think why so many of her family had gone away. It wasn't much fun being the youngest, specially by five years, and specially when the next two above her were her brothers, (Hugh) Alec and Charles. Her nearest sister Bessie was a whole ten years older than she was, so she was no use at all. They had all gone, or were about to go. She wished her eldest brother, Harry, named after her father and grandfather Fowler, came home more often. He hadn't stayed to learn the cabinet-maker's craft, but like so many in his generation had moved on to machines; he was an engineer, interested in railway engines. One day he would be famous, get a knighthood, talk to King George about his ideas and inventions, and have a mainline railway engine named after him; he would live in a 'Hall'. But that was all in the future. Just now she would have liked him to be at home for her birthday.

Mollie lay and listened while the carts rumbled by, the horses' hooves skittering every now and then, as they slipped on the cobbles with their heavy loads. Before the last ones had finished coming down, the earlier carts were already crossing Bengeworth Bridge (now called Workman's Bridge), and the horses began their plodding progress back up to the church and beyond. Far from minding being woken up so early, Mollie was glad. It gave her time to think before the hustle and bustle of the day began. Soon, she would hear the great double doors beside the house which opened into the yard behind, being unbolted and swung on their huge hinges. The horses which delivered materials and took away the finished product went in and out through these doors to her father's cabinet-making and upholstery workshops. There was a shop beyond the workshop where customers came to discuss what they wanted to buy.

The sloping street which led down to the River Avon was called Port Street - perhaps from before there was a bridge and the river was used to bring goods to the landing wharves; they'd told her that in 1055 Edward the Confessor created Evesham a "port" or market town, so probably Bengeworth had its own market at the top of Port Street. Mollie's family lived at No.9. Mollie thought that sounded rather distinguished. When she told anyone where she lived, or arranged for a friend to come to visit, she would say almost casually, "We live at No.9. You can't miss it. You'll see Papa's shop and the big front doors beside the house. Don't forget - No.9!" The house itself had a big front door with a half-porch over the top. Like all the other houses near them in the street, they had a shoe-scraper let into the wall beside the door. It was round, with a horizontal bar across the middle for scraping the mud off one's shoes or button boots.

Chapter 4. April 7th, 1897: the Birthday Treat

Behind the house was best of all. There was an orchard, filled at this time of year with a froth of pink and white blossom which smelt gorgeous. Beside the orchard was a meadow; and alongside the meadow the path she used, to go to see Aunt Jane Small. Aunt Jane was one of her father's sisters, born a Fowler. She lived in a house she called "The Cottage" though really it was bigger than that. It was really quite a big house, Mollie thought, with very dark wood - almost black - for the cupboard doors and things, specially in the kitchen. Parts of the house dated from about 1660 - that's what they said - it had been enlarged since then. Upstairs, there was a huge landing, much bigger than their own sitting-room. The garden was rather fun, too, with extra hedges so you could go right out of sight; and roses climbing up the walls, back and front, which smelt heavenly. The back of the house faced South, so if it was sunny anywhere in Evesham, it was sunniest there. Bumble bees and honey-bees hummed in the still air round the tall hollyhocks, and butterflies favoured the buddleias and other flowering shrubs.

"Mollie," came her mother's voice,"are you awake?" 'Course she was awake, had been for ages, though the brightness of the sun suggested she had dozed off since the carts went by. She didn't answer. She wanted her mother to climb the stairs, as she knew she would today and not send Margaret the maid instead. The door opened, and in came Mary Fowler - Polly to everyone but her children - neat and trim as always, with every one of her braided hairs in place.

"Happy birthday, my dear," she said, as she sat down on the side of the bed; then, "Don't squeeze me so," as Mollie gave her the biggest hug she could manage.

"Time you were up," continued her mother. "There's lots to do today, and places to go. Thank goodness it's going to be fine,"

Mollie knew there was to be a "surprise" picnic on the river, in the afternoon; but if she knew already, how could it be a surprise?

After a brief wash with the warm water her mother had brought for the bowl on the wash stand, she hurried downstairs. Beside her place at the table were several small packages, individually wrapped and tied up with ribbon. Her sisters had gone out shopping; her brothers were down by the river, or helping in the workshop; Margaret was hanging out the washing; she and her mother were alone.

Mollie quickly ate the newly-baked bread and fruit which she had for breakfast and drank her milk. Now she was free to open her birthday parcels. Bessie had given her a tortoise-shell comb. Jen, her oldest sister, a packet of coloured threads to encourage her embroidery (she was working on a sampler). The boys, Alec and Charles, had made her a wooden toy, in the workshops; that was why they had pushed her out the other day, when she wanted to join them for a moment. She wasn't really allowed inside, on account of the sharp tools and possible splinters, but sometimes she managed a good look from the doorway. The toy had a little monkey with a red hat, made of fretwork, on the end of a stick. On a parallel piece of wood there was an orange. Both were brightly-painted. It looked as though you could pull the monkey towards the orange, so it could reach it; but every time you did so the orange shot up in the wrong direction, so the monkey never succeeded. She tried again and again, but every time with the same result. She was just feeling sorry for the monkey when she looked up and saw her mother trying not to laugh at her serious face and her concentrated efforts. She wrapped up the monkey again carefully to take to show her cousins.

At that moment, Margaret came in with the empty laundry basket. "Happy birthday, Miss Mollie," she said cheerfully and from her pocket she drew out a brightly-coloured post-card. "Happen you've never been to Kent," she said. "My auntie sent me this to show what it's like down there, so I thought it might brighten up your bedroom mantlepiece."

"Oh yes, it's lovely," Mollie responded. "Would you put it there, if you're just going up to tidy the beds, please?"

Mollie looked at her mother with bright expectant eyes. It wasn't good manners to *expect* a present, but Mother never let her down. This time she drew a small box from the pocket of her gown, and handed it to her daughter. Mollie thought it was rather small.

50

Chapter 4. April 7th, 1897: the Birthday Treat

"Go on, open it," she was told.

Inside, there was tissue-paper; when this was unwrapped, she could hardly believe her eyes. There, in the palm of her hand, was a little gold bar brooch with a single pearl in the middle. She was speechless with delight.

"It belonged to Granny Fowler," her mother said. "Now you are ten years old I think you are old enough to appreciate it and take care of it. Here, let me pin it on to your pinafore, so you can show it to the others, Take care and don't lose it. After today, it will only be for Sundays and very special days. I will unpin it for you, and look after it between times."

Mollie squinted down at the brooch. It had belonged to Granny Fowler - something that had stayed in Bengeworth. She gathered up her other presents and set off up the street to No. 29. Here she reached up and pulled as hard as she could at the brass bell knob. The tinkling sound in the back of the house was soon followed by Annie's footsteps as she came to open the big heavy door.

"Come in, Miss Mollie! Miss Fowler is expecting you," and she led the way into the front sitting-room which had been adapted into a bedroom for her father's older sister, Sarah Hawkes Fowler. Aunt Sarah was seated in her wheelchair by the window, well-wrapped in a large shawl. A life of pain and disability had left her looking more than her fifty-eight years.

"Best wishes, my dear," she said in her high, cracked voice. "Thank you for coming to see us." Mollie had been coming to see them often for as long as she could remember. This house had once been Granny Fowler's house, and long ago her father had been born here. Today, she rather thought she had come at least partly for her own benefit, but you mustn't expect a present till you got it, she told herself again. Aunt Sarah searched for the package on her chairside table. She laid it on her knee and undid the ribbon which secured it. Out of the parcel came a pure white cotton pinafore, the edges adorned with exquisite bands of crochet. It was so lovely Mollie didn't know what to say, but her face said it all.

At that moment, Aunt Sue came into the room. She too had a parcel, rather bigger. Mollie kissed her aunt's cheek and said, "Good Morning", making sure Aunt Sue was watching her face as she did so, because they all knew she was very deaf. Inside the parcel was a beautifully-knitted shawl made of rainbow-coloured wool. Mollie was entranced. "Thank you very much," she cried and kissed her aunt's cheek a second time. Then she showed them the presents she had already received at home, especially the brooch which had belonged to their mother. Granny had wished it to be given to the youngest grandchild she had known, in the last three years of her life. Nancie Hancox, the youngest of them all, had not been born till over seven months after Granny Fowler died.

As soon as she could leave politely, Mollie said "Goodbye" and returned home. She still had to visit her other two aunts who were within walking distance. Her father's sisters, Aunt Bessie and Aunt Winifred, had left Bengeworth and had married over thirty years ago: one lived in Stratford-on-Avon and the other in the U.S.A. But Aunt Jane lived nearby in Beale-Cooper's Lane. To get there Mollie went through to the back of the house and down past the orchard, enjoying the sight and smell of the blossom. She followed the path beside the meadow, where the bright yellow buttercups winked at her in the sunlight. At the far end, she crossed the lane, and, ignoring the front door of the cottage, which faced her as she approached, went round the side and in through the side gate.

Aunt Jane was sitting out in the sun. Her hands were idle in her lap as her sight was poor. She heard Mollie's approach and turned her head expectantly.

"Mollie?" she called. "Is that you dear? I hoped you'd come! Happy Birthday!" Mollie returned her aunt's greeting, and settled down beside her on the garden seat. Sarah, Aunt Jane's daughter, came out to join them, bringing a tray of lemon drinks. Sarah was fully grown up and spent all her time looking after her mother and brother. She and her brother had been born in Chicago. Aunt Jane used to tell Mollie about the Great Fire there when most of Chicago was burnt down.

Chapter 4. April 7th, 1897: the Birthday Treat

For her birthday present Sarah gave Mollie a crocheted needle-case, shaped like a little hat with a silver thimble nestling in the crown of the hat, and the needles lodged in circular layers of felt, shaped like the brim of the hat. Mollie thanked her. She hoped she would one day be as good at sewing, knitting and crocheting as her aunts were.

As they fell silent, her gaze wandered to the large carved stones which lay in the garden. These were said to have come from Evesham Abbey when it was destroyed; one or two stones had been built into the house itself. Over the back door there is still an Abbey stone in the house-wall, carved into oak-leaves: the Druids' omen of peace; and the emblems for the prow of the famous ship, the 'Argo', which took Jason to seek the Golden Fleece. Mollie had read about Jason and the famous oak from the ancient temple of Dodona. It was peaceful and pleasant in the garden, but she missed her Cousin John. Where was Cousin John Small? she wondered. She'd have liked him to be there, but supposed he was working on his land outside the town. No, her aunt said, that morning John was down on the river practising with his cousin, Jack Hancox. John Small was to row number three in J.J. Hancox's boat that summer of 1897 when they were to win the race. (See p.48).

At last Mollie was free to go to the Mill, where younger company awaited her. She hurried back across the meadow, told her mother where she was going, and crossed the road from the front door. Keeping carefully on the narrow pavement with its deep curb, she crossed Bengeworth Bridge and turned to her right into Mill Street. Still on the same side, she passed the tannery and ran into the garden of Avon Mill House. Her cousin Nancie was so very pleased to see her. At not yet six-and-a-half, the eleventh and youngest of the long, double, family, Nancie lacked playmates of her own age. Her mother, Anne, was herself the youngest of the Fowlers of that generation, so there were no younger cousins; and Nancie's next sister (Catherine) Dorothy, a bit of a tomboy, chased off with their three older brothers and kept up with them, always leaving Nancie behind. Nancie had been lying by the pool watching the sunlight playing on the fountain. For company, she had Toby, the large white dog, and Dick the cat when he condescended to come near. She now settled down to hear Mollie's account of her birthday so far, and to look forward to the afternoon's picnic. After lunch they would all gather at the Mill house and board Owen Hancox's boat with their picnic hampers. The boat was called the 'Nancy', named for Owen's wife, Nancie's mother.

Both girls were happy to lie on the grass, chatting idly and enjoying doing nothing. They spoke about the school to which Mollie went, run by their distant cousins, the Misses Emily and Lucy Bomford, at Atch Lench, a few miles north of Evesham. Mollie went as a weekly boarder. The school, taking its name, Court House, from the large white building which housed it, was run with good sense and imagination, but Mollie did not enjoy it as it meant being away from home. Nancie's older brothers and sisters had had a succession of governesses when young over the years, but now that she and Dorothy were the only ones below the age of twelve they were to join Mollie at Court House School. They would all be taken in the pony and trap to the Lenches on a Monday morning, and brought back on the Friday afternoon.

Suddenly Mollie heard the hooter at the nearby tannery. "Help, I'll be late," she said and ran back along Mill Street and over the Bridge. She burst into the house, and as she did so she heard a familiar deep laugh coming from the parlour. "Harry," she shrieked. "You've come home!" There was Harry, tall and friendly as ever, her special, eldest brother, seventeen years her senior, home from his engineering career which kept him away so much. He engulfed her in his usual bear-hug and swung her up, her face on a level with his own, "And how does it feel, then, to be TEN?" he asked her. "Are you having a good birthday?"

"The best ever," Mollie replied. "And now you've come home for it, everything's perfect. Now I know why Mother said we were going to have a Surprise Picnic. YOU are the Surprise!"

Nancie in the garden c. 1897

52

Chapter 5

The Miller and His Daughter

Nancie, my mother, was born in 1890, on December 23rd, a date she would not have chosen herself, as it came so near to Christmas that one present usually did for both occasions. This she told us, more than once. As the last of a long double family, she was nearly twenty-three years younger than her oldest half-sister, Mary. Blessed with four older brothers and a tomboy older sister who kept up with them, she remembered herself as feeling left out and left behind: almost, the tail that failed to wag. Her confidence was not helped by the stringent remarks of one of her mother's older, spinster sisters who used to say, "Nancie was a mistake. Anne should never have been burdened with another child at *her* age." Anne at that time was forty-one, an age at which some, today, are starting their families. She had less than thirteen years of childbearing, compared with Joseph Hancox's wife, Elizabeth, who had twenty-five. Also, Anne survived all her childbearing and lived to be almost eighty. The spinster sister who made the remark outlived all the others until she was eighty-six.

Nancie's middle name was 'Etheldene'. How she hated it. None of us ever discovered its origin nor why it was chosen. Her father, Owen Hancox, registered her birth himself though not until February 9th, more than six weeks after she was born. He spelt her name 'Nancie'. By her own account, she was a rather miserable child, constantly trying to keep up with her brothers and sister; but no-one who knew her later with her sweetness and serenity could imagine this. She was helped by her mother who was a very sweet-natured lady; and by the affection and support she had from her own father. Later, my mother's attitude in life owed much to the care and devotion of my father.

Certainly, she had very happy, loving memories of Owen and of her childhood at Avon Mill House, Evesham, and at Warminster. She used to tell how he carved the joint at the family dinner-table; took her for walks by the river, and taught her all he knew about birds and flowers; fondled the ears of his white dog, Toby; and was amused by the antics of the cat, Dick. They always had a white dog called Toby and a cat called Dick. Nancie's sister, Dorothy, continued this custom at Broad Campden, although one cat surprised her by having kittens and had to be re-named "Mrs Richard". Nancie and her sister, **(Catherine) Dorothy**, were born after seven Hancox sons. They grew up in a house full of people and bustle, with the Mill across the yard clacking and chuntering as machines rotated and rushed back and forth. The Mill Race flowed along the length of the garden behind the trees; the fountain on the front lawn shot up in a high jet (see photo p.xiv); at the centre of family life at the Mill House, Nancie's mother remained serene, calm and caring. They must have felt wonderfully secure in their spacious home and pleasant garden (see enlarged Map p.47, photo p.xiv and picture Frontispiece), except perhaps for Owen who had the worry of the business.

Owen, as we know, had been a Miller all his life, first as apprentice at Great Alne Mill, reputed to be the oldest of its kind in the Midlands, and the only one like it still working, well over a century after Owen went there. It features in the Domesday Book. Up to 1900, the wheat was ground by the same mill-stone technique used for centuries. This was then changed to mechanised rolling mills. When the change was made to diesel, a diverted section of the River Alne still provided some of the power. For many years, Canadian wheat came by sea to Bristol and then on to Great Alne, as the Canadian grain (mixed with a small amount of locally-grown English wheat) was better suited to the particular type of bread produced. Today (July 24th, 1990), I read of the launching of the Wholemeal Highgrove Loaf, approved by the Prince of Wales, in which locally- produced flour has been mixed with (organic) Canadian wheat. Until very recently, the Mill still made flour and was open to the public. I have visited its five storeys only a few years ago and watched the milling process and the turning of the great turbine. The latest owners are developing the buildings into homes and holiday homes, but tell me they still intend to keep the machinery in working order. (see photo p.33).

Chapter 5. The Miller and His Daughter

(1) Avon Mill House (see painting (Frontispiece) and photo p. xiv), adapted for Stocks Lovell: from the front
(2) The Avon Mills, Evesham, as seen from the house (now offices)
(3) The Avon Mills and the back of the house with extra buildings, from Mill Street (See p.xii) (1989)
(4) Sketch of the Mills of Evesham done by Owen Hancox, possibly for printing on flour bags or bill-heads. View from up-river; the house is hidden by the Mills. The family boat, the 'Nancy', was used for family outings on the River Avon, such as the 'Surprise' Picnic in April, 1897

Chapter 5. The Miller and His Daughter

Great Alne Mill continued to feature in the Hancox family, as Owen's eldest surviving son **John (Jack)** went there early this century, and he and his son, Avery, worked the mill until about 1970. My mother lived in Great Alne for four years (1913-17), as I shall tell later. My mother was paid £12 a year by her half-brother, from which she had to clothe herself and provide for all her needs including presents, stamps and any travel home. She did not think it was enough. Interestingly, at that same time exactly, my father's uncle-by-marriage William Snell in Edinburgh lent him on no security, £50: more than the total for four years of Nancie's housekeeping, so that he could go to London for three months for his Final Honours Law exams. The uncle's faith - and generosity - was rewarded, as my father came first in all England in the exams. (see Part II, Chap. 8) Although none of us now alive knew Uncle William, he is always remembered with gratitude and affection.

Uncle Jack who wrote most lovingly to Nancie after she left for London, and who missed her bright presence, tells amusingly how his grandfather, James Hancox, when resident at Great Alne in his retirement, busied himself in the carpenter's shop he had built over the stables. Among other things he made a large lean-to greenhouse which finally blew down sixty years later in a gale in the 1920's. On Owen's twenty-first birthday in the Autumn of 1861, the staff at Great Alne Mill were given a dinner and taken in a wagon to Stratford Mop (the local Fair) by way of celebration.

Owen fell in love with **Catharine**, only daughter of John Avery, a needle manufacturer of Headless Cross, Redditch; they were married at Headless Cross Wesleyan Methodist Church on July 2nd, 1867. As his sister, **Harriet**, had been married to Herbert Bomford from the Mill House at Great Alne two years before, James and his wife went to live near their daughter, leaving the young couple to run the Mill House at Great Alne. Two daughters were born to Owen and Catharine: **Mary** on April 29th, 1868; and **Helen**, on June 5th, 1869.

In 1868 the Avon Mills at Evesham were put up for sale; they were advertised in the Evesham Journal on August 29th, 1868 as follows:

Evesham mills for sale

"ADVERTISEMENT - Important announcement to millers and manufacturers. The Avon Mills, in the borough of Evesham, will shortly be offered for sale by public auction. This extensive and valuable property is freehold and consists of the substantially built Oil Mills, Old Mills, the New Flour Mills, now in work, and the large Silk Mills, with the whole of the River Avon Water Power Water Wheels and other machinery; also the Mill House, Counting House, Stables, Outbuildings, several extensive walled yards, wharfage, warehouse, four cottages, the Mill Meadow, the Weirs and the fishery of the Upper Avon."

Owen decided to buy the Evesham Mills so he sold Great Alne Mill to William Spencer, son-in-law of John Elvins, to whom he had been apprenticed, and from whom James Hancox had bought the mill in 1861. Owen took a life-long and intelligent interest in milling, constantly finding ways to improve and increase the yield. He studied other people's methods, even travelling to Norway. Owen was to die of diabetes, for which at that time there was no treatment. Nancie also suffered from it (as do I). In his later years as he travelled, he always carried a small, silver fruit-knife, as fresh fruit is important in a diabetic diet. My mother made sure that the little knife which she had treasured came to me.

In Evesham from 1869, Owen and his family lived in the High Street on the corner of Magpie Lane (now called Avon Street), while the new Mill House was being built. In the 1871 Census he was employing nine men at the Mill. Two sons were born here: **Charles Owen** (19th January, 1871); and **John James (Jack)** (11th November, 1872). They moved to the new House beside the Mills and close to the River Avon, where another son, **Joseph Avery**, was born (31st December, 1874). Sadly, tragedy soon struck the family in the Mill House: Catharine, Owen's wife, contracted Typhoid Fever and died on August 11th, 1875, followed, the next month, by baby Joseph, at eight-and-a-half months old. Poor Owen, with his four little bairns, must have been devastated by this double blow.

Chapter 5. The Miller and His Daughter

(1) Anne Fowler aged 12 (1861)
(2) aged 21
(3) as an Adult

Chapter 5. The Miller and His Daughter

His housekeeper, Mrs Marsden, looked after them well, but Owen needed a wife. Two years later, he married **Anne Fowler** who spelt her name latterly with an 'e' (known as Nancy) of Bengeworth, who lived just over Bengeworth Bridge in Port Street. She was the daughter of Henry Fowler, who had bought James Hancox's original family business in Henley Street, Stratford-on-Avon, for his eldest daughter; and was himself a cabinet-maker, like James. Anne Fowler was Henry's youngest child; she had five older sisters and one brother, as already mentioned. My mother used to tell how her mother was amazed to be marrying at twenty-eight, as in those days a girl was reckoned to be thoroughly "on the shelf" if she had been overlooked and passed by to so great an age. (My own mother thought the same about herself!) Owen was looking for a mature and sensible woman to care for him and his motherless children; and he found a treasure. Owen and Anne were married in the newly-rebuilt church of St. Peter's, Bengeworth, on April 25th, 1877. The church has a tall and lofty spire, conspicuously situated at the top of Port Street, where the roads for Bretforton and Broadway divide.

My mother's half-brother, my Uncle Jack, has left a written tribute to the delight and happiness which his step-mother brought to the family. That first summer, the whole family of newly-married couple and four small children went on holiday together to Margate; Uncle Jack wrote that he, only four-and-a-half years old when it happened, remembered every detail of that wonderful time. In the following years there were too many additions to the family, so the seaside holiday was never repeated; really it was a rather unusual honeymoon, and a wise arrangement for them all to get to know each other better in holiday mood. Uncle Jack goes on to write: (my new mother) "was dearly loved by both sections of the family and she treated all alike, lovingly and strictly, with the most rigid views of her own, but always ready to allow for others having their own ideas".

William Henry (Will), the first child of the new marriage, arrived on May 16th, 1878. He was christened at St. Peter's, Bengeworth, his mother's family's church, on June 14th. Forty years later, on this same day, he was to give Nancie away at her wedding when my parents married in Purley during the First World War. **Edmund Owen (Junior)**, known always as **Ted**, was born on July 25th, 1880. Between the births of these two sons, one of the first family had had a horrid accident: Charles Owen as a boy of nine, while visiting his Aunt Harriet at Great Washbourne, had slid down a straw stack in the barn, and became paralysed from his neck down; he survived for nearly two years, but died of bronchitis (November 18th, 1880). According to Uncle Jack's description, he was "a charming, handsome boy with very dark hair". His cousin, Minnie Bebb, painted his portrait when he was eight.

On August 16th, 1882, **Charles Alfred (Fred)** was born, followed by **(Ernst) Avery**, on July 2nd, 1884. Governesses for the older children and nursemaids for the babies joined the family during these years. The 1881 Census Returns record Agnes S.M. Leys, (19) from Aberdeen, as the Private Governess; and two general servants, both called Elizabeth and recruited locally. Owen is mistakenly recorded as 'Edwin' (a corn Miller employing two clerks): one more evidence of the enumerator gathering his information orally, which led to errors and varied spelling, especially in the early Census Returns. This governess, Agnes Leys, who was an excellent teacher and wrote plays for the children to act, missed her train home, one Christmas, and so was *not* drowned when the Tay Bridge collapsed, and everyone on the train perished.

Court House School at Atch Lench, where Nancie and Dorothy went after their brothers had gone to Evesham Grammar School or Sidcot Friends' School, and there was no longer a governess at home, was run by the Misses Lucy and Emily Bomford. Their niece, Margaret Bomford, was also educated by them. She went on to train at Cambridge and then taught English Literature, Drama, Art and Botany. She was at St. George's School for Girls in Edinburgh for twenty-four years (1894-1918), where she taught my future mother-in-law, thirty years before I met her. By another curious coincidence, Miss Margaret Bomford, who outlived her two brothers and six sisters although she was the eldest, and celebrated her hundredth birthday, was brought to St. George's by Old Scholars for a special birthday party. I had just begun to teach there and heard that 'their' Miss Bomford was to visit. I watched from the window and saw her arrive. I knew

Chapter 5. The Miller and His Daughter

(1) Bills submitted by Owen Hancox, showing varied bill-heads (1878 and 1889)
(2) Nancie and Dorothy, taken while staying with Aunt Bessie at Stratford-on-Avon, during the move from Evesham to Birmingham (1899)
(3) Map of Henfords Marsh, Warminster (Ordnance Survey 1890)

Chapter 5. The Miller and His Daughter

my mother had Bomford cousins, some of whom had taught her, but only when my Aunt Dorothy sent me shortly afterwards the press-cutting from the 'Evesham Journal' of Margaret Bomford's Obituary did I learn that she was also 'our' Miss Bomford. I should have liked to have spoken to her. At least I was continuing what she had started: teaching English in the same Scottish School, so far from our English roots.

Owen was steadily expanding his business interests, buying Chadbury Mill in order to make special Brown Flour he called, "Avos". In 1889 he formed his business into a limited company called, "The Vale of Evesham Flour Mills Ltd", and bought the Mill at Harvington. He installed a special roller plant at Evesham to increase considerably the number of sacks per hour. He was continually trying out new ideas, and had much to worry about, not least when the Evesham Mills were all but destroyed by fire. Alongside his working life, he was also active in local and national politics as a Town Councillor in Evesham and a Gladstonian Liberal, and later a follower of Joseph Chamberlain into the Unionist Group. In the Evesham Municipal Elections of October 18th, 1879, he stood as a Liberal candidate.

Looking at Microfilm of the 'Evesham Journal' for 1886, hoping - in vain - to find an account of the fire at the Mill, I came across accounts of the meetings of the Young Men's Society, and their debates. 'Which does the more good to society: the spendthrift or the miser?' resulted in thirteen votes for the spendthrift, twelve against. On November 6th, 1886, they debated, 'In the present state of affairs, would it be safe to have a subterranean passage to be used as a railway under the Channel?' Only six were for; twelve against. The following week there was an article on 'Should railways be under Government Control?' 'To abolish capital punishment in cases of wilful murder' lost by one vote.

In 1894, the Vale of Evesham Flour Mills Co. started to bake stone-milled flour at Harvington Mills, and to send bread by passenger train to Birmingham, which proved very successful. Three years later, the Bakery was moved to Birmingham, shops were opened, and the business became the Avondale Bakery Co. Ltd.. Owen took his family to live in Church Road, Moseley (Birmingham). It must have been an unwelcome change for at least some of the family when they moved to Birmingham in 1899, although of course the larger towns were calling ambitious men of business, as the smaller towns had called their fathers in from their rural occupations, the generation before. I don't think Nancie enjoyed living in Moseley from the little she said, although she was lovingly remembered by one lady who sent her a letter of congratulation on her engagement, twenty years later. I have gleaned nothing about their school attendance nor their church adherence while they were there. The Post Office was unable to trace the address which I have for them there, perhaps because the site is now a housing estate, as with the Bebbs' house in Bristol.

Owen's health was failing, and he was worn out with overwork. Others took over the business and did badly. Owen retired from the Board of the Avondale Bakery Co. Ltd., and left Birmingham. Owen's eldest son, Jack, who worked with his father at the Evesham Mills and took over from him when he moved to Birmingham, referred to his father as "a clever and in some respects brilliant man, whose mind and ideas were fifty years ahead of his time. He was a tremendous worker, and a good and kind Father to all his children alike. He was never selfish and considered his employees as a family". Jack also recounts how, at the end of his first year as Manager of the Evesham Mills (for his father), he gave a dinner to the employees in the Mill House which was a great success. On December 30th, 1899, he gave them Roast Beef and Boiled Leg Mutton, Apple Tarts, Plum Pudding and Mince Pies, as well as Cheese, Dessert, Coffee, Tobacco and Cigarettes. They had songs and recitals "and General Good Fellowship", it says on the Menu. The men had a whip-round and surprised Jack with the present of an egg stand and a silver cigarette case, both inscribed.

When Owen retired from the Birmingham Company, he bought a small Roller Mill at **Henfords Marsh, Warminster**, a small town in Wiltshire, further down the railway line from Bristol and Bath beyond Trowbridge. In contrast to living in Birmingham, Nancie loved it at Warminster. Always responsive to Nature, she had plenty here to delight her, with the River Were flowing under the Mill and throughout the garden of the Mill House (see photo p.61). Apart from the distant noises of the Mill and the passage of trundling

Chapter 5. The Miller and His Daughter

(1) Nancie at Emwell House School, Warminster; I recognised her in an old school photo I saw there
(2) Henfords Marsh Mill c. 1900
(3) Hancox family in the garden of the Mill House, Warminster: Summer 1901 or 1902

Mary   Fred   Dorothy   Jack Smith and Anne Hancox
Owen Hancox   Ted

(4) Mill House garden in Winter

Chapter 5. The Miller and His Daughter

carts, she could listen to the music of the water, the sighing of the wind in the trees and the singing of the birds. Even when I visited the site of the Mill, and crossed the footbridges over the stream, almost ninety years after she was there, I found an unspoilt corner of rural delight; the new owners of the old Henford farmhouse told me they had seen the kingfisher and the flycatcher in the garden, the day before. Unaware, I imagine, of the severity of her father's illness and that he was dying of Diabetes; taking daily pleasure in his being at home rather than travelling away on business; enjoying having two of her brothers living and working there too; free from being away herself from boarding at Court House School, Nancie would for a brief spell be surrounded by her loved and loving family who meant so much to her. They were together.

This was the time of the greatest "togetherness" of her whole childhood. No wonder her tone softened and her face lit up when, in her eighties, she said, 'I loved it at Warminster'. It was the memory of the warmth in her voice at the mention of Warminster which sent me down from Edinburgh to try to discover what lay behind it. I found Warminster a small, friendly, rather old-fashioned town, the people very ready to talk. Danny Howell has compiled a book on 'Warminster: The Way We Were' which gives some idea of the town at the turn of the century. Nancie was there in January 1901, when Queen Victoria died. She used to tell us that when this happened, all the girls were given black crepe to wear round their hats, as well as armbands. She probably went to the private school, Emwell House School (see photo opp.). I think she is the girl to the right of the centre of the second row, with the very fair hair, a white dress, and her hands conspicuously folded in her lap. As a family, they probably went to the Baptist Church in North Row but I've had no reply to my enquiry there.

Henfords Marsh Mill lies to the South of Warminster (see Map p.58). Its recorded history goes back to 1332, when Robert Swoting "assured it to Thomas of Helmesford and Joan his wife". In 1441 a chief rent of 2s (10p) was paid to John Whissheley for 'Helmesffordesmull'. By 1637, the mill had been in ruins for many years, but was bought and re-built by Joshua Abath, who also enlarged the watercourse. By 1884, the last Mill on the site had been recently erected and had five floors and modern machinery. This is the Mill bought by Owen Hancox in 1900. Kelly's Directory for Wiltshire (1903) shows it still in use; but there is no reference to its being in use thereafter, so Owen may have been the last Miller to work it. In the late 1930's it was pulled down. My mother left a note on the back of her photo of the Mill (see opp.) to say it was "burned down as the easiest way to demolish when pronounced unsafe". She also left a photo of the family in the garden of the Mill House on a summer Sunday afternoon. On the back she names everyone and says "I'm not there as I was at Sunday School". There is also a photo of the same scene in the snow (opp.).

I have tried every source I could think of to discover what church or chapel Owen and his family attended, in Evesham, Warminster and Bristol, but found no firm evidence. Born into a Church of England family and baptised in the parish church, Owen was less than a year old when his father joined the Baptists. It is clear from his sister Louisa's Diary that she attended Baptist Prayer Meetings and played the organ for them; she was married in the Baptist Chapel and joined their fellowship soon after. My mother spoke of Sunday School, and, I think, of Chapel. A little hymn book, with her name in, written by herself, was found in a forgotten corner, when the new owners of my Aunt Dorothy's house in Broad Campden set about renovating and extending it in 1977.

In the 'Evesham Journal', 1886, I found a reference to Owen Hancox having lent his wagon for the Choir Outing of the Unitarian Church in Oat Street, and thought I had found his allegiance. But none of the family is listed in the full Unitarian Church records. My best guess is that some of the family anyway attended the Baptist Church in Cowl Street, Evesham, of which no members' records have survived. Owen's wife had come from the Anglican congregation of St. Peter's where her family continued to belong; she took her first child there for his christening. As the Baptists have adult baptism, there would be no register of infant baptisms. My mother was an Attender at the Quaker Meeting in York, of which my father was a Member. I have long been a member of the Church of Scotland. One thing the family seems to be is ecumenical, which is fitting when you consider Nancie's mother's reported comment, which Uncle Jack relates:

Chapter 5. The Miller and His Daughter

(1) Nancie aged 12 years and 2 weeks. Taken Jan 7th, 1903, in Bath
(2) Nancie aged 15½ years. Taken while visiting her sister Helen in London
(3) Anne and Owen Hancox

Chapter 5. The Miller and His Daughter

Anne (Fowler) Hancox "was a strict church-woman; but when a lady... demurred at her allowing all the family freedom of worship, she said: "My dear, in *my* Father's house there are many mansions." If one could hear and appreciate the emphasis, it was a real key to her character", wrote Uncle Jack.

In 1903, they had to move again. Less than three years were all they had in the idyllic setting of Warminster. **Fishponds Road, Bristol**, next door to Owen's nephew, Charles Bebb, son of Jeremiah II, and a very short distance from Owen's sister Louisa and her husband Jeremiah, was where Owen moved for the last time. Jeremiah II had a wholesale lamp business called the West of England Lamp Company, which Charles carried on after his father retired. My mother used to say that, when she was twelve, her father was told he had only a year to live; and thirteen months later he was dead. The photograph of Nancie, aged twelve, shows her sadness and dejection (see opp.). I did not appreciate why she looked so forlorn until I realised when the photo must have been taken. Perhaps it was about this time that she had to stay in bed for three months, as she once told me, when remarking that, since then, she had never had any desire to lie late of a morning. Owen must have felt especially the vulnerability and poignancy of his little Nancie: the youngest to be left fatherless; the one who, like him, would develop diabetes in early middle age.

The contrast between the photograph at twelve and one three years later is remarkable. At fifteen, complete with sun-umbrella, Nancie has an innocent elegance and an unconscious grace which I remember in her for the rest of her days. Her delightful cheery smile in this photograph reminds me each time I look at it of our elder daughter. (see opp.).

Owen had to set his affairs in order. His older children, including Will, his eldest son by his second marriage, were well-established, so he had no worries about them. From his first family, **Mary**, after teaching for some years, had returned in 1896 to Evesham "for domestic training", says Uncle Jack, before marrying Harold Hartley Smith, News Editor of the 'Evesham Journal'. They lived at No.2. High Street until Harold was so ill with asthma that they were advised to build a house on higher ground. Sadly, Harold, who was a gifted musical-monologist and amateur actor, died before the bungalow was finished. Mary and her son, Jack, then lived alone in "Top o' the Hill" as it was called. She became a successful journalist and artist, an inspired needlewoman and a passionate gardener. Before she died in August 1935, she had a long and painful arthritic illness. My cousin Henry says she had "chalk rheumatism", which led to two broken legs. He also described her face as one "that the world had walked over". I remember, as a child, being told by my mother that Aunt Mary, forced to lie on her back, held her embroidery frame above her head and created with her stitches colourful herbaceous borders straight onto the fabric without pattern or transfer. Mary and her son Jack feature in the garden photo at Warminster (p.60). I think Mary's husband, Harold, probably took this photo, and a number of others when Mary used to take Nancie for picnics in her car, a few years later (Chap. 6.). I have just inherited one of Mary's paintings.

Helen as a child was slightly hump-backed and had to wear a special corset to counteract this. She also became a teacher, rising to be headmistress of a Ladies' School in Stoke Newington, London. She, too, returned home for "domestic training" before marrying Montague J.C. Davis on April 12th, 1894. Montague had come to live with the Hancoxes at Avon Mill House, Evesham, to help run the business. On his engagement to a daughter of the house, he moved out as befitted a Victorian Gentleman; subsequently he set up a jewellery business in London. Their daughter, Doris Helen, only five years younger than my mother (her step-aunt), was the only child. They lived in Rondu Road, Cricklewood, London, where Nancie visited during her teens, as several of the old photographs show. In 1920 they moved to The Red House, Fenny Compton, (between Banbury and Leamington Spa) where they created a beautiful garden, with lily pond etc., which I well remember. Doris later moved to a much smaller house in Fenny Compton, now owned since Doris's death in 1971 by a cousin who welcomes me there, and has helped with the family search. Helen died in 1931; Montague in 1937.

John James (Jack), "the iron man", Henry calls him, the only surviving son of the earlier marriage, pursued a most successful career in milling, working initially in various

Chapter 5. The Miller and His Daughter

first-class mills to gain experience: ahead of his time in trying out new techniques and inventions. He has left a full account of his family and his life, in an individually-typed book from which I have gleaned many details - and a few quotations recorded here. For a while he returned to run the Avon Mills at Evesham after his father went to Birmingham, in 1898, carrying on the philanthropic traditions. He was also fully-engaged in rowing in regattas on the River Avon, and helping to inaugurate the Evesham Gymnastic Society supported by John Small and other cousins. He had spent four years at Prince Henry's Grammar School, Evesham, winning the Head Prize in both Lower and Upper School. In 1887, for the Queen's First Jubilee, he helped his headmaster (Reverend Seeley Poole) to make fireworks from old exam papers, cut up and wound round wooden "cores" and pasted on. The "stars" of the rockets had individual parachutes so that they would remain high in the air after the main explosion. He was deputed to set off the main rocket on the Bell Tower at Evesham, on that occasion; he says that at one juncture there was momentarily a sea of fire on the Tower top for a few seconds, but no damage beyond scorched beards.

Jack won the Workman Scholarship for University training in 1888 as his cousin Harry Fowler had won the first one awarded in 1885. He went to Owen's College at what is now Manchester University, passing in as the youngest man there. But he wished to follow a commercial career, so did not finish the course. Among the Mills he started or helped to start were Frost of Chester, Whitworths of Wellingborough and Marriages of Chelmsford. He was involved in experimental work on a new Purifier at McDougalls of Manchester and advised on breakdown jobs including one at Llansantffraid in Wales. Jack was only eighteen years old at the time, but he never told anyone that. He left Evesham Mills in 1902 for Great Alne, where his father had first been apprenticed. There he married Kate Stephens of Winchcombe, whose grandfather lived at Tregenna Castle, St. Ives, Cornwall. (This later became a hotel where Nancie and William used to stay in the 1940's each year). Jack and Kate had a son, Avery. Jack remained at Great Alne for the rest of his life handing on the Mill to his son. Sadly, Kate died in 1913, when Avery was nine, which was why my mother went to run the house and look after her brother and nephew at that time.

From the second family, **Will**, the engineer, worked in various companies both near home and abroad: with the White Steam Car Company in Cleveland, Ohio, U.S.A., and for a Tool Company in Waltham, Massachussetts. He had responsible posts at Coventry in the car industry for Mr. Siddeley (later, Sir John, and then Lord Kenilworth). Will retired to the village of Priors Marston, Warwickshire. His wife, Annie Louisa (known as Nancy) Trickett, was descended from the Triquettes of Haddington Hall, Scotland, so my cousin tells me. They were of Huguenot origin. Georges Trickett, great-grandfather to Annie Louisa, married Elizabeth Watt; and Annie's mother told them that she and James Watt of steam engine fame were cousins. Annie's father was called William Henry, the same as her husband. Will and Nancy had a son, (William) Henry, also an engineer, who married Laura (née Yates); they had a daughter (Marion Elizabeth) and a son (Mervyn Henry), both now married. Laura died in 1981. Will was a crack rifle shot and very disappointed at being rejected in World War I. Probably it was through him, whom she loved dearly, that Nancie became interested in rifle-shooting. I was startled to find the photo of her, with other girls, practising rifle-shooting (see photo opp.). Will was also a very good judge of old glass which he collected, being quoted by others as an authority. Again, this may have been what sparked off my mother's interest. She used to pick up small pieces of old glass in the little antique shops in York, in the 1930's, choosing whatever appealed to her, not as collectors' items. She acquired so many that when we came to divide them between the three of us, we each had a substantial number; my share, added to a few pieces of my own, overfills the glass-fronted display cabinet which my father bought Nancie to rescue her collection from a long, high shelf above the fireplace. By 1903, Will, at twenty-five, was well-established; he was the only one of Nancie's own brothers to be in England for most of her life; and he was a great comfort to her. He was a dedicated church worker, and during the 1939-45 War an active member of the Home Guard.

Ted (Edmund Owen junior), on leaving Sidcot Friends' School, went to Birmingham to help his father with the Avondale Bread Co. Ltd., until they all moved to Warminster, where Ted sold the flour they produced, and his brother Fred ran the Mill. **Fred** (Charles

Chapter 5. The Miller and His Daughter

(1) Owen Hancox at the end of his life
(2) Ted: studio portrait, Manitoba, Canada
(3) Rifle-practice at Evesham, 1912. Nancie on extreme left

Chapter 5. The Miller and His Daughter

Alfred) won a scholarship to Mason's College, where his cousin, Harry Fowler, had done so brilliantly a few years before; but he moved to Warminster when he was needed and had to forego his College place. He and Avery had stayed on as boarders at Evesham Grammar School for two terms when the others moved to Moseley, Birmingham, so that Fred could sit the Scholarship exam. Before the Grammar School, they had attended the School of Mrs Martin, sister to Aunt Polly (Fowler), where Avery learnt sewing and knitting; he could sew on his own buttons (useful in the Army and P.O.W. camp). When the Marsh Mill at Warminster was sold, Ted and Fred went to Canada and 'homesteaded' together in Saskatchewan. Fred sent home a postcard on their arrival in Winnipeg (see opp.). It is franked June 24th, 1903, and has a two cent stamp featuring Queen Victoria nearly two-and-a-half years after her death. Ted, whose photo I much admire (see p.65), joined the Sixth Canadian Mounted Infantry when War began. He was present at the taking of the Hindenburg Line, and sent a full account of it to his brother, Jack. Ted hurt his shoulder badly when trying to 'circus-ride' two horses at once, a foot on each. He was thrown when one horse tried to bolt and he held on to the reins of both horses. On his return to Canada, he became a Forest Ranger; after an accident when he hurt his foot with an axe, he moved to Vancouver Island and had a Grocery Store. On February 12th, 1927 he had married Mary Margaret Bell of Saskatoon. A printed card, similar to a wedding invitation, was sent out by the bride's mother, Mrs. Peter Cameron, to announce the marriage. My mother kept the card. There were no children, and the new Mrs. Hancox died not long afterwards.

Fred kept the Homestead going while Ted was in Europe, during the War. He could not volunteer as he wished to do, as he had had a punctured ear-drum, as a child, and an ulcer of the jugular vein. In spite of a successful operation, it left him deaf in one ear. When he eventually left the Homestead, he joined Ted in Vancouver Island, still single.

Avery, the last born of the seven successive sons bridging both families, was apprenticed by Jack to learn Market Gardening with Henry Field at Evesham, for three years. He worked overtime and saved every penny until he could pay his fare to Canada and have the stipulated £5 necessary for being allowed to land. Jack arranged for Avery to go to a friend in Moose Jaw, "to learn Canadian ways". Avery took up virgin land from the Canadian Government, and set off with a covered wagon and an ox team to start farming on the prairie in Saskatchewan. He homesteaded until he volunteered for the First Canadian Mounted Infantry, and was in the Battle of Ypres. Surviving after his Battalion had been wiped out, he was taken prisoner and had two years in Germany: at Hanover, and Aachen. (See photo opp.) Once, he escaped, reached the Dutch frontier, and was caught and returned. Set free in 1918, he was sent to hospital in London.

Nancie, who worked in the Bacteriological Laboratory in the King George Hospital, 1917-1919, (see Chap. 6), was told one day that someone called 'Hancox' - not a common name - was in a certain ward. Could it be a relation? She went along to see, and found her brother, Avery, last heard of as a Prisoner-of-War in Germany; last seen nearly fifteen years before. It was a moving re-union. Avery had become engaged in Canada to Vera Ledger from London who had been living in Canada with friends. She had returned to England when he was taken prisoner, hoping for his early release as he had been seriously wounded. From hospital, Avery went to his Mother and sister Dorothy in Broad Campden, Gloucestershire (see photo opp.), and there he and Vera were married. They returned to farm in Canada, but were eventually driven from their land by the droughts and dust-storms which devastated the prairie. They settled in Vancouver Island, beside Ted and Fred. They had no children. In 1949, my parents visited Vancouver Island and were re-united with Fred, Avery and Vera. Ted unfortunately had died the winter before, after my parents had to post-pone the planned visit because of someone else's illness in York. Nancie was very sad never to see Ted again after he left in 1903. (More in Chap 15).

So Owen, fathering eleven children, would have enjoyed from them all only seven grandchildren, three of them my mother's. Through the male line, two of them are Hancox; each of these has one son, but so far there are no sons in the next generation to carry on the name. I hear that other sons of Joseph (born Tysoe 1753) have more male descendants.

Chapter 5. The Miller and His Daughter

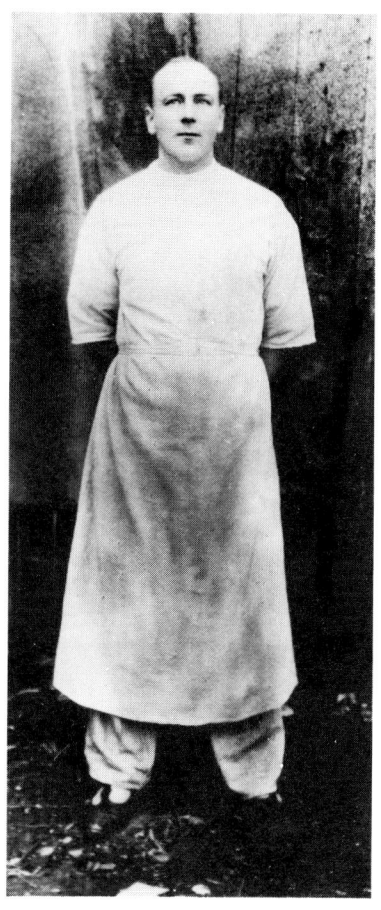

(1) Fred's card to say they had arrived safely in Canada
(2) Avery Hancox, P.O.W. at Aachen Hospital, Germany, June 1916-Jan 1918
(3) Avery and his mother, in the garden at Broad Campden (1919)
(4) Bacteriological Laboratory at the King George Hospital, Waterloo, London

Chapter 5. The Miller and His Daughter

The move from Warminster to Bristol was a harsh rending apart of a close and devoted family, not only by death, but by distance. Owen now had only his wife and two young daughters to consider. Living in a semi-detached house with relations through the wall, and his own splendid sister across the road in a very spacious old house with a large garden and parkland beyond, he had much family support. Louisa and Jeremiah Bebb reached their Golden Wedding the month before Owen died. They had a long history of giving care and devotion in a secular as well as a religious context. Owen and his wife had reached their Silver Wedding anniversary the Spring before they left Warminster. Judging by the silver mark, I'm sure that the silver table-napkin ring marked 'Mother' which I inherited from my mother, and she from hers,was probably a silver wedding present (1902) from her sons. How it must have grieved Owen to know that he would not be there to watch over his womenfolk. Nancie, at just thirteen when he died, was especially vulnerable. They were very close. Dorothy, the 'tomboy', was more resilient. She went to Art School in Bristol, and showed considerable talent. She finished all but the last term of a five-year course before being called home as her mother was ill. Dorothy looked after her mother in Stratford-on-Avon, at Top Farm, Weston Subedge, (see photos opp.) and finally at The Mount, Broad Campden. As I write, I have on the wall in front of me a really splendid large still-life, painted by her. The oranges and cherries glow and look good enough to eat; the draped material is gossamer-thin and translucent; you can feel between your fingers the tasselled edge of the tablecloth. It is as good a still-life painting as any we have seen. It is dated 1907, so she could not have been more than nineteen.

After Anne Fowler, Owen's widow, died in 1929 just before her eightieth birthday, Dorothy stayed on in the house in Broad Campden until she died in 1977. She kept hens, ducks, geese, bees, and at one time, goats. Rabbits too - I still have some gloves I made from skins she sent me. She had worked in the Land Army at Newstead Abbey (once the home of Lord Byron, the poet) near Nottingham, during the 1914-18 War, and was always successful at growing things: flowers, fruit, vegetables. Although so different, Nancie and Dorothy were always close. They wrote to each other weekly for over fifty years, addressing each other by old childhood nicknames: Peter (Nancie) and Jumbo (Dorothy). Dorothy was a straight-forward, no-nonsense person. When her older brother recorded that she "went as a pupil of Miss H. - to Aldington Lodge to learn flower gardening", Dorothy added a characteristic note of her own: "pupil to Marion H. - what rot. I was not taught a thing, only how to water the cucumber frame - just a general help, mostly housework!"

Aunt Dorothy was always a pleasure to visit with her rich Gloucestershire 'burr', so unlike my mother's voice, her salty comments and her throaty chuckle. Because of headaches and for many years dizziness brought on by Ménière's disease (of the middle ear), I remember her always wearing an enormous beret stuffed with cotton wool all round the back, to keep her head warm. She had this on day and night, removing it only to replace the cotton wool, and presumably when she took a bath. For what I think was about the last twenty or more years of her life, she received visitors lying on her divan bed in her sitting-room, beside the fire, the windowsills covered with plants, a miniature garden, and a fish tank in good working order which cast a green light over the room. She was tended by a neighbour from the village who was very good to her, and gave her even more care and attention than she was employed to do. The front door was *never* locked. In Summer it stood wide open all the time, protected by a porch with brightly-coloured stained glass windows. Inevitably the garden became badly-overgrown and the new owners found the little lily-pond only when their small son fell into it.

The chief impression I had of my mother's middle childhood was of a great and irretrievable loss by the death of her father. Three of her brothers who had been living at home had also gone. The pleasant, country world of Corn-mill and running water was lost, also for good. As I write this, I see suddenly and for the first time, the significance for her of the little stream ("beck" as it was in Yorkshire) which ran through our garden when I was a child; and her intense excitement when she saw beside it a rare bird such as a kingfisher, or a snipe. I remember especially the snipe. They were echoes of the happiest years of her long-lost childhood. Her ties with her mother were always close. One day, when my mother lay dying, always calm and never complaining, my sister saw she

Chapter 5. The Miller and His Daughter

appeared to be talking to someone, and she was smiling. When asked who it was, she replied very simply, and with no sign of surprise, "I was talking to my mother". She kept all her faculties to the end. I am heartened to think she felt her spirit growing close to her mother's; hers is not the only instance I have come across, and I look forward to knowing my mother once more when my turn comes.

I had no means of knowing how long Nancie and her mother and sister stayed on in Bristol after the stark date I have on her father's death certificate: April 27th, 1904. Nor even when they had left Warminster. Then I received the large bundles of photos and letters which had lain untouched for over fifty years: first in our attics, and later in my sister's storeroom. I searched through them and found many clues; but nothing about Bristol until I reached the only clue I was to find: the little blue letter.

(1) Top Farm, Weston Subedge, where Mrs Hancox and Dorothy lived until Spring, 1918
(2) A family gathering at Top Farm, Weston Subedge in 1915 or 16 when Anne Hancox was living there Left to right: Will, Henry (aged 2 or 3) and Nancy Hancox; Anne (on chair); Dorothy (with rabbit); Jack and Mary Hartley Smith; Avery (Jack's son); Nancie (with Victor, Jack Hancox's dog); Jack Hancox (with Toby) Photo again taken, presumably, by Mary's husband

Chapter 6

The Little Blue Letter

The only advance warning I had that Bristol might be one of the places closely connected with my mother's early life was an occasional reference by her to 'Fishponds' and 'Cousin Florrie'. I had no idea of the length of the family's sojourn there, having always thought of her at Evesham and, later, Great Alne near Alcester. Then I obtained her father's Death Certificate: April 27th, 1904, two days after his twenty-seventh Wedding Aniversary, at 370 Fishponds Road, District of Stapleton, Bristol. The registration of the death was made four days later by Francis (sic) Bebb, niece (by marriage) of the deceased, residing at 368 Fishponds Road, and entered as 'Present at the Death'. Frances (née Wall, a widow named Robins when she re-married) was the wife of Charles Bebb, the only surviving son of Jeremiah Bebb and his wife Louisa, Owen Hancox's sister, who lived in nearby **Ridgeway Park House**.

I assumed that once her father was dead, Nancie and her mother had returned to their own part of the country. I found that, later, they were living in Stratford; there is a photo of Nancie standing at the gate of 24, Evesham Place, Stratford-on-Avon, looking quite grown-up. Owen Hancox had drawn up his Will still in Evesham, on 26th October, 1894, by which he appointed William Spencer, the Miller from Great Alne, and Geoffrey New, his Evesham solicitor, to be his Trustees. They were instructed to call in his Life Policy and sell 'The Limes' and any other possessions for money; to invest all moneys; and to pay the income from the investments to his widow for the rest of her life. Money could be used to advance any of his children in life as approved by his widow; and when she died, the remaining estate should be divided between his surviving children. The witnesses were Henry Fowler, Upholsterer, Evesham; and Joseph Godwin, Miller, Evesham. Henry was his brother-in-law, of course, and Joseph was his tried and trusted senior employee at the Mill who had started with him at Great Alne in 1857, moved with him to Evesham, and was exactly the same age. The will is longer and more complicated of administration than that of his father, James, so Probate was not granted until 15th December, 1904.

There were also three photos of Nancie with school-mates: two, of the girls in her year in successive years; and the hockey team (see photos opp.).Which school in Stratford, I wondered? One very small letter (without envelope) on pale blue linen-type notepaper turned up among the scores of notes, photos, press-cuttings etc., which my mother had kept. Clearly headed with an address in Bristol and dated, it thanked Nancie for her services as secretary of the St. George Secondary School Hockey Club, and spoke of her "excellent efforts". The writer was Gertrude Price who became a long-time friend, and was later headmistress of a large school in Southport. She was Captain of the Hockey Club; the date was February 28th, 1909. The missing envelope (with address) would have told me for sure whether the Hancoxes were still in Bristol at that time. The letter told me that Nancie was apparently at the St. George School, Bristol, until at least the end of the Autumn Term in December 1908, a few days before her eighteenth birthday. A note of thanks to her had been passed by The Hockey Club at their meeting early in the Spring Term, 1909. She kept her hockey stick, until she died; I remember it.

The hunt was on to ascertain the whereabouts of this school and to confirm her time there. I arranged to go to Bristol to 'search', and I enlisted the help of the City Archivist. In the Records Office, I was supplied with some old School Registers, and huge volumes of H.M.I. (School Inspectors) Reports. I found four St. George Schools in Bristol: all unfamiliar to me. I worked my way through the volumes supplied; consulted reference cards; ordered Xerox copies of a brochure (1894), issued to launch the most likely 'St. George' School; and its Jubilee Number (1944). The photographs of this school building (see photo p.72) were impressive: a huge block, several storeys high, situated on the South edge of St. George Park in the district of that name east of the City Centre. The school at that time was called the 'St. George Higher Grade and Technical School'. It promised tuition in the Elementary Section in Scripture, Reading, Writing, Arithmetic, English Grammar and Composition, Geography, Elementary Science, Theory of Music,

Chapter 6. The Little Blue Letter

(1) Nancie's class; she is 2nd from the right, back row
(2) Second year Girls, 1906-7. Nancie is 2nd from the left, back row. She (alone) is wearing the hockey team costume: navy blue serge blouse and skirt; light blue sailor collar and tie
(3) School Hockey Team, 1906-7. Nancie seated, 2nd from right. She played left half.

Chapter 6. The Little Blue Letter

(1) St. George Higher Grade and Technical School, Bristol (1894)
(2) Nancie's Attendance Sheet (1903-1909)

Chapter 6. The Little Blue Letter

Singing, Drawing, Manual Instruction, Military Drill, French, Algebra, Physiography, Hygiene, Shorthand and Book-Keeping. The girls would also have Needlework and Cookery. Accommodation was planned for 250 boys and 250 girls, all of whom must undertake to complete each year's course, once they were offered a place. Fees 5d. per week in 1908; school hours: 9 - 12.30 and 2 - 4.30.

In the Science and Higher section, the subjects taught were Maths, Chemistry, Physics, English, French and Latin Grammar, etc., and a good number of technical subjects. The aim was to offer a four-year course of Higher education, and to insist that all parents who enrolled their children would keep them there for the full four years. The Jubilee Number of the School magazine details the long and determined struggle by the largely-uneducated members of the local School Board to build and launch the school for the benefit of future generations of local people: to be financed jointly by the Bristol Education Authorities and private subscription. It is a triumph for the vision and perseverance of the representatives and the people of the district of St. George.

After my concentrated morning's work at the Record Office, we set out to find the school, still not sure it had been my mother's. I had consulted old maps of Bristol at the National Library of Scotland Map Room in Edinburgh, and had found Fishponds Road leading to Fishponds village, Ridgeway Park House and Ridgeway Cemetery; and St. George School within St. George Park. Nearby was the Free Library. When we reached the site of the school, the building rose high above the road, almost gaunt in its aspect. (See opp.). Along with the feeling of triumph at having located it came the anguish of noticing that the bottom windows were all boarded up and the whole place had a dejected and abandoned air. We drove on a few yards, wondering what to do. "Ask that lady there", said the friend who was chauffeuring me, so I did. The response was immediate. The passerby was a former scholar who remembered the school with great affection. "I'll take you to where the school has gone, if you don't mind my coming with you in the car?" She directed us to St. George High School (as it now is) less than a mile away. The pupils - all colours and ages - were just changing classes on what seemed to be the first day of the new school year. I watched the Headmaster, Mr. Morgan, direct a small very new pupil to her next class. When I told him what I wanted, he took me to his study, brought out a huge School Register from 1894, and within thirty seconds showed me my mother's "page": date of starting (May 3rd, 1903), and of leaving (January 23rd, 1909). She had gained the Oxford Junior Leaving Certificate in 1908, when in the sixth year (see opp.). Of all the discoveries I have made in tracing my mother's movements, the main events of her life, and the influences on her, this was, I think, the most exciting find, because I had arrived in Bristol only the night before knowing nothing at all of these five extra years; in one day, the desert of her school days as far as I was concerned had blossomed; and I could see and understand how she got her good secondary education.

Encouraged by this success, we drove to Ridgeway Cemetery, where the Crematorium Authorities had warned me that we were unlikely to find my grandfather's grave as the place had at one time been vandalised. The letter from the Crematorium said, "I should like to think you might be successful, but I must say that I feel you will be taking on a very dificult task". The nearest graves as I entered the Cemetery were relatively recent, but as I walked round the curving path, they rapidly got older. I saw '1910', and then at once a large white-ish stone clearly marked: 'In Loving Memory of Edmund Owen Hancox, born Stratford-on-Avon, October 9th, 1840. Died April 27th, 1904. At Rest'. When you have searched and travelled to find something like your grandfather's gravestone and been warned by the authorities that you have set yourself what they think is an impossible task, there is a great feeling of peace when you find it, and of having reached the end of a journey. You may have noticed that Owen's birth-date as given here is wrong by a month; it is curious that someone at some point mis-remembered it. (Readers of my first book may remember that I also found my other grandfather's gravestone in Sunderland without any difficulty; but its state was so poor that I had it replaced by a new one).

A member of the Baptist Church in Bristol found out for me that Owen's funeral was conducted by the Reverend W.J. Penberthy, at that time a minister in the Bristol East Circuit of the United Methodist Free Church. No membership lists of this church survive,

Chapter 6. The Little Blue Letter

(1) Ridgeway Park House (with Louisa Bebb in foreground)
(2) The hall, stairs and black oak banisters
(3) Boating on the River Avon "about 1911". Nancie (left) and Dorothy (right)
(4) Dorothy and Nancie

Chapter 6. The Little Blue Letter

so I have not been able to pursue this clue any further. Within a few minutes, my friend found the Celtic Cross put up for Jeremiah and Louisa Bebb. It is intact and tells us that Jeremiah died April 10th, 1912, aged 85; and Louisa died September 4th, 1919, aged 87: at exactly the same ages as my father and mother. Their nearby home, Ridgeway Park House, in part of whose grounds the Cemetery was built, has a long history. It features in early documents, e.g. as Ruggewaye (1402) and Le Rydinge (1590). In 1652 it was a Manor House (a mansion) named on all the maps. By the end of the last century it is referred to as a 'fine old Manor House: standing but rapidly decaying'. The fine cedars on the old lawn were still there; but the beauty of the Manor and its grounds were thought to have been ruined when the Rudgeway (sic) Cemetery Company acquired this portion of the estate. At one time Ridgeway House was a school attended by the famous cricketer, W.G. Grace. The house had a magnificent hall and flights of stairs with carved newels and stout spiral banisters, all made of solid black oak (see photo opp.). When the house was finally demolished (in 1938, to make way for a housing estate) the staircase was sold, to be shipped off to America.

When Nancie left school, on January 23rd, 1909, exactly one month after her eighteenth birthday, her future occupation was given as 'House-keeping'. Probably this was to learn from her mother at home, as her elder half-sisters had each done before marriage. Certainly she was very good at running a house. She trained a series of maids and cook-housekeepers for many years, and kept meticulous account books, down to the last farthing. Her teachers might have been surprised to see how much further she went than housekeeping: doing hospital laboratory work during the War; accompanying her husband to far corners of the world; receiving Royalty alongside him. I think Nancie and her mother moved to Stratford-on-Avon from Bristol very soon after she left school. I find Dorothy is living at another address in Fishponds Road, later in 1909, to continue her Art Course in Bristol; and I noticed that Aunt Bessie (Fowler) Hawley, Anne Hancox's oldest sister, bought land in Evesham Place, Stratford-on-Avon, for housebuilding.

Nancie's first post after she and her mother moved from Bristol to Evesham Place, Stratford-on-Avon, was as companion to an older relative, Miss Sarah Bomford, in Queen's Road, Evesham. Nearby was her older half-sister, Mary, a successful journalist and artist for Women's Magazines, who took her on numerous jaunts and picnics in her car, large and old-fashioned as it looks to us (see photo p.76). Boating on the River Avon and bathing in remarkable swimming costumes are also recorded (see opp.). Nancie was photogenic (like our elder daughter). She looks enchanting; how she remained unattached until she was twenty-six, I cannot imagine, although the syphoning-off of eligible young men from 1914 onwards would have had its effect. While in Evesham in November, 1911, Nancie won first prize at Whist with her sister, Mary. The prize-winning was part of a 'Conversazione' connected with 'All Saints' Festival in Evesham, which took place in the Public Hall in mid- November, 1911. Fifty years later, the 'Evesham Journal' reprinted paragraphs from November 18th, 1911 and the later press-cutting has been preserved.

When Jack Hancox's wife, Kate, (née Stephens), died in 1913 leaving a son, Avery, aged nine, Nancie moved to Great Alne to live with her half-brother, to run his house and look after his child. More photos and letters give some record of the number of family outings, visits and pleasures which many relatives and friends enjoyed together. Tennis parties, amateur acting, visits to the Perkin family in Tiverton, Devon, and elsewhere, all took place as light relief. The relatives of Jack's late wife, Kate, and of his mother, feature from now on, and suddenly I recognise names my mother used to mention of people who corresponded with her, but I'd had no idea where they fitted in. Kate, Jack's wife, had left Nancie her three-diamond engagement ring when she died. She and Jack became engaged on Nancie's birthday. Nancie, in turn, gave the ring to Daphne, Avery's wife, for their daughter Mary Hancox now grown-up and married.

There was plenty of work for Nancie, as her brother Jack was himself a very hard worker. She may have found it all a bit frustrating as it was not her own house and husband, and she could not see what the future would bring. She was short of money, although she had all her entertainment supplied within the family. And they were wonderfully supportive, including the family of Jack's late mother Catharine (Avery) of Headless Cross. Of them all, Nancie loved especially Uncle Joe (Avery) (see p.76), brother

Chapter 6. The Little Blue Letter

(1) Nancie and Uncle Joe (1913)
(2) Uncle Jack Hancox: outside his house in Great Alne, in 1938, with the cup awarded to him in 1888 when he was the stroke of the Prince Henry's Grammar school winning crew in the Evesham Regatta. Photo by the 'Evesham Journal' to commemorate the fiftieth anniversary. His blazer is that of a member of the Evesham Rowing Club.
(3) Nancie and her sister Mary out for a drive in Great Alne

Chapter 6. The Little Blue Letter

of Owen's first wife, Catharine. Joe is recorded as having been born at 7.30 a.m. on January 21st, 1839, and he lived until May 1915, just half-way through Nancie's time in Great Alne, when she knew him best. Everyone loved him. My mother spoke of him with very special affection. Jack tells how, when at the end of fifty years of helping good causes, Joe was presented with an illuminated address and a purse of one hundred sovereigns by the District, the money included pennies from many hundreds of local children. Someone had a bet that a letter from anywhere in England, addressed to "Uncle Joe, Redditch", would reach him; they tried it, and it did. (My father once had a letter - in the 1930's - from New York, addressed to William Wallace, Old York, England; it arrived easily. Not so, now. When I began this search using initially only my Granny Hancox's marriage certificate, I wrote to the Vicar of St. Peter's, Bengeworth, Worcestershire. In my ignorance, I had omitted 'Evesham'. The letter was returned to me undelivered, weeks later by the Post Office, although someone there had *added* 'Evesham' to the address, so it could perfectly well have been delivered).

After the outbreak of War in August 1914, Nancie went regularly to help at the Alcester V.A.D. (Voluntary Aid Detachment) Hospital. Nursing came naturally to her, and she would be longing to do something for the War effort. She would think of her brothers in Canada, Ted and Avery, who had enlisted and were serving in Europe. As the War years dragged on, and her brothers and friends were fighting in France, she saw press notices calling for women workers in France. On April 24th, 1917, she wrote to volunteer for paid service abroad. Conscious of her total lack of means, she asked about salary and what kit would be provided and what personal outfit required. As well as offering references for her abilities, she also said that she could produce them for "character and social standing, if required" which shows how the wording of the press notices were framed. The authorities were anxious to attract only the right kind of girl. She was asked to go for interview to The Commandant of the Reserve Detachment for Warwickshire on May 18th. Her railway fare would be repaid if she desired it.

Events moved very quickly after that. More letters (including one by Express at four times normal postage rate - i.e. 4d.! - on 29th May) offered her training in Bacteriology at the Lister Institute, in London, which she accepted; and directed her to report to the V.A.D. Hostel at No.8. Grosvenor Gardens. She would be on probation for one month, followed by a contract for six months' service at £20 per annum. At the end of the probationary month, a uniform allowance of £2.10s 0d every six months would be paid; and the salary went up by increments of £2.10s 0d each half-year, until £30 per annum was reached. There were also allowances for Quarters, food, washing, and travelling. The age limit for Foreign Service was 23-42; for Home Service, 21-48. These were the conditions for Nursing Members at Military Hospitals.

By Friday, June 1st, 1917, Nancie was on her way to London by train, to report to the Hostel in Grosvenor Gardens that evening between 5 and 6 p.m. and to start training on the Monday at the Lister Institute. The authorities were pleased that she had practical experience in Chemistry and Physics (thanks to St. George School, Bristol), as she would benefit more quickly from the training. The Express letter had asked her to reply by telegram; they were most anxious for her to start straightaway. When she received her certificate at the end of her six-weeks' training, she was living at 196, Cadogan Gardens, and she was sent to work in the King George Hospital, Waterloo, which was the largest single War Hospital under one roof in England. There she worked for an Australian woman doctor for whom she had a very high regard. She very much enjoyed the work; had she lived a generation later, she would have gone without question to University to study Science. Occasionally in later years she would remark ruefully that she was the only one in our family who was not a graduate. Her granddaughters include a nurse and a doctor.

When a room became available, Nancie moved to Ingram House, Stockwell Road, which had been taken over as a Club for educated women engaged in Government employment. She was there in October 1917 when she set out on what was to be a momentous visit to **Purley**, near Croydon in Surrey. You will remember that the youngest of my mother's brothers, Avery (named by my grandmother for the family of her husband's first wife), was engaged to be married to Vera Ledger, whom he had first met when she was staying

77

Chapter 6. The Little Blue Letter

with friends in Canada. She had returned to her parents in Purley in 1917, as Avery had been seriously wounded, and she hoped he might be returned to England. The Ledgers had agreed to take a paying guest: a young man, originally from Sunderland, who travelled up to work in a Law Firm in London. Vera suggested that Nancie should come to Purley to 'vet' the young man who was living in the same house, so she went by arrangement for tea, one Saturday afternoon. The young man liked to go walking at the week-end, his sandwiches in his raincoat pocket; and when he heard a young lady was coming to look him over, he was (so he used to say) even more keen to absent himself. But the weather was atrocious; the rain drove him back early; and within ten minutes of meeting Nancie he had only one end in view: to make her his wife and to care for her to the end of his days. This he did in full measure, arranging it even so that she might stay, provided for, in the house they subsequently built, until the end of her life.

The young man used to point out that he had been trained, as a lawyer, always to consider things very carefully before coming to a decision. On this occasion he entirely forgot his training. On October 17th, 1917 "between ten to five and five o clock" he had decided. William Wallace - for it was he - was won over by his Nancie's beauty, her open manner and her innocence. She looked at him and responded frankly and without guile or simper, unlike other girls. The lines of her face were classic, as I remember, as she kept this all her life; her eyes were large and well-spaced and her eyebrows were beautifully shaped. (see photo opp. he always carried). Her V.A.D. Uniform was very fetching, he thought; and the War-time rations (more stringent than in the 1939-45 war) had reduced her weight to under eight stone, though she was above average height. On that wet Saturday evening he saw her to her train; and she agreed to see him again. Soon after, when Nancie was given a bunch of roses, she broke off a bloom for him. The dried petals of that rose still lie in the little gold locket which he gave her as soon as he dared.

Billy, as they called him, wooed his Nancie all winter. Together, they went to the Theatre (in the cheapest seats); treasured programmes remain for 'The Chinese Puzzle' and 'The Better 'ole' or 'The Romance of Old Bill'. On February 24th, 1918, they attended a service at the City Temple, taken by Reverend Ebenezer Rees, who had been Billy's Minister at home in Sunderland when he was a boy (see Chap. 7). In his Autobiography, William records that he remembers the Rev. Ebenezer once preaching a sermon on "The most important event in life: Marriage". In his youth, William heard the saying, 'Don't marry for money; but if you are thinking of marrying, go where money is!' It is possible that, if Nancie had had a wealthy father still alive or money of her own, she might have married before she met William, but this did not weigh with him. He fell in love with her before he knew anything of her circumstances.

On Friday, March 1st, (or Saturday 2nd) Billy proposed to Nancie as they sat on a bench in St. James's Park in the evening with the traffic of London swirling round them, no doubt oblivious to the cold. He was accepted immediately; and Nancie wrote to her mother, her brother Jack and her sister Mary so speedily that, helped by the Sunday post, she received their replies by the Tuesday. Billy also wrote to his mother in Sunderland, and letters from her, his brother and his sisters packed into one envelope and sped down to Purley. Charles, Billy's brother, assured Nancie that he and Billy were more than brothers, they were 'chums'; he also encouraged her to make Billy look more respectable, and offered to loan him the price of a new suit if necessary!

The envelopes of these letters with their one-penny stamps (this rose to 1½ d. by June, 1918 and remained so for decades) are franked with the message: 'Buy National War Bonds Now'. George Ledger, Vera's father, wrote to her from his hospital bed, in pencil, on hearing of her engagement. He said, "A happy marriage is the crown of life, may you live long to wear it in your United Kingdom". Her sister Mary told her she'd be a "capable and jolly little wife" who would do all she could for her husband's comfort and welfare. She was inundated by good wishes, love and helpful advice in letters which she kept. They seem to me like a safety net of prayers and good wishes supporting the happy couple. The first letter Nancie received on her engagement, from her 'loving brother Jack' at Great Alne, reached her at Ingram House on March 4th; by the 8th she had moved to c/o Mrs Tungate, Clayton, Purley Park Road, the zeppelin raids over London encouraging her to move out of town. This meant Nancie and Billy could travel to work and back, and

Chapter 6. The Little Blue Letter

spend evenings and weekends together more easily.

The letters which Nancie kept show a continuing and loving concern from the wide circle of family and friends who had known and loved her during the years before: her mother in Gloucestershire; her brothers in the Army; and in Canada; the good folk of Great Alne and Alcester; and friends from her hospital days. Jack wrote her the most beautiful letter (from his sick-bed: "a touch of the East wind rather badly... not feeling too bobbish"), with touches of humour. He said he *knew* she could make a man happy and was old-fashioned enough to think that was the greatest happiness a woman could have. He sent Nancie's fiancé a message that he could have her for four years' trial (the period Nancie had been in Jack's house), and if he were not satisfied, Nancie could come back to him! He also wrote, "I don't think I should have had the courage to let you go, dear, if I had known how I should have missed you this winter". But Nancie had learnt to spread her wings and accept a challenge. She moved out from the loving supportive world she'd known, in one of the most delightful parts of England. She would visit them repeatedly, especially in blossom-time; but she was leaving them behind. She was on her own now - except for Billy.

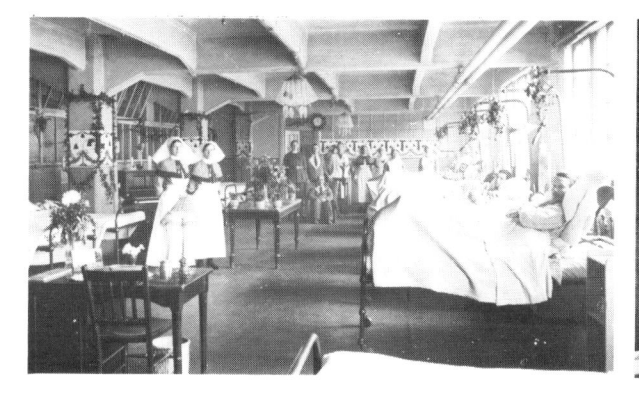

(1) William's favourite photo of Nancie as he first knew her.
He always carried a copy in his wallet.
(2) A Ward in the King George Hospital, Stamford Street, Waterloo: the largest hospital under one roof (2,000 beds) during the 1914-18 War
(3) The King George Hospital: now H.M. Stationery Office. Nancie worked here in the Bacteriological Department from August 1917 to April 1919

Part II William (1891-1918)

(1) The 'Auld Hoose' at Howtel, 1867 (see opp.)
(2) William as a young man

Chapter 7

William Wallace: Background and Youth (to 1911)

William Wallace was born on May 10th, 1891, at No.11, Stansfield Street, Monkwearmouth, Sunderland, in a one-storey terraced house, sturdily built and still there (now modernised). Monkwearmouth, as the name shows, is by the harbour, on the north side of the mouth of the River Wear; the parish still treasures the ancient church of St. Peter, founded in A.D. 674 by an Anglo-Saxon noble, Biscop, called Benedict. Biscop visited Rome five times and was inspired to found a monastery in his native Northumbria. The remains of the monastery church, rebuilt in medieval and Victorian times, stand not far from W.W.'s birthplace. Biscop brought glaziers from France to make some of the earliest glass in English history; he also brought books from Rome for the Library; and an Archchanter of the Vatican to teach the English monks how to worship in the Roman mode. St. Peter's became a centre of worship, learning and training whose influence went far across Europe.

Monkwearmouth lies in the district of Southwick, where William's paternal grandparents came in 1856, from the Scottish Border Country. I have told their story in my earlier book, 'William and Christina: One Woman's Search for her Ancestors' (published 1988): how this William (born 1831), the middle child of nine who survived (one only died - another William) was born into the house in Howtel near Flodden Field in which the Wallace family lived for nearly one hundred and fifty years. I included many illustrations; there are three photos of the Auld Hoose (built 1766) with its thatched roof and outside stone stair. Among my mother's photos, I discovered one more of the house at Howtel: taken nearly forty years earlier than the others, in 1867. It shows William's brother, Thomas, his wife, Jane, two of his infant sons, and his mother, Ann (see opp.). It gives some idea of the relative primitiveness of life at Howtel in those days, especially in contrast to life in a long-established, prosperous town in Warwickshire. Within a year or two of this photo being taken in Northumberland in 1867, my mother's grand-father, James Hancox, in Stratford-on-Avon, and her father, Owen, in Evesham, were building themselves spacious, detached, handsome dwelling-houses.

1867 is early for a photograph in such an isolated place as Howtel, but I recognise the people in it without any doubt as well as the house itself. I expect the camera belonged to one of the older brothers, who had gone away to work in Bolton and Bury (Lancashire), by the 1850's and who returned home frequently, helped by the expansion of the railways. I am including the old photo here to give a new reader a glimpse of the home of William's ancestors. Thomas (born 1833), who is in the photo, and his father James Wallace (born 1797) were merchants, supplying groceries, tobacco, etc., to a wide area of the countryside, with a baker's round as well. Our William used to go by train with his father from Sunderland to stay at Howtel, from about 1897; it left him with a lasting love of Northumberland as a whole, and the family's corner of the Cheviot Hills in particular.

'W.W.' as my father was called, certainly from 1919 onwards, also had a very special affection for his Scottish Granny, Christina (Galbraith), who stayed on in Southwick, Sunderland, in her widowhood from 1873, moving only for her last two or three years to live with her son, James, and his family in Thornhill Park. Thornhill Park is a prestigious district of Sunderland, and the Wallaces' home was a huge house, now divided into several flats. James Wallace, shipping lawyer, raised himself over twenty years from office boy to partner in the firm of solicitors, by sheer hard work and application. He had been left the "man" of the family at fourteen, when his father died in 1873: responsible for a widowed mother and six siblings, mostly younger than he was. He also died prematurely in 1911. W.W. in his turn was left, at twenty, with a mother, aunt and one younger brother and two younger sisters to care for. He was only part-trained as a lawyer, and again, in his case, he established himself in his career by prodigious efforts of

81

Chapter 7. William: Background and Youth

his own.

When James Wallace, my grandfather, died in 1911 his estate of £2,700 consisted of a Life Policy of £1,000, professional debts due to him, and the house in which they lived, when it could eventually be sold. Under the terms of a standard Will at that time, only the "income" on the estate would have gone to the widow for life. But a few weeks before James died, W.W. had persuaded him to make a new Will. He had also invented a special clause giving power to his father's Trustees to make up the income out of the capital to £150 per annum, and no more. So the six of them left were able to manage, although not easily, as the younger brother and sisters still needed to finish schooling and start on their careers.

Unlike Nancie, the youngest of eleven, William was the oldest of the surviving four. His brother, Charles, and sisters, Dorothy (not to be confused with Nancie's sister!) and Christina, were close to him in age. A baby brother, Robert Bruce, (born June 1898), lived only three months. (His father, we are told, said the baby must have found such a name too heavy to bear). In true Northern tradition, the first two boys and the first two girls were named after the grandparents: William and Christina for the paternal side from the Border Country; Charles and Dorothy (Embleton) for the maternal side, in Sunderland. Donkin was the name of James's wife, Alice, known as 'Ali'. Her father, Captain Charles Donkin, was a Master Mariner with two brigs, in which he took coal and other goods to the Middle East. In 1854, he was commissioned by the Government to take supplies to the Crimea; two years later, he took his bride, Dorothy Embleton, on a honeymoon voyage to Alexandria (Egypt) with a cargo of coal. She kept a Diary on the voyage out, during which she thought she would surely drown in the Bay of Biscay. Excerpts from the Diary are printed in my earlier book, along with a photo of Dorothy in 1891, with her infant grandson, my father, William Wallace, in her arms.

The Donkins had lived in Dock Street, Monkwearmouth, Sunderland, just up from the harbour on the North side of the River Wear, for generations. Charles Donkin was named for his own father; his father-in-law, Isaac Embleton, had been named for his. The Embletons were said to have come originally from Embleton Hall, north of Morpeth. I notice with interest that Isaac Embleton (born 1804) married Alice (Thompson) (born 1806). These are my great-great-grandparents on my father's maternal side. James Hancox (born 1804) and his wife Harriett (Cooke) (born 1806) were but my great-grandparents on my mother's paternal side. So, through the position in the family and the usually earlier age of marriage for women, one can slip a whole generation in three or four.

None of James Wallace's five sisters married. All but one died comparatively young, several of Tuberculosis (pulmonary): one aged only nineteen. His only brother, Thomas Galbraith Wallace, (born 1864) married and had three girls and then three boys. Most of them married and had family: all recorded in 'William and Christina'.

Our William Wallace wrote an Autobiography a few years after retiring for the second time. I shall use this in some of these Chapters to give an account of his early life in his own vivid words. He called his Autobiography "I was Concerned", using a saying familiar to the Quakers, whose Society he joined. He reckoned that the story of his life is of one who, seeing around him the bitter sufferings of undeserved unemployment, the poverty, and the unhappiness of wasteful industrial strife in the North in pre-1914 days, felt a passionate desire to ameliorate conditions. He had what he came to understand as a Quaker 'concern' so to establish a right relationship between workers and their employers, and to boost productivity, that the living conditions, the opportunity of employment, and the hope for the future might all be raised for ordinary men.

In his Autobiography, W.W. writes that he remembered his father as "a big man, kind, all-knowing and the embodiment of authority". His mother was "small and sweet; pretty, with fair hair which down to the white hair of her seventies, was always attractively and naturally waved and beautiful". Her second name in the family was "Soothing Syrup". He says, "whatever haps or hazards, whatever heart breaks or angers came along, her sweetness never failed to soothe". W.W. went first in Sunderland to a private "Dame's School", when he was six. There his particular school friend, Cyril Jacobs, took him to

Chapter 7. William: Background and Youth

his home in Thornhill Park, and gave him a much-valued glimpse into the life of a fine Jewish family. Next, at nine or ten, he went to Argyle House School in St. George's Square, nearby. He remembered his teachers with affection and admiration and he learnt without effort. In fact, he and his friends coasted along in the back row, as lazy as they could be until the day the form master asked for the names of those who would like to enter for the College of Preceptors exam. When Wallace put up his hand, another boy said, "It's no use *Wallace* taking it", whereupon iron entered into young Wallace's soul (to use his own words), "he swotted" for the exam and passed with Distinctions in four subjects out of eight, taking twenty-third place in all England. No-one in the school had ever reached such heights before. 'Billy Wallace', as the head-master called him in announcing the results, was on his way. His father wished to send him away to Boarding School, but his mother would not hear of it, perhaps because she had lost a baby not long before. So, instead of such advantages as he might have gained, he had all the years of his growing-up at home with his family.

They moved from Stansfield Street to Sorley Street on the South side of the River; from there, they attended the Grange Congregational Church (now the United Reformed Church and with another name), a mile away. When they went to live at No.1. Argyle Square in 1897, his father having by now qualified as a solicitor and become a partner, the church was less than five minutes' walk away, and William started Sunday School: every Sunday afternoon at 2.30 pm. Morning service was at 10.45am; evening service at 6.30 pm., for those old enough to attend. His father received letters on Sunday as there was then a Sunday delivery which William collected for him after morning church, and then took on as directed to another partner in the firm. Although it was not a "Scottish" sabbath, and they could do what they liked within reason, the boys were "almost reconciled to getting back to school on Monday", because they disliked Sunday so much. In this, they resembled James's cousin George at Howtel, thirty years before, as told in 'William and Christina'.

The Minister who made the most impression on William was a Welshman, the Reverend Ebenezer Rees, to whose sermons he listened for about fifteen years until he was twenty-one. No wonder he took Nancie to hear him in London, the week before they became engaged, in February, 1918. About this Minister, William wrote, "the true Christ-like spirit of the man shone through like a benison". By example, he taught the virtues of Courage, Compassion and Courtesy, which W.W. thought outshone all others. The two sermons which W.W. records as having particularly remembered were on "The most important event in Life: Marriage"; and "Here lies an honest man", a text which W.W. saw on a small gravestone (without name) in a churchyard in the Shetlands, and wrote to tell the Reverend Rees about it.

The house in Argyle Square was three storeys high, and the "square", which was really a gravelled drive with gardens, had gates at each end which had to be opened if a horse-driven cab or carriage needed to pass. The growing family of two boys, two girls, resident aunts and domestics, needed the extra room. In the yard behind the house they played 'constant cricket', the great art being to avoid breaking a window. At the back of the house, adjoining the 'back lane' (typical of that time and district), were an earth closet and a coal-house. The one was emptied in the dark of the night by men who were heard but never seen; the other was filled in daylight through a hatch high in the wall by a man specially employed to shovel up a whole ton of Best Household Coal. The coal cost about 14s.6d. (less than 75 pence) a ton; the man was paid 6d. (2½ pence) for shovelling the ton of coal.

W.W. noticed at this time, he remembers, the bare feet of so many working-class children, literally blue with cold in the winter. He reckoned it laid the foundations of his interest in social economics and social justice: the beginning of his 'concern'. The earth closets of his childhood also stimulated his interest in improved housing conditions. His mother, at Argyle Square, had two maids: a cook-general earning 5/- a week, and a housemaid who got 4/-. They slept in the back attic. The train from Sunderland to Newcastle used to stop on a bridge over the poor area, and small ragged children in the street below used to sing for pennies to be thrown out. James Wallace, no doubt remembering his own childhood, was one of the passengers who used to throw coins out.

Chapter 7. William: Background and Youth

In W.W.'s childhood, even middle-class children played in the street, as well as the park. In their seasons they had skipping, spinning tops, "booling" hoops, marbles, and a game with an oblong piece of wood with pointed ends called 'Kitti-Kat', as well as cricket, football etc... Often they had to make do with a football made of newspaper tied round with string. Indoors they sledged downstairs, either on a tea-tray or a wide wooden board. His sisters had narrower boards. The curve at the bottom of the stairs was not easy to manoeuvre. They did not 'skate' downstairs when their father was at home. (I am suddenly reminded that I was introduced to this game at my aunt's house in Sunderland by my cousin, one day in the 1930's, when the grown-ups had all gone to our great-Aunt Meggie's funeral). They also made models from penny coloured cardboard sheets, and put on shows, at home, with an improvised curtain and a conscripted audience. These were not always the success hoped for.

Another source of entertainment came from their cook's husband, a Coldstream Guardsman who fought in the Boer War. When he came home he kept them enthralled before the kitchen fire with tales of fighting in South Africa, how the brightly-coloured uniforms of the British made a marvellous target until khaki was used to shade in with the yellow-brown veldt; how the British troops built circular 'block houses' encircled with a double ring of vertical corrugated iron sheets between which there was a foot of sand or earth. The guardsman said (and they hoped it was true) that when the Boer bullets pierced through the outside sheet of corrugated iron, they were turned back by the sand, and returned exactly to the original marksman. A great childhood hero was Baden-Powell, founder of the Boy Scout Movement, whose dedication to camping may have inspired my father to take it up with great delight when old enough.

From his early days W.W. also records the street-sellers with their distinctive calls who passed by outside the nursery window: local fresh herring at two for 1½ d.; oranges at twenty for 1/- (5 pence); brown bowls and other ware carried on the head of "a lady dressed mainly in a shawl"; street performers; the hurdy-gurdy man with his monkey on the organ holding out its cap for contributions; and Dancing Bears. In the Argyle Square house, before 1907, they had an electric 'phonograph', on which they could record themselves singing and then re-play the round cylinders. It was actually his father's 'Dictaphone' for dictating letters and briefs: already in use in the first few years of this century. W.W. remembered singing 'Daisy, Daisy, give me your ranserdoo', not knowing what a 'ranserdoo' was but not liking to ask the maids in case it was indelicate.

Two episodes which W.W. recorded give some insight into his treatment by his parents when he was a child, beyond their concern for his education and a sound religious upbringing. One summer night when he was about four, he was playing with friends along the street and went into the house for a moment. His father, who was there alone, working on papers, called out, "Will, time you were in bed." Will asked if he might tell his friends and went back and continued to play, probably thoughtless rather than a deliberate ruse. Half-an-hour later, his father's tall striding figure appeared. Without a word he lifted his son up in one hand and carried him back down the street at the end of his extended arm. William felt so humiliated, he never needed the same lesson again.

On the other occasion, when he was anxious to join the local Cricket and Football club as a junior member at the age of twelve, he saved for a long time and had only 5s.6d. The annual subscription was 10s.6d. He asked his father to make up the difference one Saturday breakfast-time (not a good hour to choose) and was refused out of hand. To ease the pain of refusal, his mother took him to the main toy and sports shop to buy a cricket-bat with his 5s.6d. It was not, at that price, a real bat, only moulded deal stained to look like a bat. At lunch-time, his father presented him with a brand new 10s.6d. membership ticket, and asked for the 5s.6d. Of course it had gone! But somehow the bat was exchanged for a real one, said to have cost only 6s.6d. With hindsight, William guessed it had really cost much more as it lasted him for as long as he needed it. He was not a good batsman, but was always a (slow) bowler. Only in 1907, when he was sixteen, visiting the Franco-British Exhibition in London with his father, was it discovered that he was extremely short-sighted. That is why he was a poor batsman.

Keen always on football - though he would rather play than watch - he once went to London, alone, to see Sunderland play in the Cup Final at the Crystal Palace before

Chapter 7. William: Background and Youth

Willie Wallace's Certificate of Merit in Scripture March 8th, 1901 (measures over 14" x 10", made of cardboard, and in full colour)

Chapter 7. William: Background and Youth

Wembley was thought of. His pocket was picked and his return ticket and reserve money lost. He walked from Crystal Palace to King's Cross, and was allowed onto the train when he told his story. That got him home, though without anything to eat and drink since his morning sandwiches. In Sunderland he played right-half successively for different teams up to the outbreak of War in 1914; sometimes against local teams of coal miners. There was much unemployment amongst coal-miners at that time and the miners used to collect coal from the beaches and waste-tips to take home for fuel or for sale. They used to sling two heavy sacks of coal over the cross bar of an old bike and wheel it back from Silksworth Colliery. W.W. used to see them "looking weary and underfed" pushing the bikes up a steep hill near his home and at times he helped to push. His talk with the miners increased his interest in social and economic problems; and he was told long afterwards that he was remembered as "the lad who offered cigs to the miners".

He and his friend, Billy Campbell, (who later suffered so from arthritis) took to cycling together to explore the surrounding countryside: forty miles each Saturday afternoon throughout the summer with a 6d. country tea, en route. When he finished his London Matric exams in English, French, Maths, History and Latin, in summer 1908, he asked his father if he could visit his relatives in Edinburgh for the weekend. His father agreed; but instead of giving him money for the train fare or a stop for a night on the way, said he had a bicycle and it was only one hundred and fifty-three miles each way. So, on a very old-fashioned, heavy bike, on rough roads without tarmac, he managed the ride between 5 a.m. and 7 p.m., arriving more dead than alive. Three days later, he returned again in the one day. Later, he used to wonder if this had strained his heart.

Through his father's connections as a shipping lawyer, he was able to go on trips overseas on small coal tramp steamers of 700 tons: first from the River Wear (Sunderland) to Rouen, Northern France, with coal at 7s.6d. a ton delivered to the Rouen Gas Company and covered by Insurance; next from the River Tyne (Newcastle) to Leith in a small passenger boat, and so, joined by his Edinburgh cousin Arthur Snell, on to the Shetlands. On the return journey the boat called at Kirkwall (in the Orkneys) where they bathed in Scapa Flow "before Winston Churchhill discovered it for the Fleet in the 1914 War".

In 1910, he and his friend, a medical student - later a Professor of Surgery in Newcastle - walked from Gilsland in Northumberland to the Lake District, and camped on the south shore of Ullswater with other medical students in a bell-tent. It was here that he was to take his bride for their honeymoon in 1918. On the earlier visit they returned by walking over Helvellyn and the Honister Pass to Lorton; next day they walked to Caldbeck via Skiddaw (3,053 feet high), but as it was still early they pushed on to the next village. Here, all beds were taken as it was the Annual Show, so on they had to go to Carlisle: thirty-seven miles in all, with heavy packs. He wonders if they anticipated the Outward Bound Movement which came later.

As he grew up William enjoyed cricket and football and was drilled in a local Military Drill Hall by a Sergeant Major. He learnt to swim, though he reckoned he nearly drowned on his first visit to the Municipal Swimming Baths when an enthusiastic stranger threw him in at the deep end. (But W.W. was always one for embroidering a story to make it more dramatic). One year, in his later teens, he and his brother Charles and two other friends decided to bathe at the seaside (Roker) from May 1st to Christmas Eve. They kept to their programme but found it bitterly cold, and swore Never Again! One only of the friends stuck it out with him until Christmas Eve, the man who was later crippled with arthritis for the rest of his life.

W.W. was working at school towards the London Matric exams of December, 1907, preparatory to taking the London LL.B. when his father suddenly decided in June of that year that he might not live too long, so he arranged for his son to start on his five-years' Articles in his firm. W.W. himself wanted to be a doctor, at least in part from a desire to ease the suffering he saw around him. But he says, "one couldn't argue with a bearded Victorian parent"; so he had to leave school early to work in his father's office. Instead of continuing at school until his exams, he had to go to night-classes and prepare for the papers after a full day's work. At this time he was still wearing an Eton collar and knicker-bockers.

Chapter 7. William: Background and Youth

In the early years of this century, the British pound sterling was the great international standard of currency, based upon free exchangeability in the form of actual gold. There could be no "inflation" in terms of currency with this arrangement. A skilled workman earned twenty-five shillings (£1.25 pence now) per week; a low wage would be fifteen shillings. A pleasant new two-storey house with garden in a model village - such as the Joseph Rowntree Village Trust built - could be rented for four shillings and sixpence per week. Flour was 10d . a stone; cheese 4d. per pound. Milk at 1½ d. per pint compared with one shilling in the late 1960's when W.W. wrote his Autobiography; and thirty new pence now, only just over twenty years later: the price multiplied six times. Income tax was 1s.2d. in the pound (just over five per cent). Electric trams had replaced horse trams. Some people had motorcars, though James Wallace took his family for country drives in a horse-drawn landau. Some, including the Wallace family, had telephones: James's office number was 11; the home one was 234. Britain was still the world's greatest exporter, the pioneer in industrial development (with its economic strength in the North); the map of the world was covered with the red of the great British Empire.

William always had a deep and abiding love for Sunderland: 'a remarkable town' he called it, 'little known to the rest of Britain and to the Southrons in particular'. It had the deepest coal-mine in the world; when he was a boy, it was the largest ship-building port in the world. And alongside, it had a most interesting harbour with long shapely piers and miles of smooth yellow bathing beaches with Parks and Promenades. Roker Park football team "never out of the First Division for nearly seventy years" at one point, was a source of great joy to him. I remember he followed its fortunes all the days of his life; Saturday evenings were brightened for him, even in his eighties, if Sunderland had acquitted itself well that day. In Sunderland also as a growing boy, he noticed the poverty around, particularly the bare feet of some of the children, blue with cold. He had a growing resolve to do what he could in his own life to alleviate such distress; it was no coincidence that he worked to improve housing and to help unemployment even before he met Seebohm Rowntree and went to work under him in order to use the opportunities to carry out his dream. He also developed an interest in the theatre, in the form of the local music-hall, and used 6d. of his articled clerk's allowance of 5/- a month to visit the new Moss Empire Music-Hall every Saturday night for six months until he had had enough. But he remembered Marie Lloyd and the many songs of the music hall and continued to go when someone special was playing at the theatre, including Gilbert and Sullivan.

When he was sixteen, his father took him on his first visit to London. There was a pea-soup fog so he could not *see* Trafalgar Square, the stone Lions and the Nelson Monument. They stayed at a hotel in Holborn, and during breakfast on the first morning he saw what he thought was a kind of "Poole's Myriorama", that is, moving pictures, on the dining-room wall. Then he realised it was a mirror reflecting the unbroken stream of two-decker horse-drawn buses passing down Holborn. There was much to wonder at. Even at sixteen a boy had not seen it all.

At the office he learnt all the jobs in turn, including book-keeping and typing. He used to copy letters, often in his father's flowing hand, by inserting them in a Letter-Book, interleaved with wet rubber sheets and put through a press. Sometimes he typed all day if a big Brief for Counsel had to be done in a hurry. At the end of two-and-a-half years he passed his Solicitor's Intermediate Exam at the first attempt. One day, he had to take a cheque for £3,000,000 to the Bank.

James Wallace had for some time been established as a well-known shipping solicitor, highly regarded for his ability and his integrity. He was a good advocate but tried to resolve a client's case by negotiation rather than litigation, if possible. One ship-building client asked him to issue a writ forthwith for £20,000. James asked for forty-eight hours to see what he could do. At the end of the time, he handed the client a cheque for the full amount, together with an account for five guineas. The client, used to paying 10% commission, was speechless. Soon after, he returned with a very fine gold watch, sovereign-case and gold chain, with this inscription: the name of the donors and the date, and

"Presented to James Wallace Esq., in appreciation of his ability and character".

Chapter 7. William: Background and Youth

The watch is still in the family.

James's health deteriorated, and it fell to W.W. to watch when mistakes were made. He had a small room with a small window and an inter-connected telephone between him and his father, so in this way he kept an eye and learned to take responsibility. William's own words tell of his father's death, and his own anguish.

"Soon after I was twenty, in October 1911, my father took gravely ill, with double pneumonia. I sat with the nurse through the last night with him and as the morning came I watched him die; the strong able much-loved father who had seemed to a boy, quite understandably, to have almost the quality of permanency. He had lost his father and become head of the family at fourteen. He had begun under far greater handicaps than I ever should. He had achieved not only an outstanding position in his profession but a wide respect. He was of utter integrity. He could get on with all classes and conditions of men. He would stand no nonsense: he was a fighter and proud to be the descendant of fighters. But he was always kind and generous; he would, for example, never hesitate to waive a fee to poorer clients, like an old family doctor with his poorer patients; before the Poor Man's Lawyer was invented, at any rate in the North. For myself, he had, indeed in some ways, brought me up hard; but it had always been intended for my good, as I recognised. From my earliest recollection of sitting on his shoulder, he had been kind. Now that tower of strength had fallen and I felt strangely alone. I had to break the news to my mother and aunt and to the young family. I had to make the funeral arrangements and, as part of this, to register his death. As a final blow, some unintended wording in the doctor's certificate involved an inquest quite unforeseen by him. The Coroner, of course, had known my father and respected him. For the rest of that day I followed the Coroner round his listed inquests in his area (always just missing him) to see if he could overcome the difficulty in the medical certificate; or, if not, to arrange the inquest with as little hurt to my mother as possible. We had no cars in those days. I walked all the miles and caught the Coroner finally near 10 p.m. when I was near exhaustion, after two days and nights without sleep. Next day I led the Coroner and his jury to "view the body" and gave evidence. The following day I led the mourners as I have described in the Introduction. Then on the same afternoon, with my Uncle William Snell, from Scotland, one of my father's executors, I sat and arranged who should carry on his business. I myself couldn't do this even in form because I hadn't qualified; I was still an Articled Clerk. I was an executor but couldn't legally act because I was under twenty-one. But, boyish still, I was head of the family; my teenage, indeed, was clearly ended."

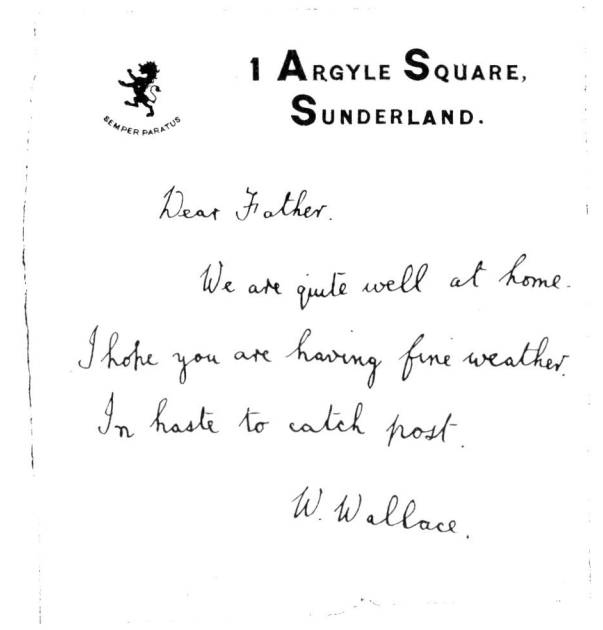

1 ARGYLE SQUARE, SUNDERLAND.

Dear Father,

We are quite well at home.

I hope you are having fine weather.

In haste to catch post.

W. Wallace.

This little letter was among my father's papers: no indication of date or destination. Why did his father keep it? "Semper Paratus" (Always Ready) was James Wallace's Notarial seal

Chapter 8

The Law: London Beckons (1911-1918)

W.W. had now to shoulder the responsibilities of a family man, and he was only half-fledged. With the example of his father behind him, and before him the task of supporting his mother, aunt, brother and sisters, and launching the younger ones into independent lives, he set about his affairs. Speedily, he found them a much smaller house nearby. It had been empty for a while, so he bargained for a rent of £26 per annum plus rates, which left them with a little more than £2 per week for gas, coal, clothing, medical fees and food for six. Charles, his brother, was at an excellent 'Higher Grade' School where the charge, if any, was nominal; nine months later, Charlie left school and gained a free Scholarship to Skerry's College in Newcastle-upon-Tyne to be coached for the Civil Service. His sisters were at an excellent private school, where the distinguished and charming headmistress, when he diffidently asked if she would excuse a quarter's notice, flatly refused to let them leave. She wished them to continue without payment. W.W. records that one thing he has noticed in life is how much true kindness there is in private life, if not always in public. I see him then as an appealing young man: small, but courageous. His father was known and respected in the community, a leading figure in the maritime world of Sunderland and the church. Dorothy and Chris, his sisters, both had intelligence and bright out-going personalities who were a credit to the school. The headmistress also had a kind heart.

So, on £2 per week, they settled down to adjust to the new life in the small terraced house: a house still there and looking rather gloomy on the day I went by in the rain. A great contrast to the home they had left, which until a few months before had sheltered all of them, as well as father, grandmother, relatives and domestic staff. If they could manage for that first year, W.W. would by then begin to earn. He had looked forward to joining his father as a partner in the firm; but now he was relieved to be able to arrange for his father's former solicitor-managing clerk to return to take over, and to have his Articles of Clerkship transferred to him. He now had to make sure he passed his Solicitors' Final exam at the first opportunity in the following June, 1912. At that time, it was the custom for an articled clerk to study at home, aided by correspondence courses. The one outstanding agency for coaching then was the firm of Gibson and Weldon of Chancery Lane, London. Luckily the fee for this twelve-month course had been paid during James Wallace's life-time, so his son completed it early in the New Year, 1912.

At that point London beckoned for the first time. Gibson and Weldon wrote to say that they had found W.W.'s work for their course quite outstanding. If he could go to London for their three-month final course they thought he had a good chance of First Class Honours. The Honours Exam of the Law Society was a separate, optional one taken immediately after the ordinary Final by only a small minority of candidates. Usually only a handful of these achieved First Class Honours; sometimes, none at all. Gibson and Weldon's estimation of his potential was gratifying. Had his father still been alive, he could more easily have gone. But how and where was he now to find the necessary money? In those days you took delivery only of those things you had saved for and could pay for. It would cost at least £50 to cover extra class-fees, travelling and the very simplest accommodation. All he had was £17 in the Post Office Savings Bank, from birthday presents in the past. There were no scholarships outside the Universities. Yet First Class Honours, apart from personal satisfaction, could lead to a chance to re-establish the family fortunes.

The one person who might help was his Uncle William Snell, a Treasury official in Edinburgh, whose wife was sister to William's mother, and who had been his father's executor. It was to his family that W.W. had gone to stay on the incredible bike-ride. The two families had always been close. The surviving family photos of William and his father, and William and his maternal grandmother (come North to see her daughter, Mrs Snell) were taken at Moffats of Edinburgh on their visits there. He appealed to his Uncle to lend him £50, his only security being the total value of up to three prizes he might win:

Chapter 8. The Law: London Beckons

£37.10s.0d. His Uncle said he didn't think much of his security, but he admired his spirit; he enclosed his cheque. Uncle William also said he had friends in Finsbury Park who would offer William an attic bedroom and board for £1 per week. This made the scheme just possible, so he set out for London.

Page after page of law books filled his days. He reckoned he had already read about forty thousand pages before going to London. Once there, he read more than one thousand pages a week in revision. Classes in Chancery Lane took up four or five mornings a week; otherwise he read law from breakfast to midnight, six days a week. On Sundays, he visited an Aunt, Miss Snell, sister to the uncle who had lent the money, who had a school at Chingford, in Essex. He used to get a return ticket by tram or bus, as far as he could for 6d., and walk the rest. There was no fire in his attic bedroom, but it was a fine spring and he could always use a blanket. When the days got warmer, he lay on the grass in Finsbury Park to read. He had pledged his success as a security, so he had to succeed. He reckoned this gave him an unfair advantage over the other candidates. In one set of Test Papers he was top with 76/80; in another, he got 119/200.

The Final exams involved two days on the Pass exams, a day's break, and two days on the Honours. He felt he had done well in the Honours, but had he done sufficiently good papers in the Pass exams to be considered for Honours? That was how the system worked, and his knowledge of practical law was unorthodox, in shipping and commercial law. He returned to Sunderland, knowing he had passed, but waiting to hear the result of the Honours Papers. He had arranged for a friend's brother to send a telegram with his results. His colleagues in the office handed him a telegram congratulating him on gaining SECOND CLASS Honours. When they saw his crestfallen face, they handed him the real telegram, which said: "You are First in First Class Honours and have been awarded the Clements Inn, Daniel Reardon and Clabon Prizes..." His gamble appeared to have come off.

Two results quickly followed. One was his first taste of publicity when he answered questions truthfully and naively, such as saying he had even read law in his bath, which led to an appropriate headline in the papers. This made him anxious to avoid press comments in future. The other was that his prizes were to be in book form, so could not be used to repay Uncle William. This would mean a debt hanging over him for years. (It also meant he built a very large set of book-shelves to hold all the books. I now treasure the book-shelves and find them very useful). Six months later, he was awarded the Scott Scholarship of which he was unaware. It went to the top candidate in all four Final exams in one calendar year and was worth £150 in *cash*; the loan was instantly repaid. I have, hanging on the wall behind me, the Certificate which says W.W. came first in First Class Honours in the Law Exams of June, 1912 (see p.95 for the article published in "Law Notes" for September 1912 about his success).

W.W. then had an offer from a distinguished firm of solicitors in the City of London to take over the remaining two or three months of his Articles of Clerkship and to pay him meantime. The salary would be £100 p.a., which he thought insufficient to reflect his First Class Honours. He explained that he would have to send home £50 p.a. so they raised it to £125 p.a. and he accepted, reckoning he would gain useful experience in a well-known City firm. For his work he had to wear a silk hat and morning coat; in it he lunched daily at an Express Dairy as cheaply as possible. He took rooms in Purley Vale, Surrey: bedroom, sitting-room and attendance for ten shillings a week; extra for food or firing. Out of his forty-eight shillings a week, he sent £1 home and manged on the rest. His brother, Charles, joined him a few months later, taking a post in London at fifteen shillings a week and sharing the rooms in Purley until he moved into his own bed-sit. Before the end of Charles's working life he was a Director of a world-famous Company in Birmingham. Dorothy became a teacher, and Chrissie worked in the Bank. All of them subsequently married.

In Purley, W.W. became friendly with Mr and Mrs Scott, who were "Geordies" from the Tyne and proud of it. They went long walks together over the Surrey hills on Saturday afternoons. He went regularly to Purley Congregational Church (where he was eventually married). His interest in social and economic problems was growing, encouraged by people he met, books he read, meetings he attended. Arising from his concern about the

Chapter 8. The Law: London Beckons

poverty and hardship witnessed in Sunderland, he had corresponded with people like Ramsay MacDonald in a search to learn more about the problems and ways to help. Now, in London, he became a "Poor Man's Lawyer" (at Mansfield House Settlement in Canning Town). In those days, the work was unofficial and unpaid.

His enquiries about social conditions and efforts to ameliorate them led him to the Fabians, where he heard and met Sidney and Beatrice Webb, G.D.H Cole, Bernard Shaw and others. He corresponded with H.G. Wells, one of his youthful heroes, whose every book he read. He yearned for "the establishment of something (he) could accept as social justice". The legal work he was doing in London and the future it offered did not attract him. His mother needed him at home. He was offered a managing clerkship in Newcastle-upon-Tyne by Charles Shortt, brother of Edward Shortt K.C., the then Liberal Home Secretary: salary c. £150. As he could live at home, this was worth much more to him and his family, so he gave a month's notice. At that point the Senior Partner in his firm in London died, leaving £50 to each of the staff still there and who had been with the firm longer than six months. The son approached W.W. to say that, although he was legally entitled to the £50, he hoped he would want to disclaim the legacy; but W.W. reflected on the disproportionately low salary the firm had been paying him anyway, and the need for the extra money at home, so he did not comply.

He returned to Sunderland in Spring 1913, glad to be back with his family and friends, and enjoying the firm in Newcastle. He also resumed his outdoor interests, including camping, and bought himself a small circle tent. He went with his cousin, Arthur Snell, on a Norwegian vessel taking coal to Viberg (later Viipuri) in Finland (then part of the Russian Empire) and returning with Finnish timber. (The Swedish Captain, the Finnish Steward and the Norwegian Chief Mate - who spoke English well - looked after them on the voyage). Once landed, William and Arthur took train to St. Petersburg (now Leningrad), where no-one spoke English or German, so that, lost and bewildered, they ended up at a ridiculously expensive hotel, unable to communicate with anyone. They had earlier found the British Embassy at 3.02 p.m. but it had shut at 3 o' clock. They saw drunks pushed into the gutter and left to lie there; they visited the gold-domed St. Isaacs, the Kazan Cathedral, where the worshippers approached on their knees up the long flight of steps and along the (pew-less) nave. At the end of the church coloured tapestry pictures were carried past, no doubt to cater for an illiterate congregation. They explored the city on foot and took steamer trips on the River Neve: restful and cheap (one old penny for 75 minutes). After two or three days at the hotel, they found a hotel clerk who did speak some English. If they settled up and left immediately, they could just manage the bill. They had hoped to discover something about living conditions under the Czar, but this was not easy when no-one spoke to them, nor, according to William, seemed to notice they were there, both in St. Petersburg and at the Finnish islands where they unloaded pit-props over the side, and W.W. and Arthur went ashore through a large Russian military camp. The Sentries had fixed bayonets, but they let the English youths come and go at will for several days. No-one asked for papers; once a sentry appeared to present arms as they passed. (See p.94-5 for W.W.'s 1913 Passport).

Finding still no outlet for his interest in social research, and having read "Poverty: A Study of Town Life", by Seebohm Rowntree (B.S.R.), he wrote on impulse to ask his advice. The letter, W.W. thought later, sounded priggish; but he included it in full in his Autobiography because it led to the whole of the the rest of his life. I shall include it here:

>   23 Otto Terrace,
>   SUNDERLAND,
>   9th February 1914

Dear Sir,

I am nearly 23, and an admitted solicitor. I qualified as such two years ago, and at my Final took first place out of six hundred candidates. For years it has been my ambition to spend my life in social work - that is to say in some work having as its direct object the raising of the conditions of the people.

Chapter 8. The Law: London Beckons

Most men seem to spend their lives in an effort to keep themselves in comfort till they can respectably die. I feel I am rapidly drifting into this self-centred attitude. I have nothing in my occupation nor my surroundings which tends to make me do anything else. I have at present a good situation, and I have no doubt that if I remain in my profession I will achieve what the world calls success, but I believe that it will in reality be failure - failure to see the best that is in me for the highest ends.

You will wonder, Sir, what possible reason I have for writing to you in this strain. My reason for writing to you rather than to anyone else is that from what I know of your life and work I shall find you not unsympathetic. I am writing to you as one of the leaders of social reform in this country to ask you to give a "lead" to a humble would-be recruit. What I wish to know is this, Sir - I am capable and reliable and a very hard worker if I am interested - can you suggest to me any sphere of work in which I could find an opening and into which I could put not only my brains but my heart - or if you cannot do so, can you suggest anyone to whom I could apply? There must surely be a place for me if I can find it. I am prepared to give up all hopes of being wealthy in the future if I can find a life work which I can look back on and feel that it has been worth while.

Will you, Sir, in the circumstances, forgive what must seem to you my presumption in writing.

       I am,
       Yours faithfully,
       W. Wallace

B. Seebohm Rowntree, Esq.,
YORK.

He was invited immediately to spend a night at The Homestead, York, B.S.R.'s home. B.S.R.'s Secretary wrote to tell him to look out at York Station for "an old shabby bay horse" which pulled the carriage, as the best horses were away with the family on holiday. He was advised not to bring a dress suit as they would not be dressing for dinner, with the family away. This was as well as W.W., as no doubt B.S.R. guessed, did not own a dress suit. The solicitor to the Company and to the Rowntree Trusts at that time was also at dinner to help size him up. B.S.R. told him he had no opening, but would remember him.

In March, 1914, W.W. was again invited to go to London by a Senior Partner in a very distinguished law firm unknown to him, who had in his year also been first in the Law exams. He offered two months' salary for a sea voyage such as he himself had needed to recover after the exams, provided W.W. stayed with his firm for at least a year afterwards. Regretfully and gratefully, W.W. refused. Soon after, a London family solicitor of Lincolns Inn offered him a job which he accepted, partly because he saw no particular prospects with Mr. Shortt in Newcastle; partly because his brother Charles now had a post at the Head Office of Barclays Bank in London and he would be glad to be with him again. Conditions at home had eased, and, chiefly, he hoped to find more scope in London to continue social research in his spare time, and if possible to work for a degree in Economics at the London School of Economics. War was about to break out, but few of his generation had given it a thought.

At the outbreak of War in August, 1914, W.W. faced a dilemma: aware of the suffering in neutral Belgium where the German troops had marched in, he could not resist his own pacifist ideals. Although not yet a Quaker, that was where his sympathies lay. His ideal of the peaceful brotherhood of man fought with the historical courage of his Wallace ancestry and the great sword in the Wallace Memorial at Stirling which his father had shown him as a small boy. He could not voluntarily shoot to kill another human being. All his Wallace instincts were to fight the injustice of innocents being brutally killed just across the Channel; but he had a widowed mother and large family responsibilities. His was a problem which faced many of his age, and older, at that time.

Almost at once, there was an appeal for motorcyclists to volunteer as Army messengers in France, so he went to the Recruiting Office in Westminster straight away to be medically examined, passed and given the King's shilling. As he was leaving, someone

Chapter 8. The Law: London Beckons

noticed he was wearing glasses, so they tore up his papers, took back the shilling and sent him back into the street within the hour. But for the belated eye test he could have been killed at Mons or taken prisoner for the rest of the war.

Guns were mounted where he had bathed at Sunderland; invasion was envisaged as a possibility, at least in the North. His mother felt very much alone with both sons in London. Mr. Shortt, his former employer in Newcastle, invited him to return with a view to partnership eventually, and with help in transferring his brother Charles (who was medically unfit for the Forces) to Barclays Bank in Newcastle. He was glad to accept. At Christmas 1914, he visited London to try to enlist in the London-Scottish, hoping their eye-sight standards might be lower; but again he was rejected. (Walking down Whitehall afterwards, he saw Winston Churchill standing on the Admiralty steps. Winston gave him personally his well-known scowl, which W.W. interpreted as "Why are you not in khaki?" W.W. longed to explain).

His only consolation for not being accepted into the Army was to be able to drill with the Officers' Training Corps on the Newcastle Town Moor, directed by an old friend who had become Adjutant of the Durham University O.T.C. at Newcastle. Curiously, the eye-sight test for the Officers was less severe, so he paraded in black coat, striped trousers and a bowler hat until his uniform came through! From time to time he tried to volunteer, but was rejected. At the end of the O.T.C. training he was sent for trial by the Cavalry, but having never before ridden a horse was not surprised to be thrown, once they reached the gallop. He was not accepted for the Cavalry! In Spring 1915 he passed the officer's eye-test (for an infantry commission), but was questioned on grounds of his heart. Sent to see Sir James MacKenzie, the distinguished heart specialist in Harley Street, he was told he was suffering from "Dilatation and hypertrophy of the left ventricle of the heart", and was advised he might die if he carried a heavy suitcase. His life was saved, while friends and comrades, half-trained and half-armed, were destined for unmarked graves round Ypres. This was the end of his volunteering for the Army. He carried many suitcases thereafter and lived to a good age.

The North-East coast was not without war incidents: shelling by the German Fleet which delayed his train from Sunderland to Newcastle one morning; and a Zeppelin raid over Sunderland which he and his brother watched one night from out in the open. But for the most part they were able to resume their pre-war activities and made full use of the little tent he had bought the year before, packing it and the Primus stove, tin mug and plates, and ground sheet and a camping eider-down onto their two bicycles. In London in 1913, he had become the Northern representative on the Council of the Camping Club of Great Britain. In 1915 he bought a rectangular tent, "some six feet square" with separate fly-sheet and jointed poles for easy transport. It could sleep four, and he, his brother and two friends who were civil servants in reserved occupations, cycled thirty to forty miles out to the village of Blanchland or nearby to spend Saturday nights there all through the summer. There were no restrictions on lights at night; the huge steel works at Consett, a dozen miles away, lit up the night sky and all around, every few hours. Their friends were fighting and dying in France, and there was nothing they could do to help them.

In the Summer of 1916, W.W. and Charles camped for three months in the cycle tent in a field on the Tyne above Riding Mill, travelling into Newcastle each day to work. They found a large Sunday School Treat boiler for making tea, in the field, and converted it into a steam cooker, using firewood for heat, and nesting aluminium pans for cooking a two-course meal. That same Summer he and Billy Campbell did a cycling tour of Scotland seemingly untroubled by war. The only danger envisaged for the travellers was that their bicycles must be insured against war-risk for the sea-voyage they went on from the North-East coast of England to Aberdeen. A submarine might sink them, so they must pay 15/- per bike; but no-one suggested that they should not go, nor that their own lives should be insured. They pedalled against a strong westerly gale from Aberdeen, via Balmoral, Glen Shiel, Pitlochry and so to Oban. At Oban the wind turned; and they rode back against an equally strong east wind to Berwick.

In his spare time, William wrote a thriller, some short stories and a Prize essay for a competition on how to provide a world free from War. Only the essay received honourable mention; the others remained unpublished. He continued to try to do objective research

Chapter 8. The Law: London Beckons

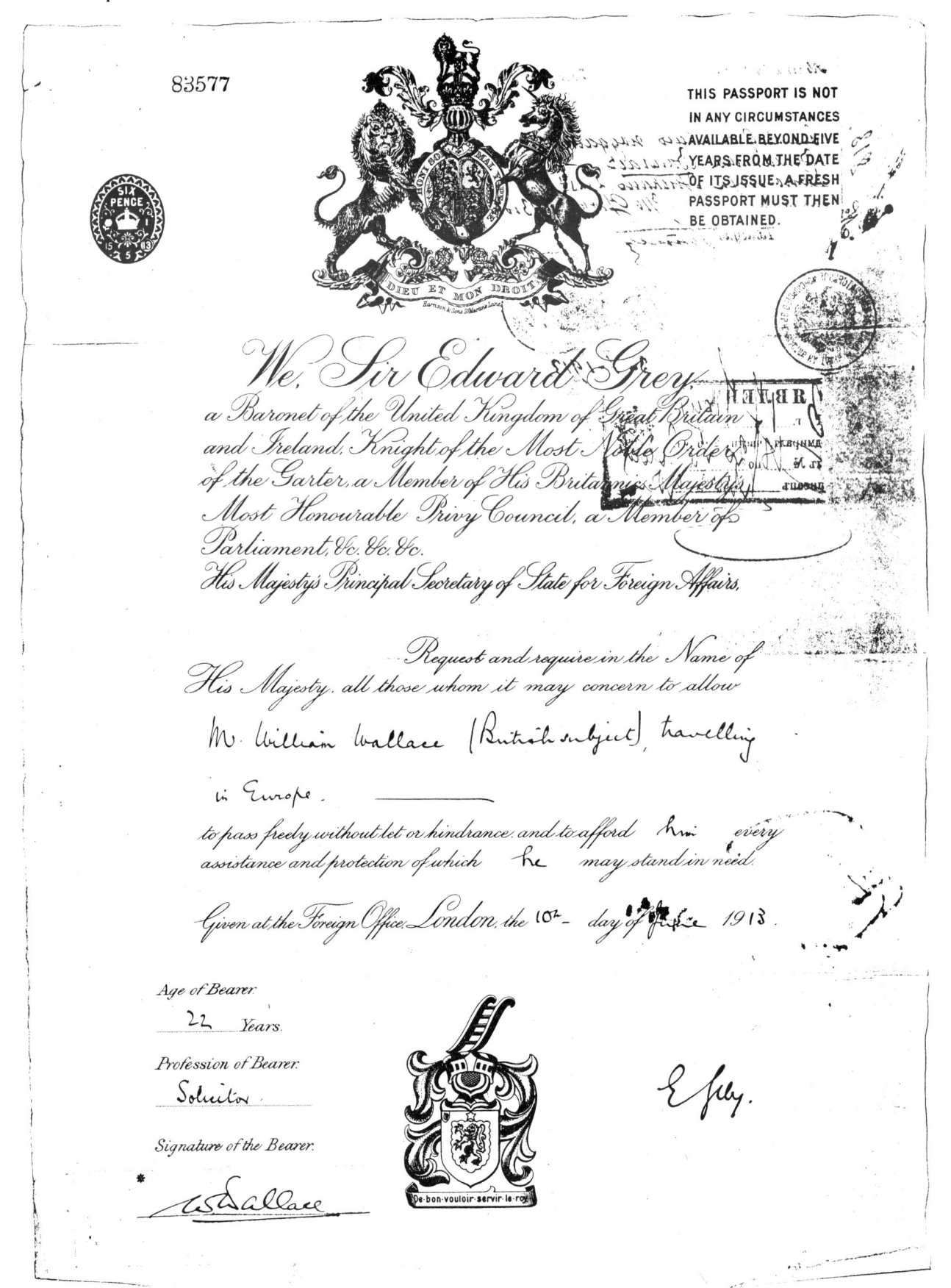

83577

THIS PASSPORT IS NOT IN ANY CIRCUMSTANCES AVAILABLE BEYOND FIVE YEARS FROM THE DATE OF ITS ISSUE. A FRESH PASSPORT MUST THEN BE OBTAINED.

We, Sir Edward Grey, a Baronet of the United Kingdom of Great Britain and Ireland, Knight of the Most Noble Order of the Garter, a Member of His Britannic Majesty's Most Honourable Privy Council, a Member of Parliament, &c. &c. &c.

His Majesty's Principal Secretary of State for Foreign Affairs,

Request and require in the Name of His Majesty, all those whom it may concern to allow

Mr William Wallace (British subject), travelling in Europe

to pass freely without let or hindrance, and to afford him every assistance and protection of which he may stand in need.

Given at the Foreign Office, London, the 10th day of June 1913.

Age of Bearer: 22 Years.

Profession of Bearer: Solicitor

Signature of the Bearer: W Wallace

William's pre-War Passport

Chapter 8. The Law: London Beckons

into social conditions and social problems. The Steel Union offered him the post of assistant solicitor, but he refused because it had political implications and he wanted objective research.

Conscription was introduced. W.W. was classified B2, "fit for clerk-ship abroad". He asked to be treated as a volunteer. As this was being considered, Seebohm Rowntree wrote to him in May, 1917. Rowntree had been appointed by the Prime Minister, David Lloyd-George, to take special responsibility for post-War Housing in the newly-created Reconstruction Committee, and he wanted W.W. to join him; but it seemed that the Reconstruction Committee would have difficulty in adding to their Staff anyone eligible for military service, even in a low medical class. It looked a hopeless proposition and W.W. was bitterly disappointed. He wrote and told Rowntree how he was placed. The Committee agreed to appoint IF the Tribunal approved. After further consideration, the Tribunal agreed that W.W. would be exempted if he either continued with Mr. Shortt OR did work of national importance. Mr. Shortt offered him an immediate partnership and future with them. The Ministry of Reconstruction offered one year's work only, with no security beyond. Another difficult decision: the most difficult personal choice he ever faced, he said. But his friends were risking their lives at the Front; and here was a chance to do the sort of constructive work for his fellow-men which he had sought. When appealed to, B.S.R. said he would be more *sensible* to return to Newcastle.

W.W. wrote two letters, one accepting and one refusing the Committee of Reconstruction post. He took both to the letter-box on the corner; measured his feelings as he attempted to post each one; and dropped in the acceptance. Basically, as his letter said, his principal feeling was that when his friends returned from the war he wanted to be able to say that he had not just kept his old position and added a new (commercial) appointment as well, which was part of Mr. Shortt's offer. Just as he was about to join the Reconstruction Committee, Lloyd George abolished it, and created a new Ministry of Reconstruction of which B.S.R. was not a member. It was nearly the end of his chance to pursue his dream. But instead he was appointed to the staff of the new Ministry. In August, 1917, he arrived at the office of the new Ministry, where he was joined by another young man also newly-come, a master at Repton School who also wished to do some constructive work. (Later, this man became the well-known publisher, Victor Gollancz; he was negotiating to publish W.W.'s Autobiography when he suddenly died).

London had won again.

William's pre-War Passport (part of other side)

Extract from 'Law Notes', September, 1912

With his capacity for steady, earnest work, his power of concentration, his determination—he tells us of his conviction that any man of ordinary capacity, if he will only make up his mind with sufficient determination that he will do a thing (if he possibly can), can do that thing—his intellectual ability and sound common sense, there can be no doubt about Mr. Wallace's success in the profession.

Part III William and Nancie (1918 onwards)

PASSING BY

Andantino moderato — Words by Herrick / Music by Edward C. Purcell

There is a lady sweet and kind,
Was never face so pleas'd my mind;
I did but see her passing by, And
yet I love her till I die!

(1) 'Passing By': the song William liked to sing to Nancie
(2) Photos taken on the Camping Honeymoon by Ullswater, 1918

Chapter 9

William and Nancie Together (1917-1920)

I have already told, at the end of Part I, how William and Nancie met at the home of the Ledger family in Purley in October, 1917. William was then their lodger, and Nancie went down to 'inspect' him as Vera Ledger was the fiancée of Nancie's brother, Avery. William had left London because his hostel accommodation had been unsatisfactory and lonely, and the "big bangs" and the fires from bombing of the Docks outside his windows was distracting.

Here are William's own words describing how he remembered his Nancie looked when they first met:

"She was dressed in what at any rate I thought was the rather fetching V.A.D. uniform. She was slender, with the softest honey-coloured hair. She was actually as pretty as a picture; my brother a quarter of a century later recalled her, in a letter, as "the daintiest little V.A.D. of the last war": a fellow-director of mine, slow to express judgements, said, many years after, that when he first saw my wife, Nancie, in York in 1919 he said to himself "A perfect piece of Dresden China!" But I didn't stop to analyse this then; if ever. What struck me first was that she was just a perfect English maiden, and I use that term advisedly, though she was then, like myself, twenty-six years old. The first thing I noticed was that she had the sweetest voice; with just a happy trace of the West Country. But, more: she had the most clear and direct eyes, of a friend; something new in my experience of girls in those days. Many other things I found later, for example, the shapeliest legs in the world, concealed by her long uniform skirt. But it was far more than enough: I was irretrievably in love".

All the time I knew him, W.W. liked to sing to his Nancie the haunting little song "I did but see her/Passing by,/And yet I'll love her/Till I die". (See opp.). His obvious devotion to her ran like a golden thread through all our lives. When we were very small, I can remember him chivvying us to get into the car when going for one of our picnics; at the same time he would wait patiently for her, saying, "Your mother is not to be hurried". He had a quick temper which was occasionally roused, but it was over as soon as it started, in a flash. He bore no grudges.

The wedding took place at Purley Congregational Church on Friday 14th June, 1918. There were no photographs so far as I know; but as Nancie kept her wedding dress ever afterwards I know what it was like: of simple style, but made in a lovely green-and-blue (peacock coloured) shot silk taffeta. W.W. was not fully recovered from a bad bout of the particularly virulent 'flu which swept the country in 1918, killing many. He told us once that his knees were knocking during the ceremony, though whether from the 'flu or the occasion, he wasn't sure. Nancie's mother from the Cotswolds, her brother Will who travelled overnight from Coventry to give her away, and William's brother Charles were their only guests. Together the five of them travelled up to London and had their Wedding Lunch in the refreshment room at Euston Station, before the honeymoon couple set out for Penrith en route to a camping holiday in the Lakes. They stayed their first night in a very modest Temperance hotel in Penrith. W.W. wrote 'It was there that I first saw her soft silky hair, to her waist, and could only stroke it'.

Next day they took the steamer to Howtown on Ullswater with the small tent and equipment and their baggage. They were put down alone on the pier with no visible means of transporting themselves and their luggage to the camp-site two miles away. W.W. as we know wasn't supposed even to carry one suitcase. Providence, he said, intervened and sent the only carrier's horse-drawn cart to take them and their things to within walking distance of their camp-site. It was the deserted lake-side where he and his friend had camped, years before. There was the solitary tree he remembered, and the little wood with a stile. Drinking water was available from the farm half-a-mile away, and Lake Ullswater at the tent-door, for bathing and washing up. The week before had been gloriously sunny; one letter after another which wished Nancie "a happy honeymoon" had

Chapter 9. William and Nancie Together

commented on it. Unfortunately the weather broke and it rained every day, clearing up only in the evening when they went walking together. It poured so much one night that the wife of the farmer in whose field they were camping could not sleep for thinking of them out in the storm. She insisted her husband go down to the tent to invite them back to the farmhouse into a dry bed.

W.W. was a very experienced camper, and he cooked the meals on the Primus Stove. To be sure that Nancie could manage the camping he had taken her at the Whitsuntide week-end to a camp in the Surrey Hills and let her try a night under canvas with bracken heaped underneath the ground sheet. She found it at least tolerable, so on their honeymoon they were even more alone than most. Loving the countryside as Nancie had always done, she must have been very happy (see photos p.96 taken by W.W. of Nancie in pyjamas and bathing costume by the tent, radiating happiness. W.W. had his camera with him, photography being another long-term interest of his; he developed his own film).

Nancie was twenty-seven-and-a-half when she married. Until she met 'Bill' as she always called him, she told me she had decided for some years that she was truly "on the shelf", as all her contemporaries were either married or resigned to being "old maids". She must have been very adaptable. She took him on trust, and he never let her down. He worked so hard and conscientiously that one War-time Christmas when we lived near Colwyn Bay, she broke down and wept when he said he must work on his (Ministry of Food) papers on the afternoon of Christmas Day; but he provided her with pleasant and beautiful homes, principally the house at Strensall which they built together and lived in for over forty years. They were never rich, but never in want. He provided for us all, making sure especially that we, his children, had the best possible gift from them, beyond loving, caring, sensible parents, and that was the best education they could obtain for us.

After ten days in the tent on their honeymoon, they went to Keswick for a few days; and on the last day he "walked (his) poor little wife to the top of Scafell Pike (the highest mountain in England) and down into Langdale for the night". Could this be why, ever afterwards, when the rest of us were keen walkers, my mother would say she did not mind walking for a *purpose*, but had no desire to walk just for the sake of going for a walk!

As W.W. records in his 'Autobiography', they took one another "To have and to hold, for better, for worse, for richer for poorer, in sickness and in health, to love and to cherish, till death us do part, according to God's holy ordinance" and thereto they plighted their troth. After fifty years, they were still active and enjoying each other's company. (See photo for Golden Wedding on front cover). Some time after the Golden Wedding, he once said to me, "If I have sixty years of time with Nancie, I shall be content. I couldn't ask for anything more". He died less than a year short of the sixty years since the day they had first met.

Nancie's relatives and friends were surprised and thrilled when she got married. For some reason they had not expected her to respond somewhat suddenly to a complete stranger from another part of the country. She would not be coming back as they had expected to Great Alne or Evesham or Stratford-on-Avon. They wrote most loving letters on her marriage, and after the birth of Jean, her first child, two years later. She kept these letters; they must have meant a lot to her. As her relatives and friends heard of her husband's progress in his career, they acknowledged that Nancie had done rather well for herself.

Her brother Avery, P-O-W at Limburg am Lahn (i.e. on the River Lahn) in Germany, did not hear of her engagement until May. He wrote to her on 18th, sending the card to their mother's address. It reached Weston Subedge only on July 26th when it was forwarded to Nancie at the home they had bought at West Wickham in Kent: Wyncroft, Grosvenor Road. Avery wrote to send her his best wishes and best love. It was through his fiancée that Nancie had found her husband. Avery also wrote that he had been up all night with a "man who is very bad". His little khaki card, headed 'Kriegsgefangenen-sendung', reeks of the Prison Camp. Avery wrote again on June 15th. He had heard the date of the wedding two days before, so was able to think of them on their wedding day. "You are lucky people and good luck to you", he wrote. How he must have wished it was he and

98

Chapter 9. William and Nancie Together

Vera who were getting married.

Somehow, a wrongly-printed card was sent out in error on their marriage. It gave their new address correctly, but it gave their name as 'Mr and Mrs William Galbraith Wallace'. Charles was the one who had 'Galbraith' as his middle name, not William, but the initials 'W.G' stuck for a long time. Several correspondents addressed their letters to Mrs. 'Galbraith Wallace'. One long-married friend from Great Alne wrote a few days after their marriage looking forward to their Golden Wedding; and advising that one thing only made a happy marriage: goodness. One letter from young Avery, Jack's son - sent too late to catch them in Purley on 14th June - was forwarded to the house of the farmer who owned their honeymoon field, so now I know exactly on whose land they camped. William and Nancie revisited the site thirty-four years later (see photo p.102). I hope to go there too, one day, though I think it will have changed after over seventy years. (I have now been; and it remains the same, except for more trees, as in 1918).

In July, 1918, Nancie's cousin, Florrie Hall, from Fishponds, Bristol, whose bridesmaid she had been in 1909 (see photo p.1) scolded her for the "tremendous shock" of the news of her marriage, as Nancie had apparently not written about her engagement. It was Florrie who inherited her grandfather's estate (Chap 2), and who then lived with her great-aunt Louisa Hancox at Ridgeway Park House, from 1900. Florrie was to be in London a few days later, and hoped to see Nancie; but she would be disappointed as Nancie had gone North to meet her new mother-in-law in Sunderland.

Nancie was issued a Certificate on 21st August, 1918, under the National Registration Act, 1915, by Bromley Rural District Council. It certifies that her occupation was "Household Duties", no doubt what the authorities expected as the newly-married couple had moved into their house in West Wickham. Nancie did not sign the form. She was travelling to London every day to continue her work at the King George Hospital. On November 15th, a letter was sent to Nancie at the Hospital about her War Service Bar; she had already clocked up thirteen months' service there; and the four hundred and eighty hours she had worked at Alcester, while still with her brother Jack, would count towards her Second Bar.

In January of that year she had ordered household linen from Larne in Northern Ireland: towels, and table napkins by the dozen or bundle; she kept the bill (with a 1d. stamp on its receipt). She had sent some beautifully embroidered hankies to Gertrude Price (of the little blue letter) for her birthday on January 24th, and kept Gertrude's letter of thanks. Perhaps the hankies also came from Northern Ireland, and she embroidered them. Nancie enquired about further training and exams she could take to help her with her hospital work; she was sent a form to fill up for a Scholarship. But in March, 1919, they told her that the only exam she could take would be a degree in Science. This she obviously could not do in her generation as she was now married. Although not unusual nowadays, and only difficult when I was a student, it was impossible for her. She had the brains to take a Science degree, and would have enjoyed it. She kept the form along with those early letters; but from now on her course would be the more homely Domestic Science, at which she was superb.

For the first year or so of their marriage while living at West Wickham, W.W. continued to work at the Ministry of Reconstruction which he had joined in August 1917, where his brief was to suggest "how best to work out a post-war policy covering house-building and rents". He worked on this with his usual thoroughness, writing memoranda, urging the government to spend money on emergency post-war housing; the Treasury and the Local Government Board vetoed it. Two Committees were set up to tackle the problems of Rent Restrictions and Financial Assistance, and W.W. was appointed Secretary of both. He strongly recommended that, instead of the subsidising of all houses because some could not pay the rent, wages should be made sufficient to pay economic rents for suitable houses. (Assistance to be given only to those who were unable to pay and these should be kept to a minimum). This was the main recommendation of the Majority Report of the Rent Restriction Committee.

The outstanding problem with post-war housing was that the rents of the working-class houses were being restricted during the war to 1914 figures by an Act of 1915, at least until the end of the War. Building costs were soaring. Private house-building for renting

Chapter 9. William and Nancie Together

would be uneconomic and so not undertaken. Two things therefore should follow: rents should, in the right way for the right period, be controlled; the state must bridge the gap between abnormal and post-war costs. W.W. and others who agreed urged that this should be done; but the Treasury and the Local Government Board strongly opposed it. W.W. was not popular with the Local Government Board. As so often when help was urgently needed - in this case to provide homes for returning heroes - what was provided was too little, too late. In 1917, W.W. suggested an Excess Rents Tax on pre-war rents, and urged the development of Housing Associations which have gradually become more widely accepted and implemented since then.

In his capacity as Secretary of the Rent Restrictions Committee W.W. was summoned to meet Lord Hunter whom he had so far never met, at the Athaneum Club. Nancie was with him that evening, so they waited in the vestibule. Lord Hunter appeared, talking to a friend, and telling him he was apprehensive about taking on the Rent Restrictions job. The friend replied, "Don't worry. I understand you have got as Secretary the ablest young man in the Ministry." W.W. glowed at this quite unexpected recommendation and Nancie was impressed.

After my father wrote this Report it was expected that a formal note of appreciation to the Secretary would be included; but when the Chairman, Sir Donald Maclean, was asked about this, he simply asked why my father (who had tried several ways to join up, in vain) was not in khaki; and no paragraph of thanks was included. This man's son, Donald Maclean, defected to the Soviet Union in 1951. "Patriotism comes in different guises", wrote my father.

W.W.'s knowledge of the provision of suitable housing and his life-long interest in it was very useful when he became Chairman of the Joseph Rowntree Village Trust (created in 1904 by Joseph Rowntree to provide housing and do research). Fifty years after he wrote the Reports for these two committees, he commented that the conditions, the problems, and the suggested solutions were virtually unchanged. One of the themes of his Autobiography especially relevant here was Bagshot's "pain of the new idea". He had contemplated using this title for his book, so strongly did he feel about it. He was also Secretary of a small expert committee on the classified list 'The Neutral Tonnage Committee', which dealt with the necessary steps to be taken in connection with neutral shipping after the War; and he was Acting Secretary to the Local Government Committee, whose task was to reconcile the Majority and Minority Reports of the Poor Law Commission. One side was led by Beatrice Webb "very attractive and supremely able, chain-smoking cigarettes in a long white cigarette holder which she used rather like a conductor's baton to emphasise her points to the Chairman", wrote W.W.

At the end of his work for these committees, W.W. was offered the O.B.E. which on the spur of the moment he gratefully declined, feeling strongly that he "wouldn't like to meet his friends who had joined up, in the hereafter, with an O.B.E. for service in civilian clothes at home". He always felt that this was the right decision for him; and it was a long time before he realised the importance of the first step in the highly organised "Honours System", and that often later honours were built on the earlier ones received. Perhaps he did himself a disservice; but he never regretted his refusal. He could not accept such an honour when so many of his friends lay in Flanders, and he had been prevented from fighting beside them. Much later he was given the C.B.E.

Inevitably, when hostilities ceased, the Ministry of *Reconstruction* was axed, which I have always found a particular irony. Many lost their jobs; W.W. was saved only because he had worked on Housing, and was needed in that capacity. At this point, he was then invited personally by Neville Chamberlain (later Prime Minister until 1940), at one time Chairman of the Birmingham Housing Committee, to join the Birmingham Town Clerk's Office and become Secretary of that Housing Committee. He was also asked to become Secretary of a Liberal Research organisation, but he felt this would lead to a political career which was not what he sought. A day or two later Seebohm Rowntree phoned and asked him to go to the Cocoa Works (as we always referred to Rowntrees in those days). W.W. said he was delighted to accept, but that he knew nothing about Cocoa. "Neither do I," was the response. "I want you to deal not with cocoa, but with Co-Partnership." When W.W. asked no questions about the job, the salary or the conditions, B.S.R. said, "I must

Chapter 9. William and Nancie Together

tell you about your new post, and the salary. Come across and talk to me!" "Across" turned out to be No.10 Downing Street, the Prime Minister's house, so W.W. walked round from his office in Whitehall and within twenty minutes all was agreed. Later he received a letter confirming his post as assistant to Seebohm Rowntree who was then Labour Director at Rowntrees. It was W.W.'s only real contract of service with Rowntrees from 1919 to 1957. He was to begin on May 1st., 1919, at a salary of £400 (The government had raised his £300 per annum to £350 in Summer, 1918, after his marriage). The Chief Civil Servant in charge of him encouraged him to leave for York, but wrote to express his regret "that the public service should lose so promising a man".

On May 1st, 1919, William and Nancie did not go to York, but to her mother's house near Chipping Campden, in Gloucestershire, which seemed to them after their War years in London, like Paradise. Seebohm Rowntree had decided that W.W. should begin his employment with Rowntrees by having a holiday after his rigorous time in London. He could see the young man had been working too hard - a family failing, I fear. So they went to this delightful house half-buried in honey-suckle and old-fashioned roses which I remember very well. It is situated at the side of a steep track, little used in those days. I have mentioned it already as the house where Nancie's sister, Dorothy, went with their mother to live in 1918; and where Dorothy stayed until she died in 1977.

At this house, only the end wall (without any windows) faces the lane, and in those days privacy was complete. Heavy evergreens grew at the little entrance gate, which had stepped flagstones up and round towards the front door. It was a secret approach with a very special atmosphere of anticipation and sudden surprise, as I remember it all through my childhood. All along the length of the house, the garden was built up a steep bank, so that the rockery climbed high above the dining-room window. Only from upstairs was there any view of the garden from that side, although at the back the ground sloped away down into the field and one could see the buildings of the village, including the old Quaker Meeting House. At the top of the garden, away from the lane, was an orchard; round the garden hedges, brambles climbed in great profusion; at the far end of the house from the gate, beyond the back kitchen, was the little extra building with the Earth Closet: not really welcomed by those of us not used to it in the 1920's.

William and Nancie took walks in the surrounding country to Stow-on-the-Wold, Broadway, the Slaughters and the Swells and to the Windrush River, whose name they took for the house they later built. Soon, W.W. started work on the papers he had taken with him, sitting in a deck chair on the lawn. I've come across a Diary for this period and was puzzled at first by numbers, ringed round, on every day. Then I realised he was noting down the number of hours worked while in Broad Campden. It starts with small amounts over the first week-end (they arrived on a Thursday), but soon settled to seven or eight hours daily, with only occasional exceptions. In the first week there would have been time for the walks he mentioned; he did only 18¼ hours. Soon, he was recording forty hours a week: even forty-seven.

His brief at the beginning of his time at Rowntrees was research into Co- Partnership, and the possibilities of implementing this at the firm. He set out to discover the special experiences in profit-sharing in other businesses; and then to consider how to develop further the "spirit of partnership" within the Rowntree business. He read every book and report he could find which dealt with the subject. He bought paper and prepared long schedules divided into twenty-seven columns in order to include all available information; he drafted a questionnaire.

After a few weeks, B.S.R. asked if W.W. felt "able to face a little work". They returned to York in June; and W.W. arrived at the Cocoa Works carrying not a briefcase, but a *suitcase*, filled with schedules done in six weeks of "idle holiday". He started as he meant to go on; all my life I remember him best, working on his knee at home: in the sunshine out-of-doors when possible, otherwise beside the open log fire in the sitting-room. (See photo p.138 (2))

William and Nancie did not have a home of their own for nearly a year after they arrived in York; they had rooms in the house rented by Miss Stockley (a retired Rowntree employee, known always to us children as "Tockie") in the Rowntree Garden Village of

Chapter 9. William and Nancie Together

New Earswick. The village is about a mile further out from York than the Rowntree factory and William went to work by bicycle. New Earswick was founded in 1904 by Joseph Rowntree for the building not merely of houses and Schools, but of a community. "The Trust was conceived as an experiment in social welfare", wrote W.W. in his Preface to the account of the history of the first fifty years of the village, "One Man's Vision", (published 1954). "It would not have been possible without the friendly co-operation of the residents there". The lovely gardens round every house, the splendid schools for every age, the Folk Hall for meetings, parties and entertainments, the Quaker Meeting House and the provision for the elderly and infirm: all these came later. Trees were planted along the roads, appropriate to their names: Poplar Grove, Cherry Tree Avenue, Hawthorn Place, etc.. Even in 1904, the first houses were built with their 'backs' to the front road, if necessary, so that the living-rooms faced the sun. The village had its own modern dairy farm (White Rose Farm, run by Carl and Bea Sorenson), sewage disposal works, and a brick and tile works. The farmhouse is now a home for the elderly; the tile works, a nature reserve. A Village Council was formally constituted in 1907 to discuss and decide all relevant aspects of this self-governing community. All houses were rented from the Trust.

In April, 1920, William and Nancie were most anxious to move into their own home, as their first baby was expected in June. This was the house next-door to "Tockie" (see photo p.106), the first in the village geographically: the end house of a row of three with big windows on three sides and the village beck running through the garden. This is where the kingfisher and snipe and many other birds delighted Nancie, as mentioned earlier.

Firmly entrenched in this end house, in Spring 1920, was a "sitting tenant" who refused to leave. When William went to interview him, desperate to get Nancie into a house of her own, the tenant tried to bluff his way, although he had been given permission to rent the house only over the Winter. He tried to quote the Rent Restriction Act as evidence that he could not be compelled to leave, but he was speaking to the wrong man. W.W. told him that he himself had drafted much of that Act and it applied only to *un*furnished houses. The tenant withdrew from the house at once; and William and Nancie moved in just in time for my elder sister, Jean Galbraith, to be born there on June 22nd, 1920.

A monthly nurse called Janet, long known to my mother as she was companion to my mother's Aunt Sue, came to York from Evesham to assist her. The proud father took photos, now blurred with age. The pram stood under the apple tree by the side lawn and the washing fluttered in the back garden over the gooseberry brushes. The pram was wheeled out round the village. One day, so a family story goes, they were walking with the baby when they met the splendid Scots lady who worked in the Village Estate Office. It is said that she looked at the baby and then at its parents, and said, "Isn't she beautiful?" She again looked at the baby and then at its parents, and said, "Isn't she intelligent?" She looked at the baby and then at its parents, and said, "Isn't it *Wonderful?*" If you can hear the tone of incredulity in her voice at the third remark, you will realise why we laughed.

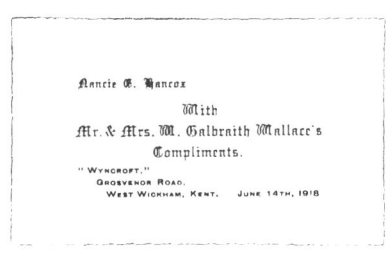

(1) The Wedding Card (the 'Galbraith' was a mistake!)
(2) Return of Nancie and William to the Honeymoon Camping site, April 1952
(Note: the stile and the wood were still there)

Chapter 10

William at Work (1919-1931)

William was a man of commitment and dedication, whether to his wife and family or to his work. Whatever he did, he did it with his whole heart. Small in stature, but generous in heart and mind, he was a professional: all must be done to the highest possible standard. In this way he approached the subject of profit-sharing and its application to the Rowntree business. His work for, and interest in, Co-Partnership lasted for the rest of his life. He was a member of the Industrial Co-Partnership Association (I.C.A.) from its inception; found among its members some of his best friends in industry; and served on its Executive Committee. He attended the great majority of its conferences and meetings for over fifty years and spoke at many.

In 1953. he succeeded Lord Amory as chairman of the I.C.A. and chaired the large conferences held annually at Oxford and Cambridge in alternate years. (He and Nancie managed to turn these into family occasions, too, as they visited us at the same time, both in Oxford while we lived there, and later further North as they drove by). He records how at one Conference, John Speden Lewis (of the John Lewis Partnership) disagreed with something W.W. had said, and told the Conference that any employee of his Company could send an anonymous letter and have it published in the Company Magazine; whereupon a shop steward from Rowntrees stood up and said that anyone at Rowntrees who had a grievance would not express it anonymously, but would go and have a talk with Mr. Wallace (then Chairman of Rowntrees). W.W. much enjoyed his years as Chairman of I.C.A. and resigned most reluctantly, perforce, on being appointed to the Restrictive Practices Court, as he was not allowed to hold both offices. But the I.C.A. then made him a Vice-President, so he was very happy to continue to "belong".

Co-Partnership, also known as a profit-sharing scheme, is linked with employee-shareholding. W.W. always thought of it rather in the wider sense of working together in a spirit of partnership which may well produce employee-shareholding as a by-product of that spirit. In 1919-20, he enquired into all ascertainable experience of all ordinary employers in the United Kingdom up to July 1920. In 1919, he had also enquired into all schemes, continued or abandoned, in what was then the British Empire, and in the United States of America; (though the American material was not used). His material was widely discussed, including by an informal Astor/Rowntree group which met at Hever Castle, the home of Lord Astor, in February 1920; and continued to meet, either there or at Lord Astor's home in London. W.W., a member of this group, was asked to write a Report on their conclusions, which he did.

As a result of this work towards a profit-sharing scheme at Rowntrees, it was discussed first by the Rowntree Board and by the Ordinary Shareholders. Next, it went to the Central Works Council and others, including representatives of the unions concerned. In 1922 it was introduced by the Company to take effect from January 1st, 1923. B.S.R. inaugurated week-end Ballioi Conferences of Works Directors, Managers, Foremen and Forewomen, in Oxford. W.W. spoke at many of these, over the years: first in 1921, and certainly in October 1932 when I was taken as a convalescent after an appendix operation to Oxford with him and my mother. I was taken to the evening session to hear him speak. I remember the occasion, but nothing of the content, and rather think I fell asleep. B.S.R. asked W.W. to write a book based on his research into co-partnership and profit-sharing, and his conclusions. He could not find time until he retired from the Chairmanship of Rowntrees when he had a few relatively free months before he began his sittings in Court in Autumn 1958. *"Prescription for Partnership*, was published by Pitmans in 1959. It summarised what he still thought held good in the field of profit-sharing. This book was selected as an "Ambassador" book by the English-Speaking Union. The I.C.A. described it as "the best general study of co-partnership in practice yet published", and circulated copies to all relevant libraries. W.W. reckoned that the book was the climax to his interest in industrial relations which had first led him to throw up his profession over fifty years before, to deal "not with cocoa but with co-partnership". He believed passionately in

Chapter 10. William at Work

creating the best industrial relations possible.

One of the other aspects of employment which exercised the mind and heart of W.W. was Unemployment Insurance. As a lad he had been touched by the hardships of undeserved unemployment in his home-town of Sunderland. In 1920 he and others had anticipated a possible slump, and felt that the question of unemployment insurance was urgent. A concerned group, including B.S.R., W.W., leading Trade Unions, and with the particular interest of the Prime Minister, Lloyd George, tabled certain far-reaching proposals which were issued anonymously to the Press on January 11th, 1921. These proposals included the statement that the rank and file of workers believe that improvements bring unemployment and that additional production aimed at providing increasing employment may damage those already at work, and so they resisted. Those in work cling to the 'Status quo' and impede progress. W.W. called this lack of acceptance of change, "the pain of the new idea", and noted that it continued decade after decade. He reckoned it could take fifty years for some new ideas to be welcomed and implemented.

The essential proposals - in 1920 - were that the rate of benefit in Unemployment should be 50% of the average earnings of the insured person; with 10% extra for a dependent wife, and 5% extra for each dependent child under sixteen, provided that the total benefit did not exceed 75% of average earnings. Industry, under these proposals, would be compelled to create a wages equalisation fund, and employers would be given an incentive to eliminate every removable cause of unemployment. Unfortunately, the Coalition Government of 1921 was not prepared to accept these proposals. Our economic history and progress since then would have been very different if it had. Rowntrees in 1920 adopted a Supplementary Benefit Scheme to bring current state benefits broadly up to the levels suggested, as have certain other firms since. The need for reform of unemployment benefit, and the fact that Trade Union restrictive practices arise at least in part from the pain of unemployment has been a theme repeatedly expressed by writers in 'The Economist' and elsewhere. After the necessary fifty years, as W.W. said, the new idea becomes less painful and can to some extent be accepted.

Although W.W. does not write of it in his Autobiography, I know from his personal correspondence files that he made strenuous efforts to help a wide variety of people to obtain some employment during the lean times, both in the 1920's and 1930's. He was frequently asked to help, and it really hurt him to have to say, 'No'. Rowntrees themselves had schemes for finding alternative work for some whom they had to dismiss when they were overmanned, as I mention later on.

In spite of the many calls on his time, W.W. kept up a lively correspondence with his family in Sunderland, responding to any request for advice or help. His mother wrote to him frequently and at length, her words seeming to hurry across the page anxious to bring all her love to her "dear ones"; these letters he kept. Both his sisters and his brother were married during the 1920's. W.W. also kept in touch with his own friends from his boyhood, and in particular with an old friend of his father whose last years were struck by tragedy. The graphic account of the happenings in letters by a hand not very used to writing make very moving reading. My father responded as best he could with help and comfort.

At Rowntrees, when W.W. began work there as personal assistant to B.S.R., Joseph Rowntree, though in his eighties, was still Chairman. B.S.R. acted as Deputy Chairman and also as Labour Director. The history of the Company could be said to go back to 1695 when Mary Tuke was born, daughter of William Tuke, a Quaker and a Freeman of the City of York; a blacksmith by trade. When Mary was thirty and unmarried, she decided to start in business in York as a grocer. The York Company of Merchant Adventurers did all they could to oppose her. In 1733, at the age of thirty-eight, she married, and three years later her husband became a Merchant Adventurer. In 1746, when her husband had been dead seven years, Mary took her nephew, William Tuke, into the business which he inherited when Mary died in 1752. Tea dealing became their speciality; manufacture of cocoa and chocolate began only in about 1783. Not until 1862 did the name Rowntree become associated with the business when Henry Isaac Rowntree took over the cocoa and chocolate side from Tuke and Co.. In 1869, he was joined by his brother, Joseph, whose name has become world-famous for good organisation and

Chapter 10. William at Work

lifelong philanthropic works.

The thirty employees of 1872 had grown to 6,932 by 1924, five years after W.W. joined the firm. When he left in 1957, there were, at home and abroad, altogether about 20,000. In Joseph Rowntree's time, Joseph Rowntree looked upon each of his staff as a personal responsibility, and they knew it. In 1890, he bought twenty-nine acres of land on the northern edge of the city of York to build a new factory, and moved from the old second-hand premises near the river. In 1956 as Chairman and on behalf of the Company, W.W. handed over to the City the site of the old factory, with sufficient funds from a Rowntree Trust for it to be maintained as a Riverside Garden forever. Rowntrees became a limited company in 1897, but it continued to be a family business for many years, with members of the Rowntree family among its executive directors.

Wages, hours and conditions of work were very good. Joseph Rowntree always put adequate wages to the rank-and-file as the first charge. There was a Quaker sense of responsibility for welfare. All this appealed strongly to W.W. He, too, believed in the worth of each individual. He wrote:

'For my part I share still with Joseph Rowntree and his son the thrill of the words of John Milton -

"Lords and Commons of England, consider what Nation it is whereof you are, and whether ye are Governors: a Nation not slow and dull, of a quick, ingenious and piercing spirit..."' He also wrote, in "Prescription for Partnership": 'my own Prescription for Partnership in industry is very simple: just sincerity, a respect for the other man's point-of-view and consideration for his interests, a recognition that we have the nicest chaps in the world; basic courtesy, and a desire to do justice'.

B.S.R. said to him when he began work at Rowntrees:

"We have just finished a war claimed to be fought to establish democracy. It is therefore up to us to seek to establish the principles of democracy so far as practicable in our business. As personal assistant to me those therefore are your terms of reference."

In line with Joseph Rowntree's feeling of fatherly obligation to his workers, in 1906 he announced a Scheme for a Pension Fund. It was based on current money wages which allowed for rises in the cost of living. There was no distinction in eligibility for membership between 'staff' and 'work people'. The employees could choose individually the amount of pension for which they would subscribe, within certain limits. "Back-service" was met by a personal gift from Joseph Rowntree. Once the Scheme got going, the Company contributed pound for pound with employee-members. By 1946, the maximum allowed was two-thirds of their basic wage, less a deduction fixed in relation to State benefits.

Joseph Rowntree also introduced in 1917 a Widows' Benefit Fund, believed to be the first of its kind, the whole cost of which was broadly borne by the Company. When he presented the proposal to the Board, Joseph Rowntree asked them to accept the principle before discussing the cost.

A five-day standard working week of 44 hours was introduced early in the 1920's, so everyone had Saturdays free. The first Works Psychologist was appointed in 1922 and began with vocational testing to help in more accurate selection, initially with girls applying for factory work. The tests quickly justified themselves.

In the years of serious trade depression following 1920, the Rowntree Company's 'Supplementary Unemployment Benefit Scheme' was greatly valued. There were, inevitably, redundancies, and W.W. was a very active member of the Unemployment Committee empowered to help a redundant employee to move as necessary and be established in a small business of his own. One business started in London went on to produce good rubber hot-water-bottles to retail at half-a-crown. The Committee also found suitable openings for their ex-employees with other employers.

The 'principles of democracy' which W.W. had been told to establish within the Company found their form in the Works Councils made up of representatives of all sections and grades in the firm. W.W. was a member of the Central Works Council for all his years at Rowntrees (1919-1957), from newly-arrived assistant to B.S.R., to Company

Chapter 10. William at Work

Chairman: the longest continuous membership at that time, and perhaps at any time. When the Council, in 1923, were reviewing Works Rules, a shop steward noted anxiously that no provision was being made for disagreement among the Council members. B.S.R. suggested that the members should try trusting one another always to find agreement. They did, and it worked, though sometimes it took quite a time to agree.

Another innovation at this time was an Appeal Committee. Any worker who felt he/she had been unfairly treated in being subject to suspension, dismissal or other disciplinary action, *provided* this did not affect performance of work, had the right of appeal. The Appeal Committee consisted of equal numbers of workers and management, with a Chairman appointed by all the members of the Committee, not by the management. This was very unusual then.

The Profit-Sharing Scheme was nearly still-born. It had been planned during the boom conditions of 1919-20, but by the time it was due to be launched, the long trade depression of the Twenties had begun. They kept the Scheme, but between 1923 and 1938 only two distributions of surplus profits were made: 2% in 1929, and 2½ % in 1936. But every year B.S.R. tabled the figures, and explained to the elected Profit-Sharing Committee what was happening and what steps were being taken by the Directors; he also answered questions. Later on, the workers benefited greatly from the Scheme, as profits rose.

One small incident related by W.W. gives some insight into the workings of this large "capitalist" firm. The Purchasing Director, a hard-headed Yorkshireman, who was also both wise and kind, had negotiated a big contract for supplies of an essential cocoa material to run for a substantial period at a very keen price. All went well for quite a time; but then the seller asked for an interview to tell them that the market had gone against him, and he was ashamed to say he must file his petition for bankruptcy. They asked him how much he was losing per pound (on thousands of tons) on the deal. "Just short of a penny", he replied. The Purchasing Director suggested that, if W.W. agreed, they would add 1½ d. a pound to the contract price, which would save their supplier's business. The visitor was overwhelmed with gratitude and relief. Some years later, in a time of shortages, this particular supplier made sure that Rowntrees got their share.

W.W. was first involved at Rowntrees with the fundamentals of good industrial relationship; it was that which took him from the legal profession into the business world; he wrote that it was the happiest period of his working life. He also wrote that this part of his story sets out experiments in social and industrial relations made from the 1920's onwards and still relevant to Britain's urgent present-day problems, at the time he wrote. We could still learn many lessons from them today.

Flooding below the garden of Pyrmont. The triple tree trunks were our favourite "Notchy Nook" for playing by the Beck

Chapter 11

Nancie At Home (1920-1935)

'Pyrmont', the house which Nancie and William occupied in New Earswick, was named by Joseph Rowntree's wife, whose family were connected with the German spa town: Bad Pyrmont. The name is still on the little old gate at the end of the front lane where we used to run up to catch the red 'Cosy Car' bus to school in the 1920's. Initially the house was No.5. Poplar Grove; later changed to No.16. Western Terrace.

William and Nancie were delighted with their new home: pleasant and spacious, with large windows to south and west and the garden on three sides, it was very attractive. As well as Tockie, next door, they had the family on Tockie's other side, the Kays, who were a support and stay to all of us through all the years we knew them. The young couple had also become members of a small and friendly community. The village had its own social life, with meetings, parties and entertainments in the Folk Hall which was the social centre, as well as the place where different religious bodies: Roman Catholic, Methodist (until they built a Chapel in 1927) or Quaker, met. Playing fields, a bowling green (for men and women) and tennis courts were all provided for the use of the village. Nancie and William were quite keen tennis-players; Nancie had a strong underarm service. They used to enjoy pleasant summer evenings at the tennis-club, escorted by the baby in the pram, and later occasionally by Jean and me.

From 1918, there were special parties to welcome home returning ex-service men. Whist drives, Pensioners' parties, May Queen Carnivals (from 1921), with floats and side-stalls, when everyone dressed up, ran races and had tea in the Marquee; and teams for football, cricket and even mixed hockey: all these took place. Meetings for Girl Guides, the Women's Guild, Orchestral, Dramatic and Musical Societies and many more were strongly supported by the village members. Nancie and William took part in many of these activities. Nancie was President of the Women's Guild; she was also elected to the Village Council, of which she later became Chairman.

She was a very active member for some years of the New Earswick Dramatic Society, which had frequent productions. Surviving press-cuttings are full of complimentary remarks by the drama critics: in November, 1923, in "Tilly of Bloomsbury", Mrs Wallace's portrayal of Lady Marian Mainwaring was "a well-sustained and capable interpretation of a somewhat difficult role, and was very commendable"; in another production she "played the none too attractive part of Blanche Sartorius, with great skill, her acting being admirable throughout"; in November 1926 she was "conspicuously successful, acting with ease and distinction"; in February, 1928, she was "good, very" as the mother in a well-known comedy of the time, "The Lilies of the Field": the one hundredth and seventy-seventh play acted in the Folk Hall since it was built in 1907. Just before Christmas, 1929, she played a leading role in "The Quaker" as a Quaker mother who never faltered in her faith; and in April, 1932, she appeared with the York Settlement Community Players in York, as Mrs Stockman in Ibsen's "An Enemy of the People". It was reviewed in "The Yorkshire Herald", "The Yorkshire Post" and "The Northern Echo", who in particular praised Nancie for her performance as the Doctor's wife. This is the only one I can remember seeing and I recollect only one line from it. The other notables from the small Swedish town, who were unanimously against the doctor, raised their glasses and said in unison, "Your health, doctor". I sensed the hypocrisy and the sinister intent, at the age of nine and a bit; and *my* mother was the doctor's wife!

In 1925, at the New Earswick Village and Carnival Show on Saturday, July 18th, a First Prize was won by "Mrs *M* E Wallace"; for Exhibit No.68 in class No.61. Tantalisingly, there is no indication of what the prize was for. Only a large, bright pink card with a patterned edge remains, but it gives us a glimpse into the number of classes open for competition and the numbers of exhibits entered.

All the extra activities and commitments beyond his daily work at Rowntrees which William undertook and which took him away for evenings and week-ends or longer were

Chapter 11. Nancie at Home

bound to impinge on Nancie, but she was content to be at home and to have the care of her children herself. Whenever he was away in those early days, occasionally staying with her relatives in the South, she wrote him loving letters; and he kept them. In them, she refers to their first baby as "the fossil"! One letter from Nancie tells him that Jean, aged about three-and-a-half, was looking anxiously on the letter from her father for the little bears he always drew for the children; they were rather like ginger-bread men: two-dimensional, and flat on their backs. (See opp.).

Fortunately, neither Nancie or William was a party-goer nor did they need the bright lights of a city. They had no 'wireless' until they moved to Strensall, fifteen years later, and I don't think they had the telephone, certainly not at first. Relatives came to stay, especially William's as they lived fairly near and could come directly by train. The collection of small brown photos taken and developed by William show that his mother and aunt and sisters came from Sunderland, and even his mother's sister (with her daughters) from Edinburgh, whose late husband had lent William the £50 to help him get started. They all came to see the new home and the babies. Photos also show that William and Nancie took Jean to Broad Campden in 1920 when she was six-weeks-old, to stay with her Granny Hancox; and again in 1921. The following year, they holidayed in Wensleydale in North Yorkshire, and also Hutton-le-hole, a small and beautiful village on the Yorkshire Moors, where we went often, for picnics and occasional holidays, especially once we had a car. (Photos see opp.).

Weddings were a theme even in the children's play. On holiday once, in Hutton-le-Hole, Jean and I organised a double wedding (see photo opp.) between her Teddy, Edward, and my favourite doll, Pamela; cork-filled and with her underclothes printed on her in mauve and white, she was decently-covered with dresses, one of which I made and even embroidered. My teddy bear, Billy, was married to Jean's favourite doll, Marie (pronounced as in 'Mar-mite'): a rag doll, made by my mother to compensate Jean for having a baby sister. Marie had a flat face, with embroidered nose, mouth, eyes and a single kiss-curl on her forehead. She was much-loved. As the years went by, Marie gradually grew fatter and fatter as she was recovered when her 'skin' frayed and the stitched mouth, etc., wore off.

My mother was gifted at needlework and handicrafts. While at New Earswick, she went to Arts and Craft classes in York in the afternoons. One of her embroideries was a Jacobean fire-screen which stood in the hearth throughout each summer, and is still treasured. She also carved long strips of wood to attach to the book-case my father had made as a young man to hold his law prize books. These were to match the design on the sideboard, bureau, etc., which William had ordered when they were first married from the successors to the old Guild of Handicrafts in Chipping Campden. It was "all nicely carved in pre-1914 timber," he recorded. Nancie did leatherwork at the classes: a folder for my father's writing things, and leather-topped stools with large coloured designs: Jean's, a witch in a red cloak, on a broomstick; mine, a rabbit with a blue jacket and big yellow trousers, striding along. Later she embroidered tapestry cushions for each of the ladder-backed, rush-seated chairs (also from the Campden furniture workshop) with patterns chosen by the different members of the family. Most were flower designs; mine, at my suggestion, she took from a simplified design like a child's drawing of house, garden, man and woman, and the motto 'Home Sweet Home'. She also encouraged me to stitch a large sampler at the age of nine, with the Alphabet, numbers and a picture of Red Riding Hood and the Wolf. When I reached the final stitching of the grandmother's cottage, the three huge blue fir trees and the flowers at the bottom of the picture, I was glad it was finished. My mother also went regularly to the York Women's Luncheon Club at the de Grey Rooms, once a month, on a Friday. Sometimes, from Strensall, I went with her.

My father used to read to us, as he did later for his grandchildren. He bought first editions of each of A.A. Milne's books as they came out, so we grew up knowing about Pooh, Piglet, Kanga and Eeyore, as well as the Beatrix Potter stories, and many others. "Little Folks," a large annual, and, later, the Japhet and Happy Annuals from Horrabin's strip in the "Daily News" or the "News Chronicle" come to mind. He also sang to us, especially to lull us to sleep. One of my sweetest and most lasting memories is his singing

Chapter 11. Nancie at Home

Glimpses of Childhood: 1. W.W.'s little bear 2. Before the front door of Pyrmont: Aunt Annie (Snell) on left; and her sister, Granny Wallace 3. Granny Wallace with Aunt Meggie (left) and Jean (hugging Marie), Hilary and Ian 4. Ian, licking out a cake-mixing bowl (Garage in the background) 5. Nancie, with Hilary and Jean 6. Nancie with the children and all their dolls (1930) (Jean has bandages on because she had swollen glands) 7 and 8. At The Mount, Broad Campden: in 7, Nancie with Hilary and Toby; in 8, Granny Hancox with Jean and Hilary, 1924. Hilary appears already to be "reading" 9. Pamela and Edward Bear's wedding at Hutton-le-hole

Chapter 11. Nancie at Home

the song "Golden Slumbers kiss your eyes, Showers awake you when you rise. Sleep, pretty darling, do not cry, and I will sing a Lullaby" until I fell asleep.

William's brother, Charles, and his sister, Chris, had stayed at Pyrmont in 1923, perhaps to see the new baby (me), born in late November, the year before: as dark as my sister was fair, and with hair as curly and thick as hers was fine and silky. I was meant to be a son, much hoped for; but long afterwards, indeed at my father's funeral, our neighbours of those years, the Kays, told me that after his initial disappointment, he soon forgot it, and ever afterwards I could "wind him round my little finger" as we used to say. In June, 1927 as I shall tell, they got their long-desired son. William built a sand-pit in the garden, and erected a swing. We had a little tent on the side lawn, and pretended to go camping; we swung in a hammock; we bathed in the backyard in an old, iron, two-handled tub, and had the garden hose sprayed over us. By the back door, we sat and shelled peas, and top-and-tailed gooseberries: more companionable occupations than watching T.V.. After my brother was born, they found me under the gooseberry bushes looking for babies. A maid, when asked where he had come from, had given the stock answer often given to children in those days, "Found under a gooseberry bush".

Milk was brought to the back door twice daily by a man with a pony and cart, as were other necessary fresh foods. The fishmonger called at our house, and in due course took away from us more than he brought, as he married our maid, Lily. On Mondays, Mrs Magson took away a large, cheap (because it was light to carry) suitcase full of washing which she returned later in the week. The travelling suitcases in those days were usually made of heavy, solid leather. Miners, en route from Jarrow and other depressed areas further North hoping to find work, came on foot to our back door, and were given mugs of tea and large sandwiches. Even as a small child, I sensed how it hurt my mother to see them so reduced, and so far from home. Without work, they could not feed their families. Travelling salesmen also came - sometimes to the front door. They, too, carried heavy suitcases bulging with embroidered and 'lace' table-cloths, etc., from (as I remember) Cyprus, Malta, India and further East. Often my mother purchased something, perhaps because she was sorry for them, as she could embroider well enough herself. Once she bought a white blouse with vivid 'Hungarian' embroidery which she wore for years.

Nancie followed the fashions as she bought or made new clothes; the waistless dresses, (or rather, dresses where the waist appeared to be at the knees), the cuban heels and the cloche hats are there in the photographs. The only striking, almost irreversible, change I see is that between 1926 and 1928 she cut off her wealth of glorious fine silky hair. "Bobbed" hair may have been fashionable; attractive on some people it was not. How could William stand it?

Originally 'Pyrmont' had gas fires, and gas lighting too, I think. They found me one day when I was still at the crawling stage, seated before the gas fire (unlit) in my parents' bedroom. I was admiring my handiwork: a pile of broken incandescents which I had taken out of the gas fire. My brother had similar tendencies. Finding a hole in the mattress cover, while supposedly resting in his cot, he teased out the horsehair until he had enough to make a haystack. Later, he took up farming.

One Autumn I was put to sleep in the spare bedroom where the apples were temporarily stored. I ate one or two (though told to leave them alone); they were horribly sour. Foolishly, I told my sister, and she used the knowledge for her own ends. For some time, she made me do whatever she wanted by threatening to tell what I had done. "Remember the little green apples", she would say. "I'll tell". I put up with this for a while until suddenly one day I said, "Tell her, then". It was a valuable lesson: my mother was not cross and I learnt that to own up was better than being afraid.

I woke once in the night to a very loud thunderstorm, and I was very much afraid. I must have been between four and five. In the midst of my fear, I said a prayer, and all was calm inside me; and I fell asleep. Another lesson learned. At about the same age I took part in a play, put on at the Folk Hall. I was a 'Tiny Tot' lifted onto the stage wearing a white cotton nightie and a pink dressing-gown. I had to repeat some lines after the teacher and stand in the centre of a ring while others danced round me. I embarrassed my mother, and made the audience laugh, by poking my finger at my favourite little boy, Dickie Pelmear, each time he passed me. A few years later, we watched annual

Chapter 11. Nancie at Home

performances of Gilbert and Sullivan operas very well done by the local amateur G and S group. They were wonderful. I remember especially 'Iolanthe' with the men in the chorus wearing grey woolly wings to match their wigs as peers of the realm. We were also taken to the pantomime in York, to the Circus, and to the early wild life films.

In these early days, to ensure the legal status of the private roads in the village, barriers were placed across the ends of roads once a year on June 1st, and those wishing to take a vehicle past had to pay a toll of one penny. We also paid one penny to be ferried across the dip in the road just beyond Lock House, between New Earswick and Rowntrees, where the River Foss used to flood over so that we could not walk by. A man with a pony and cart got us across dry-shod. The Beck also flooded in the village until major work was done to drain off the water through culverts. The open ground between our garden and the tow-path of the River Foss, and the railway line, also flooded sometimes (see p.106); even the front gate was occasionally under water! (See p.113). When the floods receded, everything was covered in rather smelly mud: the "unforgettable, unforgotten river smell" that Rupert Brooke, the poet, noticed at Grantchester.

A horse and cab was the only transport until an occasional bus service started. The first motor bus was an old Ford wagon with a canvas awning. It had long wooden forms screwed to the floor, facing each other across the bus. Each time a passenger wished to get in or out, the driver had to dismount in order to fix some steps to the tailboard. This bus ran only on Saturdays and cattle market days. There was also a small bus, the Yellow Peril, which ran on Saturdays only. In the mid-1920's, the Cosy Car Service began to run single decker red buses: 1d. to Rowntrees, 1½d. to York, and 2½d. return. The alternative was to walk the mile from New Earswick to the tram terminus at the Cocoa Works, which I believe my mother often did. She also, I think, had a bicycle at first, but with two small children and no way of carrying them on their bikes (as we used to do in the 1950's) it was time for William to consider a car.

At the side of the back garden, beyond the sand-pit, the Trust had built a brick garage. In Summer, 1926, my father brought home a second-hand Clyno car, with touring roof and celluloid side-flaps (the one in which they were to have the accident in the next Chapter). It was his first car. He once told me that, having 'beached' the car safely in the garage the first time he brought it home, he said a little prayer of thanks. (This might have been partly relief at having driven it without mishap, with only a handbook of instructions to guide him. No driving tests, nor schools of Driving Instruction in those days). In this little car we all went to a Camping Site called Broadsands Bay, near Torquay, for our summer holiday that year: my parents, my sister and I, and our nursemaid, Hilda - and the camping equipment. Here my father put his camping experience to good use, cooking on a primus stove, and seeing to all the arrangements. It was a memorable holiday. (See photos p.113).

On the return journey, when we stayed at Broad Campden with my Granny, as we had on the way down, I left behind there a remarkable doll called 'Bluebell', made of bright blue feathers with a celluloid face. She was sent on afterwards. But another (soft) doll called 'Waggy Joan' because I had squeezed her neck so hard that her head lolled sideways, was left at a picnic place at Gunthorpe Bridge, near the Fosseway. She was never seen again. My mother made me a substitute, but I found her too hard to be loveable. I never liked her. I cut open her tightly-embroidered mouth, to try to make her smile, and when my mother had darned the opening, the poor thing looked like the radiator on the Cosy Car bus. I'm afraid I also attacked with scissors the hair of a rather special china doll which my father brought back from Germany in the 1920's. The doll has a beautiful face, and his eyes close and his tongue moves. I have discovered that he was made in about 1911 and would have been more valuable if he hadn't got a tiny chip near his eye. I called him Michael. I had another precious baby doll with a china head whom I christened Elizabeth. She was bought for me at the York Gala on Knavesmire. She fell out of bed, broke her head and was thrown away, to my lasting sadness.

In summer 1927, my father took Jean and me camping for a week on the top of Filey Brigg; he cooked for us, washed and dressed us, struggled with the tangles in my hair, and took us bathing in the sea. Once, after bathing, he rubbed me down and put my vest on before retiring behind a rock to dry and dress himself. On his return I was missing,

Chapter 11. Nancie at Home

lured away by the sound and sight of a distant cricket match on the sands which I was happily watching though inadequately clothed. When we returned home, there was a baby brother in the family cot. He was not a very strong baby, and smelled of cod liver oil. He had a number of illnesses as a child, and was nursed lovingly back to health by his mother who had a special skill. He grew up able to do more physical hard work than most, and is still doing it. My father had taken Jean and me (and Mr Kay and his youngest son) to camp, so that the house would be quiet for the birth. It must have been an ordeal for him to be so far away from Nancie at this time. He could not be contacted quickly, and he would be very concerned about her.

When Nancie was pregnant with Ian in 1927, she developed diabetes and had to diet for six months. By taking care she was able to recover from this, and remained free of it for another ten years and more, until she put on weight considerably in the late 1930's. She then lost about two stone in a short time; and had to diet throughout the War, as I shall tell. I watched her do her injections, she was very brave, and by meticulous care she kept herself well, for our sakes as well as hers, for many years. When I developed diabetes, she wrote me a comforting letter, saying that, except for growing older, she had enjoyed better health once she was diagnosed than she had before.

Nancie's health was rather fragile. Our local doctor, Dr Gaynor (see photo opp.), a dear man, was our family doctor until he retired in 1932. He brought each of us into the world; he saw us through various childish infections; he treated Jean for a lengthy bout of "swollen glands" and avoided an operation on her neck which would have left an ugly scar; he removed my tonsils and adenoids when I was four (operated at home on the scrubbed kitchen table, with ether dropped onto a flannel over my face to anaesthetise me); he guided me into a York Nursing Home in 1932 to have my appendix out; he attended my brother Ian through more than one crisis; and he encouraged my mother all along.

In response to an anxious letter from my father in June 1932 wondering whether he could safely take my mother for a touring holiday, Dr Gaynor wrote a lengthy reply, the gist of it being that Nancie should go away, even though there was some risk. She used to tell us she had been diagnosed as having a "weak heart". In this letter, the doctor writes that he assumes she is suffering from lack of condition in the muscles of her heart...due to an unnoticed attack of flu. What she needed was Rest; and stimulation. He did indeed refer to her 'weak heart' which could easily be damaged by strain, physical or emotional. He recommended that she spend much of the time lying down, including being in bed by 8.0 p.m. and having one and a half hour's rest after "a very small middle day meal". It appears that Nancie had been resting on the doctor's verandah - at least this is something the doctor considered by way of a rest cure - but he thinks a holiday would be better. He had already given my mother some champagne (Moet 1921) from his own supplies, and he advised William to have some with him, both in the car and in the bedroom, though he did not anticipate it would be needed. Cold air on the face, he thought, should be tried first as a heart stimulant before resorting to the champagne!

Six months later, Dr Gaynor wrote again, in reply to W.W.. The doctor was trying to retire but finding it difficult as he still lived in Hall Cottage in the heart of the village. He told W.W. he was prepared still to see patients by appointment, either at his home or theirs; but he did not reckon always to be available in an emergency. Because of my brother's medical history, my father had to find "someone else for the post of family physician" whom Mrs Wallace would not hesitate to call. The agreed figure for attendance was 12/- per head, per annum. One of Dr Gaynor's maxims often quoted by my mother was, "Never stand when you can sit, and never sit when you can lie".

In 1925, William had taken Nancie on holiday to Cannes in the South of France; and early in June 1929, they went to Switzerland to Lake Lucerne; and returned with brightly-coloured labels stuck onto their suitcases. My father sent me a picture post-card from Switzerland of a gnome painting the white spots onto a red toadstool: one of my most treasured possessions for years. Otherwise, the holidays were modest: the summer Ian was one, we went to Embleton, a small sea-side village on the Northumbrian coast, north of Alnwick. (See photo opp.). Embleton made a deep impression on us. Jean and I, nearly 50 years later, each driving alone on the same day found ourselves near Embleton,

Chapter 11. Nancie at Home

1. Camping at Broad Sands Bay (1926): Hilda, Hilary and Jean; Nancie sitting in the tent 2. The Clyno Car did Trojan work 3. "Sense of Responsibility" 4. Much better, now 5. Nancie with Ian, at Embleton (1928) 6. Dr. Gaynor (1948) outside his garden hedge: 16 years after he retired 7. Roker (1929): Mollie Kay (left) and Flo next to Nancie (on right), Ian and Hilary 8. Sometimes, the front lane even was flooded

Chapter 11. Nancie at Home

*1. Hilary outside the boarding-house at Sandsend, painting Sandsend Ness (prob. 1933) (Photo, as were most up to that time, taken by W.W.)
2. Hilary got a camera in 1934, but was not as good as Dad! Jean and William in a pool at Hutton-le-hole 3. Hilary and Jean in party-dresses: mine was apricot taffeta, Jean's a pale blue. Our satin shoes were dyed to match. The dresses were for a Christmas party we gave in the Folk Hall, 1932
4. Out for a picnic, 1933. (Jean away at Ackworth) William loved to wear his London University blazer. 5. Jean, Nancie, William and Hilary, bathing on the Northumbrian coast, 1934 6. Travelling the old way: the ferry at Ballachulish*

Chapter 11. Nancie at Home

and on impulse visited it, arriving at 4.30 p.m.. We had neither of us been back since 1928. I reached the house where we had stayed; Jean, aiming for the same house, took a wrong turning (as I had nearly done) and arrived on the coast a mile away. We heard from each other later that we had been so close in what was an extraordinary co-incidence.

The following year we stayed on the sea-front at Roker (see p.113.), the seaside part of Sunderland. My Granny Wallace was still alive and in Sunderland, as were two aunts and a Great-aunt, so no doubt we went there so that we could enjoy each other's company; and because both William's sisters had recently had their first child. My Granny Hancox in Broad Campden (born Anne Fowler) had died in the Spring of 1929, in her eightieth year. Perhaps that is why my father took my mother away for an exciting and unusual holiday that summer. I remember she was very upset when her mother died. With us in Roker was the maid we had for many years and loved dearly: Flo. She came to us as a girl from Ashington, Northumberland, at a time of desperate unemployment there; and stayed with us until she married, in 1931 from our house. Jean was a bridesmaid. She also came with us to Sandsend, near Whitby, our next holiday-place. Four summers running we went there staying in a boarding-house on the sea-front, building sand-castles, and paddling and exploring among the rock-pools where the sand ends. On the rocks we found ammonite fossils; with the sand, another holiday-maker, an engineer home from East Africa, built a huge model of a railway engine, perfect in every detail.

The second year in Sandsend, we joined forces with a friendly family from Sheffield. One day, we devised a silly game of trying to splash each other by throwing stones into the stream that flowed out from the Valley behind and crossed the sands to the sea. (There is a stream at either end of Sandsend, both flowing under a road bridge and under the railway viaduct, high, high above the village: gone now). By ill-luck, a stone Jean threw hit the boy from the other family on the back of his head, and we had to take him to the doctor. My father was very distressed. He kept saying, "An inch either way, and Peter could have been killed!" I have just come upon an exchange of letters between W.W. and Peter's father. W.W. had offered to pay the bill for Peter's two visits to the doctor; this was refused though with gratitude for the offer. W.W. apologises for delay in writing, and says: "The fact of the matter is that I simply have no time whatever for private life at all, and particularly private correspondence". (1931) Some of the reasons for this will appear in the following Chapters.

Relatives and friends came to see us, by the day or to stay, while we were on holiday at Sandsend. There are photos of us all swimming, and making castles, and boats large enough to sit in, out of the sand. We went walking in the Mulgrave Woods behind, and were taken to Whitby to buy the then popular jet (shiny black, made into necklaces and jewellery). At Easter 1934, we all went to Keswick to join my father's brother Charles and his family. We re-visited places Charles and William had known and loved; together we all climbed to the top of Skiddaw (3,053 feet high). My father had to hold onto me as the wind was so fierce he thought I might be blown away. Ian suffered from ear-trouble in 1933 or 34, and the doctor forbade him to bathe or paddle at the sea-side, so we holidayed for the next two summers on a farm in Northumberland, away from the coast.

Once my father had the car, we were taken for picnics on every available Saturday, as Rowntrees had their five-day week. We went into the beautiful unspoilt countryside of North Yorkshire, to the beech woods carpeted with bluebells or primroses, and the moors purple with heather, according to the season. I was teased for years afterwards because apparently I used to gaze at the passing scene out of the car window, and remark hopefully and repeatedly, "Nice place for a picnic, Daddy!", probably just wanting to *be* there.

I don't remember any wet Saturdays, though there must have been some, and other days too. The attic at the top of the house was our playroom. Here, we had a house made by our father of plywood, big enough to get into. We had many treasured toys. Jean and I divided the room down the middle, each imagining we had a kitchen sink against the long window at the end. There we played 'house' as the two "Mrs Greens". We had a little, cheap gramophone given or lent by someone presumably as my parents did not have one until they bought a radiogram in 1935. On this we played sentimental records, lent by

Chapter 11. Nancie at Home

one of the maids, such as "Romona" and others like the ones in "Pennies from Heaven".

The roads were almost deserted in those days, especially along the country lanes. My father always drove. He had arranged for my mother to have driving lessons, but on a summer's evening when she was out with the instructor, she was very late back. As time went by, he was sure she'd had an accident... had been killed. The car had only broken down or had a puncture, but when she saw the state he was in, she said she wouldn't ever drive again. And she didn't. She would probably have made a good driver. I found her driving licence, the other day: June 27th, 1930 - June 26th - 1931. It was not so usual for women drive then; but Nancie had been driven about for years by her sister, Mary, before she even met her Bill.

My sister and I went to school in York to the Mount Junior School, now the Carlton House Hotel. We took the Cosy Car bus from the end of our front lane up over the railway line where Mr Potter, who had, as the result of a railway accident, a hook instead of one of his forearms, opened and shut the crossing gates. Usually, our driver was Harold, a man with a face as red as his bus. The bus took us to York station, from which we walked up to school. It was always a scramble to get me ready in time. Sometimes I missed the bus, and began to walk. Almost invariably I was then offered a lift in the car of a family who lived further out in the country. As the car went all the way to school I would arrive before Jean, which was hard on her; but there would not have been room for us both to have a lift, as the car was an Austin Seven. We kept our bus money in purses hung round our necks, and surrendered them only when playing games or gym. Mine anyway was a handsome one in tooled leather which my mother had made at her classes.

Celandines grew - still grow - along both sides of the front lane to the house: probably the first flower I really knew, and forever a favourite. From seeming entirely green, they would open their circle of fingers, the colour of melted butter. On picnics we found their giant cousins: Kingcups or Marsh Marigolds. Pale wood anemones were another favourite although they went utterly limp before we got home. Great drifts of bluebells in the beech woods; the lace of cow parsley along the roadside verges; sweet-smelling primroses on moist and mossy banks: all delighted us; and our mother knew all their names.

As a pre-school child, I was taken to stay with each of my aunts in Sunderland soon after they were married and before they had their first child: to Auntie Dorothy, with my nursemaid, Gerty, in 1925; and to Auntie Chris, perhaps the following year, as I can still remember vividly seeing a motor-bike catch fire when I was out in my push-chair. Someone rushed out with sand to douse the flames, but I dreamt about it for a long time afterwards and it frightened me. I think I must have had a close, kerbside view! One of the uncles hired or borrowed a magic lantern, and showed me pictures on the wall while I was being bathed before the fire. We were also taken to an aunt in Sunderland for breakfast on the day my father drove us into the hills from York, to watch an eclipse of the sun as it rose, through smoked glass.

All our holidays were good ones: those at the sea-side (1927-1933); on the farms in Northumberland when we were old enough to help with the harvest, and be taken to Lindisfarne, the Holy Island, and to see the Auld Hoose of our forebears (now modernised!); and on our visits to Scotland. As we got older, we went further afield on holiday, though never abroad as a family. Inspired by a school-friend at The Mount whose family lived in Scotland, we joined them on the Island of Arran, embarking with the car from Ardrossan. There, we enjoyed swimming, boating, tennis, picnics, and good company. It was so good we went a second time, the following year. In 1938, our parents took us to see the Glasgow Exhibition, and on to a holiday in the Highlands.

My father arranged his annual leave in the early years of the 1930's so that he could join us for only part of our seaside or farm holidays. His other two weeks he kept for taking Nancie and two much-loved friends on a touring holiday to the North of Scotland in late May or June. They stayed en route at Rockcliffe, north of Carlisle; they went as far as Arisaig and Mallaig and the White Sands of Morar, and sometimes to Gairloch and Lairg, even, in 1934, to Durness, in the far north-west of Scotland. We were left at home in the care of others, although as Jean and I went to boarding-school, from Spring 1934 only Ian was at home. Once, when a former maid and her new husband were in charge, he called us out of bed to see a bat they had found drowned in a crock of egg-preservative. I was

Chapter 11. Nancie at Home

terrified of what I thought was an ugly little beast, and have found them repulsive ever since! Yet I don't mind spiders and have often been called by school and college friends to remove them.

By 1931, my parents had joined the York Golf Club at Strensall, so they had some close acquaintance with the area long before they bought the land on which they built a house, only a couple of hundred yards from the golf course. They used to go out to Strensall from New Earswick in the summer evenings and play together; but never in competitive golf, nor did they use the club-house to have a drink. They took Jean and me to see if we thought we would like to learn, once we were old enough; but I immediately found it natural to play left-handedly, and the thought of the price of special left-handed clubs put an end to that idea. Jean did not learn, either.

The present occupier of 'Pyrmont' has lived there since 1952. I met her fleetingly, last year, at my sister's funeral, and, knowing I would be visiting York in the near future, she invited me to stay with her. I accepted gladly. It was a fascinating and moving experience, as well as a delight to be with the family who now live there, to return to the house where I was born after a fifty-four-year interval. So much of it was exactly the same, especially in the garden: the froth of remembered bluebells; the orange-yellow Kerria (japonica) beside the garage; the little orchard where, unbelievably now, I once got lost among the unscythed grass; the two lawns, one with an apple tree beside it, in which I remembered my mother once embedded mistletoe seeds, and the other with two bushes by the path: roses, now, not the lilacs we had, which once were damaged in June when unprecedented snow weighted their blossoms and broke them. The currant and gooseberry bushes, the vegetable plot and the fruit trees were in the same places; the sandpit, dug for us so lovingly by my father, had been needed no longer, so was filled in; and the tree by the side gate which grew tiny, wizened but sweet-tasting red apples, had long ago served its time.

The village stream, the Westfield Beck, runs as before through part of the garden and beyond the orchard fence. Although there is a footbridge across the Beck into a small extra piece of garden (called the 'plot', and named as such when a small extra charge was made in the rent in the 1920's), in our time there was a locked gate and a high fence so that we would not fall into the water and be drowned! Until a few weeks ago, I was unaware that tragedy had come to the Beck, probably before my parents went to 'Pyrmont'. In a short typescript (found among my father's papers) headed "Recollections of New Earswick from 1915", by a resident, I learnt that a mother in the village had once drowned her baby in the Beck. I know nothing of the circumstances, except that sympathy and compassion prompted the Women's Guild Committee to organise a house-to-house collection to pay for her defence. I am now better able to appreciate the locked gate and the high fence. When my sister and I were old enough, we had a favourite spot beside the Beck, below an old, notched tree, which we called 'Notchy Nook'. (See p.106.). Access to it was from the orchard over the fence. Inevitably, one day, when I climbed over, my kilted skirt (Wallace tartan, of course) caught on the fence and tore. I got into trouble with the management, although I don't think I was made to mend the tear that time as I was on other occasions.

We each had our own small garden 'plot' no more than a couple of square yards, along the concrete path between the back door and the vegetable garden. Here, my brother, sister and I grew marigolds, love-in-a-mist and sweet-scented stock from penny packets of seeds from Woolworth's. Escoltias and nasturtiums too. One year, we decided to make ponds in our little patches and had access to cement to fill in the bottom of the holes we dug. I worked at mine with a will, finished first, and amused my mother by going round triumphantly, announcing loudly, "I've concreted my bottom!"

Inside, the house was more spacious than I had expected, as I had thought it would seem to have shrunk. Each time we returned from boarding-school, we used to go round saying, "Isn't everything tiny!" Now, coming from my own home and not from Ackworth, built as a Foundling Hospital, it was all the right size. The same red quarry tiles on the hall floor welcomed me in at the front door, after we had climbed the few steps onto the narrow terrace which runs round the outside of the house. Family photos were always taken on these south-facing front steps (see pp.109 & 113.). The kitchen, where we had

Chapter 11. Nancie at Home

spent many hours drying dishes and gossiping with the maid by the glowing black-leaded range on winter evenings, now has, of course, a modern cooker and a stainless steel sink; and no maid. Outside the back door, instead of the old-fashioned 'mangle' against the neighbour's fence, there is a way through to what was 'Tockie's' house.

I was given my old room to sleep in, the one in which I had once been incarcerated for six weeks because the doctor could not be sure that a rash I had was not the dreaded scarlet fever. Rather than let me be sent away to the Isolation Hospital, they hung a sheet dipped in disinfectant over my door; my mother changed into special clothes before entering the room; and she nursed me herself. I was rather bored, I got tired of the Tiger Tim frieze which ran round the walls repetitively: I can see it now. I was taught to knit, though with teazle wool which split as one worked with the old-fashioned sharp-pointed needles. Cut-out paper dolls with clothes to take on and off, puzzles and books to do and read: all were supplied and all were burnt afterwards. My father sent a message that he had almost forgotten what I looked like and was going to put up a ladder against the window to climb up to see. I don't remember whether he did; but I heard him mowing the lawn in the summer evenings. There have been some slight structural alterations, to the house to add wash-hand basins and improve the bathroom; otherwise, no change. Over the head of the bed in which I slept was a print of Ackworth School, seen from the colonnade of the girls' wing. I felt very much at home.

As you can see in the photograph, opposite, the curved sitting-room window is eight panes wide. Through it, we used to watch the setting sun, looking across the road to the fields of Sorensons' farm, now The Garth. We used to visit the farm on occasion and were even taken to be shown the bull. Carl and Bea Sorenson (see photo opp.) were lovely people; the village was lucky to have them. In their private life, they were not so lucky. Their only child, a beautiful daughter, Anne, who married into the Rowntree family, was killed in a tragic flying accident (her husband was piloting the plane), leaving two small motherless children.

W.W. bought a Kastner-Autopiano with Music Rolls, known as a Pianola, in 1924 from Pentlands in Edinburgh, on the recommendation of his cousin Arthur Snell, at a cost of 98 guineas. He cashed in 3½ % Conversion Loan stock, held through the Post Office Savings Bank in London, and used other Savings as well to pay for it. He took advice both from Arthur Snell and from their Uncle Willie Donkin who was a Piano Specialist in West Jesmond, Newcastle-on-Tyne. The piano stood at right angles to one end of the window, its back away from the wall. The space behind sheltered our toys when they were not in use. Later, Jean began piano lessons and I soon followed.

The house William and Nancie built at Strensall incorporated the main features of the New Earswick house, especially in the sitting-room: the brick fireplace with built-in seats at either side; the long mantlepiece high above (at picture-rail level) where the early purchases of old glass were well out of reach of the children; the windows in every room looking onto the garden. Nancie had an argument with the architect about the new house at Strensall, which she won: she insisted on the sitting-room and dining-room windows being low enough for her to see all her garden *while she was sitting down*. The architect told her it would weaken the walls in a hundred years' time. She responded that she wanted to see her garden during the years she was there (and they were many); in a hundred years, she would be gone.

At New Earswick they had two long low-slung basket-work chairs, in the early days, with long cushions in them, covered as I remember, with William Morris-type material in blues and greens: popular in the 1920's. These chairs stood either side in front of the brickwork chimney-piece with its two inglenooks. Nancie embroidered matching cushions for the alcove seats. Here, William worked on his knee by the fire in the evenings (even in the next house where he had his own study), writing lecture notes, preparing for his external degree exams, discussing his ideas and getting advice sometimes from Nancie. He wrote that *together* they chose the title of the famous pamphlet: *We Can Conquer Unemployment*: discussed in the next chapter.

In the dining-room in our day stood the long book-case which William had made, usefully holding a great many books. At an early age, I found Plato's "Republic" and other works on the early Greeks, left, I suppose, from my father's studies for his

Chapter 11. Nancie at Home

(1) Pyrmont, New Earswick (taken 1985). "Tockie's" house on left, with flat roofs over the upper windows
(2) Bea and Carl Sorenson (1947), who ran the White Rose Dairy Farm
(3) The corner where we caught the bus to school (our front lane at extreme left); entrance to The Garth (bottom right). The level crossing was where Fred Potter lived: the snow-covered roof of the Lock House is just visible over the crossing.
(4) Hilary (centre top with mop of hair) had dancing lessons with Mrs Schwabe in New Earswick

Chapter 11. Nancie at Home

correspondence course for his degree in Commerce (Chap. 12). Was this one spoke in the wheel which turned my interest inevitably and increasingly towards the Ancient Greeks so I always wanted to learn their language, and have been teaching their history and culture for nearly thirty years? In the bureau drawer in the dining-room they kept the stock of sweets from which we were allowed one each after lunch. Rowntrees made a special line in those days of large round sweets: the upper half of white peppermint, the lower half of dark green jelly. I was delighted to learn from Christopher Milne's autobiographical 'The Enchanted Places' that he too remembered the same sweets and the same ritual of a sweet each after lunch.

Other memories come back when I think of 'Pyrmont'. Bonfire night, when W.W. had built a bonfire on the plot which we could watch in safety from the garden, while he lit and tended it. We were given sparklers, and other small safe fireworks to wave around. I danced round, rotating s small 'Golden Rain' or similar, guaranteed harmless. As it finished the tiny golden sparks, the inner core of the firework shot out and up the sleeve of my much younger brother's coat, burning his arm to the bone. I remember the consternation, Dr Gaynor being sent for, my feeling of guilt though I was not really responsible. However careful, as my parents always were, accidents will happen.

My parents were not forgotten in New Earswick after they moved and were frequently invited back, sometimes for my mother to open a fête or a bazaar; often for my father to attend or officiate at a function in connection with his long Chairmanship of the Joseph Rowntree Village Trust. He had been interested in Housing before he came to York, and he never lost this interest. Nancie was interested, too; she was a member of the York Housing Improvement Society, campaigning for better conditions. In 1948, W.W. was made a Life Member of the Yorkshire Naturalists' Trust Ltd. Five years later, they were photographed at the opening of a week's conference at New Earswick of the British Beekeepers' Association, the connection being the J.R.V.T., and not because they ever kept bees! They were constantly involved in the life of New Earswick.

I remember my childhood as sun in the garden, picnics in the country, and tea by the fire in winter; learning the alphabet at school by putting squares of cardboard with a letter on into the correct pocket of a many-pocketed cloth banner-like apron which hung along the kindergarten wall, a different letter embroidered on each pocket; dancing round the small school hall singing 'The Wraggle-Taggle Gipsies Oh!'; holidays at Hutton-le-Hole, and later at Sandsend, beyond Whitby.

William and Nancie created a very happy home for us, full of affection. Each of us was valued individually, and they strove always to be fair. There was also a sense of security. They may themselves have been anxious at times: about our health, and our safety; about how we would manage if the bread-winner fell ill or died as there was neither Welfare State nor family means to rescue us, and this had happened in both their families; in more than one generation in my father's. None of this filtered through to us. My father must have been away a lot, judging by all he did, as described in other chapters, but my mother was at home, making a home for us. She was at the helm, and our ship (so far as we were concerned) sailed peacefully through the years.

1935 Windrush a-building (Note: builders' hut at R.H.S.)

Chapter 12

The Prince of Wales and Mr. Lloyd George (1917-1931)

Beyond the demands of his working day, William continued to pursue his interest in Economics, and his desire to work for the improvement of social conditions and the community spirit. As a result he was gradually drawn into some of the basic forward-looking movements of his time; his brains and expertise were "borrowed" by the politicians; and he met people in high places. From 1919 onwards he did a lot of speaking: in the village of New Earswick, in the City of York, and further afield. He spoke about housing, unemployment, profit-sharing and industrial relations generally. He addressed the Institute of Industrial Workers, the Industrial League and Council, and the Joint Council of the Engineering Industry. In 1921 he gave his first address (of many) on Co-Partnership at the Balliol Conference. He attended a York W.E.A. (Workers' Education Association) Tutorial Class in 1919-20 on Economics and Social Theory, and later helped to organise lectures and classes at the Cocoa Works during the winter months. As part of this he arranged a series of lectures on the Economics of Industry for the workers. Because of the Depression there was no money to pay an outside lecturer, so he took on the job himself, delivering more than a hundred lectures over two years. He gave talks to the post-Matric boys at Bootham School (later, girls from The Mount School also came) on everyday economics. This was quite a test of his enthusiasm as they took place at 8.30 a.m., and W.W. often worked late into the night (and had as yet no car).

During his early years in New Earswick William was elected Chairman of the Parish Council of Huntington, which included New Earswick at that time. New Earswick became a Parish in its own right eventually, but until it did W.W. had to keep the balance between the wishes of the two villages by his casting vote. He wrote that he found the running of that Parish Council in terms of growing friendship was one of the things he had most enjoyed. He was also asked, in 1928, to stand at one week's notice as an Independent Candidate for the North Riding of Yorkshire County Council against the sitting member (Conservative). Not surprisingly he lost; but a week later he stood against the same candidate for a place on the Rural District Council and Board of Governors of the North Yorkshire village of Flaxton. This time he won, and served for six years until pressure of business made him decline the invitation to stand yet again. In 1921 he was invited by the Labour Party to stand for Parliament in the North Yorkshire constituency; and in 1929 he was invited similarly by both Labour and Liberal parties to stand for the same constituency. Even with the offer by a prominent Liberal to pay his election expenses, W.W. declined. He thought he could do more useful work for social progress where he was.

W.W.'s interest in the academic side of Economics persisted. In 1917 he had started work for the London degree in Economics through evening classes at the London School of Economics, but he had to forego these when working for the Ministry of Reconstruction. When he was considering continuing with this degree work as an external candidate, London University established a new degree in Commerce. Also, the Metropolitan College of St. Albans offered a new correspondence course for this degree; and to encourage new candidates they offered the return of fees to the first twenty-five or so students who took their course and were successful at the first attempt. W.W. enrolled. Some of the subjects were easy as he'd been teaching them or practising them in industry. Others caused problems: 'Modern History' did not begin in 1789 as he expected, but over two thousand years earlier, with the Ancient Greeks. French at degree standard meant essay-writing, learning of grammar and a Summer School at Boulogne. But in September 1923, at the first attempt, he passed the Final and got his money back.

In 1924 he helped to form a small Business Research and Management Association from which much later in 1947 grew ultimately the British Institute of Management. W.W. was appointed a Founder-Member of the B.I.M.. B.S.R. (Seebohm Rowntree) had

Chapter 12. The Prince of Wales and Mr. Lloyd George

become Chairman of the Company in 1923, and W.W. worked immediately under him, organising and running the Business and Economic Research Department and other relevant matters; his title was 'Economic Adviser'. He was in touch with leading economists including Maynard Keynes, whose views co-incided with W.W.'s on the folly of Churchill's return to the Gold Standard in 1925. Churchill himself later admitted he had been wrong.

At the beginning of the General Strike in May, 1926, the maintenance engineers at Rowntrees asked W.W. what to do, as there had never been a strike in the Company and they did not wish to disrupt the machinery. They had no grievance. B.S.R. was consulted and he told the men they had better strike to keep in with Trade Union members outside the factory; but to try to leave important plant to run without attention for days. The machinery continued to run, and the only strike (at any rate in W.W.'s time) in Rowntrees passed off without mishap. The following year B.S.R. established in Britain the first Management Research Group of leading non-competing firms (based on what he had seen in the U.S.A.) and for fourteen years or more was Chairman of the Group. W.W. attended all the meetings as a Rowntree representative, and found them fascinating.

Towards the end of 1926, Sir Isaac Pitman and Sons Ltd. wrote to ask W.W. to write a book on Business Forecasting. This was probably because he had forecast the slump of 1921 six months before it had happened; and he had criticised Churchill's return to the Gold Standard in 1925 and forecast what in fact happened. In spite of his replying that he was no expert he was unable to offer them the name of anyone else in Britain who was; so he wrote, *"Business Forecasting and Its Practical Application"*. The book - his first - was published on 23rd June, 1927, the same day that W.W.'s only son, Ian Galbraith, was born. (Dr. Habgood, future Archbishop of York, was also born that day). It was also the birthday of the then Prince of Wales - which is relevant here. In 1940, my sister, then a student for the Bachelor of Commerce degree at Edinburgh University, was offered a copy of this book for Vacation reading. Her response, "Oh, I think there'll be a spare copy at home", startled the tutor into realising the significance of the shared surname.

William submitted this book as the thesis for a Master of Commerce degree at London University, and waited for notice of examination. I will let him tell the sequel in his own words:

"On the morning of 26th January 1928, while I was at breakfast with my wife and three small children, the post arrived. One envelope, from the University of London, was addressed to "William Wallace Esq., M. Com.". Before opening this I realised I had been granted the degree without further interview or examination; and to the mystification of my children, if not my wife, I danced round the room waving the envelope: I have always been young for my years! The enclosed letter advised me that the Senate had conferred the degree, and had expressed the hope that I should attend personally at the next Public Presentation. I had also a letter from the External Registrar expressing his pleasure.

On May 9th 1928 (missing my birthday by one day) I attended, with my wife, at the Royal Albert Hall for presentation. So far as I can recall there were some seven hundred Bachelor graduates, a few Masters and one or two Doctors.

For conferment of degrees we all walked round the Hall on a sort of raised pathway to the Dais, carrying our Caps in our left hands and our hoods over our right arms. My Master of Commerce Hood was very attractively lined in deep orange, and was apparently new and unworn as I was the first to get the degree by examination. I had hired it; and it may have been worn by H.R.H. the then Prince of Wales when the first Master's degree was conferred upon him *honoris causa* some six years before, soon after the degree was instituted. I followed directly after the procession of Bachelors. The Vice-Chancellor was Sir William Beveridge, later of course Lord Beveridge with all his achievements. Each Bachelor was presented by his Dean and knelt before the Vice-Chancellor to be invested with his Hood. I was the first of the Masters and I had no Dean, only a group of L.S.E. students who had assembled in the gallery to cheer me! As I approached Beveridge he looked at me in some perplexity and muttered "Hallo, Wallace ; what do I do with you?" I wasn't very sure; I hadn't expected to be asked for my instructions! I didn't know, as was the case, I was expected to kneel but I did know we had to shake hands. So I just muttered back "I think we just shake hands"; and without my kneeling we just warmly

Chapter 12. The Prince of Wales and Mr. Lloyd George

shook hands and I was invested with my hood. I have often thought since how amusing it would have been if the Vice-Chancellor had had a powerful microphone before him. I had been told that after this I had to put my Cap upon my head and continue my dignified way round the arena. Instead, I was so exalted by the occasion and so amused by our muttered conversation that I just wandered round swinging my Cap rather nonchalantly, until I got back to my wife, and was probably advised by her of my error! The same evening I was a guest at a small Graduation Dinner in the Grovers' Hall, entertained by the String Band of H.M. Scots Guards and addressed by Beveridge, L.P. Amery, Gregory Foster and Lord Barnham. It was quite a day".

THE PRINCE'S PARTNER

W.W. continues:
"There was an unexpected and interesting sequel. I was invited to attend the Commemoration Day celebrations at the London School of Economics on Friday, 22nd June 1928, when the Prince of Wales was to be present. I accepted in the expectation I could work this in with a Company visit to London that week. Actually, however, I had to go two days earlier for the Company appointment and felt that, even if I could be free, I could scarcely afford a special journey to be one of a large audience on an occasion of no personal significance to me; so I stayed at home on the Friday. How wrong I was. On the following morning I was quietly digging in my front garden when a newspaper representative arrived and asked me if I were "Mr. Dash". I replied that my name was Wallace. Then he explained that he was referring to the Prince's Partner, Mr. Dash. I told him I did not know what he was talking about. Then he said he was referring to the speech the Prince of Wales had made at the meeting the previous day at the London School of Economics, where of course I had been present. I told him I had accepted an invitation but had not been able to attend. Then the reporters began to gather and telegrams to be sent to Rowntrees from the Daily Mail and other papers; and it all came out.

The Prince had apparently been making a speech to a gathering on the roof of a newly-completed wing of the L.S.E. which he was formally opening and this speech was "broadcast to a great crowd in the hall of the building". He had been told I was present and this is what he was reported to have said. He said that to some extent he also was celebrating a commemoration.

> 'It is now six years since I was given the honour of becoming a Master of Commerce, but until a month back I was the only living specimen of that species. I felt it to be a lonely position, and feared that if I filled it alone I might some day end up in being preserved in a bottle. Now I am thankful to say I am no longer alone. Last month a man who bears the name of a very great and famous Scotsman got through the wire entanglements, stormed the fort, overcame all difficulties and joined me.
>
> So there are now two Masters of Commerce. I am not going to tell you the name of the one who has become associated with me in this degree I have received. He is here and you will see him in due course; but I understand he is a modest man and I hate making anyone blush. I will say his name is not, as you might think, Robert Bruce.
>
> Speaking for both of us, however, I can say we are not satisfied that there should be only two of us. Glad as I am of the company of my partner - we will call him Mr. Dash - I do not think that the old proverb that two's company, and so on, is very good or suitable in this case. One or other of us might be cut off in the flower of our youth and one would be lonely again. Besides, a deputation of commercial magnates might come along with a lot of their knotty problems, and then there would be only one thing for me to say, and that is, 'Partner, I leave it to you'. We want a lot more Masters of Commerce and Mistresses of Commerce, and it is up to you to see that they come along soon...'

Chapter 12. The Prince of Wales and Mr. Lloyd George

If the Prince had stated my name there would still have been wide publicity because all he did then was of outstanding public interest. But his reference to "My Partner, Mr. Dash" put the Press on its mettle to see who could find his partner and get the story first. For a few days almost every British newspaper featured "The Prince's Partner, William Wallace" with a photo and background. One Scottish newspaper sent me a reply paid telegram about my ancestors. Another paper referred to my "tight little curls"! Scores of press-cuttings were sent to me. If there had been T.V. then, I should certainly have been constrained to appear. Then, just as suddenly, I disappeared from any but the local Press for years and it became just a story of "old, forgotten, far-off days". But it was interesting while it lasted. I had a kind personal letter from the Prince commending my book and thanking me for a copy of it. I might add, too, that my directors began to take an interest!"

On May 31st, 1923, the Prince of Wales had visited the Cocoa Works, at the special invitation of the Works Council. He got a tremendous reception; and according to a full account in 'The Times' afterwards he was apparently impressed by the attractive and rural surroundings of the factory; the warmth of the welcome he got from the seven thousand employees, the pensioners and even two hundred and twenty children from New Earswick; the beautiful gift of a Royal Blue leather and gold casket full of varied chocolates; and his tour of as much as possible of the two hundred acres of buildings, sidings and gardens. Many other members of the Royal Family have since visited the factory, all those who came during W.W.'s chairmanship being received by him and my mother. I particularly remember Queen Mary's visit in 1938 when we were allowed to watch her arrival from an office window, and I took photos of her with my little box camera.

In 1931, William and Nancie were invited to a Royal Garden Party at Buckingham Palace (see photo p.126.). I remember my mother's elegant dress of green lace which must have been the fashion then. Whether his name was suggested because of William's connection with the Prince through the Master of Commerce degree, or because he had been doing some work for the then Prime Minister, Ramsay Macdonald, he did not know. He watched the Minister in attendance tell King George V some funny stories, out of earshot of Queen Mary; they also saw distinct signs of boredom in the behaviour of the Prince of Wales, he flapping his coat-tails as he followed his parents in their dignified procession.

B.S.R. was obviously William's first hero (after his father and the Reverend Ebenezer Rees of his boyhood). He worked beside him daily for many years. He knew the calibre of the man; and he loved him. Lloyd George was another hero. W.W. worked with him at No.10. Downing Street, especially on the problem of Unemployment; he and Nancie stayed with L.G. and Dame Margaret in their Welsh home, Brynawelon, in Criccieth, as guests of the family in 1927. W.W. has referred to L.G. as "the most vibrant personality I have met", with a special quality of mind, plus a Sixth Sense.

Churchill was also a hero. In spite of great differences in their views on both policy and practice, Churchill and L.G. had a high regard for each other's abilities. Churchill described L.G. as "the greatest Welshman since the Tudors", and once wrote to L.G., "all the rest of our lives we shall be opposed; but I am deeply attached to you". L.G., walking on the beach near Criccieth in August, 1927, was asked by W.W., "Of all the present-day politicians whom you know, which would you personally rank as 'statesmen'?" His instant, terse, emphatic reply was, "Only Winston". To many others, both are heroes for the same reason: each won a War which otherwise would most likely have been lost.

In 1927, L.G. asked B.S.R. - never a party politician, but a Liberal and a personal friend of L.G. - to help him produce a vital Report on unemployment within a week! L.G. had promised he would do this for a Committee whose recent Report dissatisfied him. B.S.R., with L.G. in London, phoned W.W. to catch the next train down from York bringing his pyjamas, as L.G. wished to see them at the House of Commons at 4.0 p.m. Lloyd George presented W.W. with a three-foot high pile of mimeographed Minutes and papers and asked him to read them and produce a draft Report for the Committee. W.W. said he couldn't possibly read them all within the few days available, but would draft a paper giving his own ideas in an objective, non-party approach. This was accepted, and W.W.,

Chapter 12. The Prince of Wales and Mr. Lloyd George

refusing the proffered first-class secretary and a small flat in Park Lane, returned to York. B.S.R. told him that L.G. would probably never thank him for anything he did, but if he approved he would just ask for something else to be done.

William worked hard all week, day and night. At 9 p.m. on the Saturday, a waiting car at Rowntrees took him to the station to put his fifty-page draft in the late post-box on the London night-mail train. He followed by train the next afternoon. In his draft W.W. had urged the imaginative use of unemployed labour for national development, to improve, for example, our roads not adequate for modern traffic. L.G. approved of the draft, except for two paragraphs, and asked for a full revised draft Report to cover a number of subjects as well as unemployment. L.G. persuaded W.W. to take Nancie to the 1927 Liberal Summer School at Cambridge. While there L.G. invited W.W. to go to Criccieth for a week or two, to write him a Report on agriculture (which W.W. reckoned he knew nothing about). W.W. refused, saying he intended to take his wife and baby son on holiday, whereupon L.G. crossed the room to Nancie and charmingly invited her to go to his home in Criccieth for a holiday, so that William could do some work for him. Thinking her husband had agreed already and not able to say 'No' to so distinguished and eminent a man, Nancie accepted. William and Nancie were given the main guest-bedroom once they arrived in Wales; members of the family who arrived later were sent to the local hotel. The daughter, Megan, was a delightful member of the house-party (as well as subsequently a Member of Parliament) and they much enjoyed her sense of fun. W.W. found her strangely like her father: "in personality, in wit and charm and drive, with her quick mind, her Welsh warmth and eloquence". (see p.126 for Criccieth Photo).

On the way home the old Clyno four-seater with cloth hood and only one door, in which we had all gone to Torquay the Summer before, skidded on a newly-wet road. It turned over, pinning W.W. upside down against the steering wheel, his knee jammed against the horn. They were soon rescued and apart from bruises and torn muscles, were unhurt. The accident had been caused by a fault in the near front-wheel brake drum.

While out shopping with L.G. in Wales my mother had bought an antique oak chest-of-drawers which she arranged to have sent home for me. I have it still. They were also taking home the gift of a huge blue-and-white dish, broken in the accident and successfully mended to stand above our dining-room mantlepiece until the house was sold in 1980. They were also sent, as a present from Dame Margaret (L.G.'s wife), an anthracite stove of hers to "keep them warm in Yorkshire". Dame Margaret had been a charming hostess and won their hearts. She and L.G. had taken Nancie out in their Rolls for drives and to visit Agricultural Shows on several afternoons while W.W. stayed behind and tried to "mug up" Agriculture for the Report he had to write. On one occasion, W.W. took Nancie and Megan for a drive in his little car. They got stuck in a flood, so W.W. got out into the water which came above his knees and pushed the car through while Megan took the wheel. Megan was silent - unusual for her - but when they got to Brynawelon she burst out with the full story, apparently impressed most of all because W.W. had taken the incident so calmly and never said a word throughout. Such self-restraint was almost incredible to a Welsh father and daughter.

Ready for the 1929 General Election, the famous 6d pamphlet, *"We Can Conquer Unemployment"* was published. The preface was by L.G. and no other name appeared on it. His picture was on the cover, standing with outstretched hands and the words, "We Mobilised for War. Let us Mobilise for Prosperity". It caught attention and sold hundreds of thousands of copies because it was Election time and the pamphlet was associated with L.G.. But its fundamental arguments were based on W.W.'s 1927 draft. The issue of May 18th 1929 of "The Nation" described W.W. as "the writer of *'We Can Conquer Unemployment'*". B.S.R. probably had the seminal ideas, and he acted as catalyst in bringing together W.W. and L.G.

L.G. was a speaker without a peer; but he could not write effectively. He held a series of week-end meetings at his house, Bron-y-De, at Churt, in 1928-9 which W.W. attended and found absolutely fascinating. There were gathered L.G.'s advisers (sometimes called the "Brains Trust") to discuss economics and policy and many other things besides. Particularly noticeable in the group and of particular interest to W.W. was John Maynard Keynes, with whom he had some interesting discussions.

Chapter 12. The Prince of Wales and Mr. Lloyd George

The title, *'We Can Conquer Unemployment'* was coined by W.W., with help from Nancie as he worked on the report at his own fireside. L.G. nearly changed it to 'The Problem of Unemployment', but W.W. records that he said to L.G., "Is it credible that you are contemplating this new title which only a Sidney Webb would choose?" L.G. replied, "Oh Wallace, old man, is it as bad as that?" So the original title was restored. When L.G. saw the mounting sales for the 6d. pamphlet, he told W.W. he had been 'dumb'. He should have demanded a farthing a copy royalty as the writer!

L.G. *did* thank W.W. in addition to asking him to do more work for him. He wrote him a personal letter to express his deep appreciation of the work W.W. had done. Ramsay MacDonald, the new Prime Minister, also used B.S.R. and W.W. to advise on Unemployment, and W.W. drafted yet more proposals. But finance was not forthcoming and unemployment rose to two-and-a-half million. Later, in 1931, the Labour Government fell, being replaced by a National Government under Ramsay MacDonald, formed to defend the pound which they then de-valued. That was the end of W.W.'s contact with politics and L.G., which had lasted from 1917 to 1931, when he had been asked to sit at L.G.'s right hand at meetings, to draft his documents and advise him on economic matters. On his study wall W.W. had a signed portrait of Ramsay MacDonald; but a wicked cartoon of L.G. by Low, signed by L.G., shared the place of honour beside it. He was told, by someone who saw it, that President Roosevelt had a much annotated copy on his desk of *"We Can Conquer Unemployment"*, W.W.'s brainchild.

(1) William took this photo when he and Nancie stayed in Criccieth with the Lloyd Georges (August 1927). Left to right: Olwen, Lady Carey Evans; Dame Margaret; Nancie; Lloyd George; Megan with puppy (kneeling)

(2) Nancie and William in London for the Buckingham Palace Garden Party, July, 1931

Chapter 13

Changes In The 1930's (1929-1940)

For the first ten years at Rowntrees W.W. found that much of his work was research, leading by stages into a share in management. From 1929 (except for work on Unemployment and the separate enquiry into British Agriculture) he worked primarily in management and wholly for Rowntrees. In 1929 when the Secretary to the Company died he was appointed in his place and so attended the weekly Board Meetings and heard all discussions of the Company's problems.

The first problem - of the slow sales of a particular product being made for an American Company - he solved by suggesting that the customer be offered double quantity for the same money. It worked. A further complication was that this product was sold through penny-in-the-slot machines, very popular then, and the supplier of *another* company of automatic machines went bankrupt. Hopeful purchasers put their pennies in these other machines, and nothing came out! This put them off using the machines alongside, so sales fell away. W.W.'s solution to this was to buy out the bankrupt company at auction for £2,000. He sold off some 50,000 derelict machines for scrap which were then removed, leaving his own machines clear. The sale of the rest of the bankrupt company's assets, and 6d. per derelict machine for the 50,000, re-imbursed him for the £2,000. Their own product then sold successfully. W.W. reckoned that the profit then made by this product over the years was, alone, more than enough to cover his total salary cost during his thirty-eight years at Rowntrees!

Rowntrees paid higher wages than most of their competitors. In early 1931 with a further and even more serious trade depression than that of the 1920's just beginning, it became necessary to arrange two successive general wage cuts of 5%. The workers had to be told that this was the only way to keep their jobs safe, and that as soon as possible the wages would be raised again. There were no strikes - the workers agreed and within about a year pay was back to the old level. W.W. offers this as a genuine policy of good industrial relations in which the employees were kept informed; and it led to a spirit of mutual trust: good for business and the happiness of all concerned.

In 1931 W.W. was appointed a Director of the Company (at a salary not exceeding £1,500). I can still recall vividly stopping our neighbour, Carl Sorenson, in his (open tourer) car when I met him about the village that morning to tell him about my father's promotion, I was so proud of him. One of W.W.'s particular functions from now on was to look forward, budget a year ahead, and be responsible for all the figures of the business (costing, statistics, budgets) other than the books of account. He was also, in time, brought into the Overseas Associated Companies, and in 1938 was made responsible for all the Overseas Companies including Eire, Canada, Australia and South Africa. He was Chairman of the Irish Company and used to visit Dublin. On arrival there in May, 1940, he reported to the authorities as he came off the plane. All they said was, "Would you mind just writing your name in the Visitors' Book?"

Selling prices fell drastically between 1920 and 1938; consumption per head per week of chocolate and confectionery rose from 4 ozs. to 7¼ ozs. Rowntree profits rose fairly steadily after the low figure of 1931.

Several changes took place at home from 1931 onwards. Jean was soon old enough to have to leave the Mount Junior School, but at that time the Mount Senior School did not accept anyone under fourteen. William took advice and visited schools, very keen that his family should have the best education available. He decided to send her to the Quaker School at Ackworth near Pontefract where Nancie's grandmother had gone in 1823. Jean went there in September, 1932, and I followed a year later. We had to adjust to huge rooms and corridors, treading stone stairs already worn into hollows by feet tramping up and down for over one hundred and fifty years. It was cold, at times bitterly cold. Huge fires, well-guarded, burnt in each class-room, but away from the hearth there was no warmth. With us we took our tuck-boxes (called "Tibbies"). I still have mine. I used to fill

Chapter 13. Changes in the 1930's

it up with materials for knitting and sewing, with writing paper, paints and crayons, and large boxes of bars of Aero chocolate (Rowntrees, of course). In it I also kept my roller-skates (a favourite pastime at Ackworth), and the fruit ordered for us by our parents every Saturday. Later, no doubt, my beloved flute. I did a lot of roller-skating and swimming in the School Baths (much improved since Elizabeth Anne Hawkes's day!) Those of us sufficiently keen were allowed to swim every week-day until the Christmas holidays. Not many did, so there was plenty of room; the steam rose from the (slightly) warmed water into the cold air as December approached until we couldn't see across the Baths. I got my Bronze Life-Saving Medal, and practised for the Silver, but a lower age limit for this of sixteen meant I left well before I qualified to try.

We played hockey - Jean was rather good - and cricket. I went for solitary walks by the stream in the fields beyond the playing fields, finding wild flowers and watching tadpoles and sticklebacks in the water. This we were allowed to do if we signed the 'Out-book' with our destination: "P.V." for Primrose Vale; and went no further. Once, our form teacher in my second summer took three or four of us for a much longer walk to look for a kingfisher. We saw it, but only after she had filled my mouth with a boiled sweet, to stop me chattering. In my last year at Ackworth I agreed to keep a 'Natural History' Diary (I think for a Competition). I observed and recorded a thousand things, especially as I was by then sleeping not in a school dormitory but across the road and down a path through a garden, in the School House, which gave much more scope. I also took on the care of an Axolotl in a tank in the school labs, and wrote about it, too. I think I won the competition; they were certainly very pleased with me and gave me a charming butterfly brooch: one more keepsake I still have.

I don't know that either Jean or I enjoyed our time at Ackworth as much as all that, but we 'tholed' it as the Scots say. We were very well taught (everything but Classical Greek which was for me a serious omission, but that's another story). I loved the swimming, and the Saturday evening lectures and recitals. I loved the huge copper-beech tree nearest the school which I was punished a number of times for climbing. To begin with I missed my parents, the house and the garden, and our Saturday picnics in the country. I was very homesick and sobbed uncontrollably for a night or two. Homesickness is like an illness. It takes over and no effort of will can stop it; but it passes. Our parents came to visit sometimes, on a Saturday, and took us out to lunch in the car. One time, on my birthday, I was confined to the 'Nursery' with chicken-pox and could only wave from the window. Another time I caught measles on the very last day of the Spring Term and so lost much of the school holidays. When I was out of quarantine from the measles, my father came to school and took me for a long drive, a sort of mini-holiday. He offered to take me away somewhere to stay for the night to extend the feeling of the holidays, but all I wanted was to go home.

Visiting us at Ackworth during my first Summer Term, my parents played tennis with us in the grounds. It was a very hot afternoon, and although I was wearing a cotton dress (no doubt inherited from my sister) I complained of heat. On inspection I was found to be wearing my full complement of winter underwear: chilprufe vest and combinations, and liberty bodice (the sort we used to button our suspenders onto). I had simply gone on dressing myself in the same garments I had gone back to school in at the beginning of the term. No wonder I was hot. My mother was both shocked and amused. When the school hairdressers cut my mop of curls, she was not amused, only angry, as it looked so frightful. From then on I had to suffer my growing hair (always very thick) for thirteen weeks as she would not allow anyone but our home barber (Mr Bradley of New Earswick, who cut it superbly for 6d.) to touch it. I really was hot: like wearing a fur hat all summer. She had another shock on a later visit after I had applied the scissors myself and could not really see what I was doing.

At Ackworth Jean and I both continued piano lessons, having learnt while in York from a Mr. Golden who lived on The Mount, near our Junior School. When the John Francis Trio performed before the school one Saturday evening, I was so taken by his flute-playing that I gave my father no peace until I was allowed to learn. First he arranged to give me a piccolo - the flute's little sister - as a Christmas present, but I was so disappointed he soon changed it for a flute. I had lessons in York; but at Ackworth I got

Chapter 13. Changes in the 1930's

up at 6.30 a.m. to practise every morning before breakfast, and I played in the School Orchestra. This continued at The Mount where lessons were possible. Chilblains which swelled my fingers until they could not bend made all playing difficult. I had them each winter at Ackworth; on my toes as well as my hands. We wore thick black woollen stockings which turned green in the school laundry. The laundry also ruined all elastic so we used to have spare lengths of elastic, which did not go through the laundry but could be worn round the waist to hold up our navy knickers: called, I think, "tummy tights". Gym tunics were short, and when the stockings and the knickers shrank there was a draught which blew cold on the tops of the legs.

From Ackworth we went each year by special chartered train or coach on unforgettable outings. One was to Malham Cove and Semerwater in the North Yorkshire Dales; another to Goathland on the North Yorkshire Moors; and in 1935 (I think) we sang in the Free Trade Hall in Manchester. The best and most exciting train journey was the shortest. Rising as usual at 6.30 a.m., we left an hour later in the dark to take train to York for the Christmas holidays. We reached York by nine o' clock and savoured each day of our return home, the holidays being long enough to break any quarantine for an infectious disease at school.

All this was part of the excellent education our parents provided - at a cost to themselves as they missed us at home. I also remember how supportive they were, my mother writing to us every Wednesday without fail and sending parcels whenever I asked for something. Her letters had the same format throughout my life. My father, whose letters were occasional, might address me as 'Dear George' (his pet name for me) or usually (until his very last letter in 1976) 'Dear Geogre', which is how I spelt it when first writing it from boarding-school at the age of ten; but my mother always wrote: 'My Darling Hilary.....Ever your loving Mummy'. And she was. Among the letters she kept was one from her mother on hearing of her engagement in March 1918. It begins 'My dearest Nancie', and ends 'Your loving Mother'. Her mother was her closest confidante. This letter is the only one which shows she had told someone about her growing attachment to 'Mr. Wallace' as my Granny refers to him. On hearing of the engagement, Nancie's mother wrote to him immediately to invite him to come to stay at Easter. One letter survives, written by Elizabeth Ann (Hawkes) Fowler to her daughter, Anne Hancox. It has neither address nor date, though must have been well before 1890 when Mrs Fowler died. She ends her letter: '... believe me to remain with best love your ever affectionate Mother'. So is the torch handed on. At Ackworth, we also had a compulsory period on Sunday afternoons for Writing Home. I never failed to write, although once at least I forgot to post my letter which provoked an anxious phone call from W.W. and a reprimand from the House mistress. My father saved all these letters. The members of staff were both kind and fair-minded, and my first headmistress anyway I loved dearly.

From about 1929, my parents had been feeling that our house in New Earswick was rather small for us. Although it had four bedrooms, a resident maid occupied one, and with three children besides my parents it meant we had no spare room for visitors. Week-end after week-end we inspected possible houses in York and the surrounding villages, especially an old Manor House about ten miles out, until woodworm was discovered in its beams. All the houses we saw had some drawback, so it was decided to build. The night before they signed a contract for land at Clifton, on the West side of the City, they heard that a civilian airfield was planned for the adjoining land. They switched to Strensall, opposite the York Golf Club of which they were members, and bought two fields with rather dry sandy soil in which carrots and sugar beet grew. Each of us laid a "foundation stone" under the corner where our bedrooms were to be, with our names on the bricks. Trees were planted, especially across the South-West corner of the inner field against the prevailing wind; and the full length of the North side against the North winds. While we were on holiday for the second Summer running on the Northumbrian farm, Roddam Rigg, Wooperton, near Wooler, in August 1935, William returned to New Earswick and moved house for us. Nancie, as was her wont, had everything well-organised. Each item of furniture had on it the number of the room into which it was to go; a plan was provided at the Strensall end, to show where all the furniture was to be placed. We were spared the trauma of watching our home being dismantled, and we returned to live in "Windrush", our spacious, newly-built, six-bedroomed house, with joy

Chapter 13. Changes in the 1930's

and expectation. (see photo opp.).

William and Nancie had been working on the new garden for many months before we moved in and this continued for many years after! My father used to say that having come to live close to his Golf Club he now seldom had time to play. Nancie was the gardener, William worked in it to please her. He helped her make the formal rectangular pond surrounded by crazy-paving and a rose garden, below the sitting- room window (see photo opp.); later, a smaller, natural-looking pond with bog garden in another part of the garden; and an Alpine 'scree' for special plants. My parents put on bathing costumes to set the water-lilies and other plants in the pools, but before they did so William dived into the formal pond at some risk as it is not very long and has a ledge for smaller plants all round. They arranged for a large lawn to be levelled and seeded, with a grass tennis court from which we got much enjoyment, especially in the first years (see photo opp.). W.W. bought an Atco motor mower, with which each of the rest of us took turns; I seem to remember him saying he reckoned he walked four and a half miles each time he cut the whole lawn, though I don't know how he counted the distance. A beautiful double pink weeping cherry tree opened its petals and then scattered them on the grass, in full view of the dining-room window. A weeping willow tree softened the brick contours of the east end of the house by the garage. (See p.xiii.).

Jean moved to The Mount School in York, as a boarder, when we returned from our holiday in 1935, to stay there for three years. I had a further two years at Ackworth and went to The Mount from 1937 until Christmas 1940. Once at School in York we were able to go home for a few hours each weekend; latterly it became the custom for us to be taken (with friends) by our parents after the Friends' Sunday Meeting and to stay for lunch and tea. Ian, who had also been at The Mount Junior School, went to a tutor in Strensall village until he was old enough to go to a Preparatory boarding-school in Westmorland before going on to Bootham, the Quaker School for boys in York.

In June 1939, W.W. went to New York on the New Mauretania's maiden voyage, mainly to discuss export possibilities and to visit the factory in Toronto. Before leaving home, he personally dug an air-raid shelter in our garden. My sister, with characteristic humour, later painted up the name 'Mon abri' (my shelter) which is what our bathing hut had been called on the holiday from which we hastily returned, a week before War was declared. (see photo opp.) Also before he left, he wrote letters for each of his children, asking us to care for our mother, should anything happen to him, so deep was his sense of foreboding. The letters were not to be opened until after his death. When I read mine after his death nearly forty years later, the tenderness and love for Nancie which it contained reduced me to tears. They had something very special between them. I remember he told us that the Americans in the United States in Summer, 1939, were in a great state of jitters about a possible War, glued to every News bulletin. He got back to Britain with a month to spare before War broke out and found everyone much calmer here. We went for a pre-arranged family holiday on a (different) farm in Northumbria, not far from Bamburgh. W.W. grew increasingly uneasy about the international situation, and brought us all home early to a week which I spent machining black-out curtains for the thirty-six windows in our house, and listening to every News Bulletin to report its contents to my father. My mother had prudently purchased a huge roll of blackout material before we went away. Some of the bigger curtains survive as dust-sheets (still with their labels, e.g. 'Sitting-room South' stitched to the corner).

Even before we were at War, small children and their teachers, and mothers and babies, were evacuated from the docks of Hull and Middlesbrough to the supposedly relative safety of North Yorkshire. Strensall was a "de-railing station", which meant that trainloads of pathetic evacuees arrived there, clutching brown paper carrier bags containing their "iron rations" of biscuits, etc., a gas mask in cardboard box slung over their shoulders. Officials had been busy in the village for some time, visiting homes and allocating the number of evacuees to each house. The method of arriving at a fair allocation was to count the number of rooms in a house (both living and sleeping), take away the number of people who resided there permanently, and the difference was counted as the "spare room" for that number of incomers. A mother and baby was a special case as they needed free access to a kitchen at all times, so the practice was to

Chapter 13. Changes in the 1930's

(1) Windrush in the early days
(2) By the new pond (c. 1937): Jean, Dorothy (William's sister), Nancie and Hilary
(3) Jean, Hilary, William and Ian on the tennis court (Easter 1946)
(4) Ian cleaning out the formal pond in the late 1950's. Jill, Nancie, Charles (William's brother), and William standing behind him
(5) One of the "rests" needed at frequent intervals. The white cotton bags, "pots", held 40 lbs. when filled. We over-filled them, carried them to the weighing machine, and had any excess put into the next bag.
(6) Jean picking peas, while Ian eats some
(5 and 6 taken by HMF)

Chapter 13. Changes in the 1930's

place them in the houses of single maiden ladies (elderly) living alone. As the village of Strensall had a large military camp within easy walking distance, and many of the mothers were neither too scrupulous nor very responsible, they very soon took to going out in the evenings to find more lively company than that provided by their hostess, leaving their baby to be looked after by the last class of person suited to the job! The elderly ladies also found that their trim, clean houses were suddenly no longer as tidy nor as sweet-smelling as they had been. There was uproar in the village; the problem was solved only because, after a week or two, the mothers took their babies home, saying they would rather be bombed than continue to have to share someone else's house in a manner which didn't suit them.

The schoolchildren settled in more easily, though many were bewildered and homesick at first. They were taken from the train to the Parish Hall and given refreshments and then taken to their new homes. I remember going with my mother to help with feeding the evacuees. On Friday, September 1st, we were working there when news came through of the invasion of Poland. Realising what it meant, I felt as though someone had thrust a sharp instrument right into me. "You've gone quite white, my dear," said one of the kindly village helpers. To our household were allocated two little girls, Lily and Audrey; also a Primary School Headmistress, a charming lady who became a close friend. She counted as three (we'd been allocated five children) and had our one spare bedroom. The little girls had improvised beds in the billiard room as we had no other spare bedrooms. My sister and I sat with them until they cried themselves to sleep that first night. Their parents came to visit them quite often at the weekend either just turning up in time for lunch, or sending a note which arrived an hour or two before they did. As food was strictly rationed, this did not make catering easy. The parents were very grateful. I've just found some touching letters from them. And a letter from the Middlesbrough evacuees thanking my parents for some "chocolate novelties". I think the children - and the Headmistress - stayed until my parents were moving to Wales, a year later. While with us they stubbornly refused to like any food except fish and chips, and bread and jam. When they went home, they asked for a cloth on the table and table napkins. I did not see them except in school holidays, as our school was also evacuated: to a large Quaker Guest House, north of Scarborough.

In the Company for months, even years, before September 3rd, 1939, they had spoken of "Wallace's War" because he had so often predicted that it was inevitable and tried to see what steps could be taken to maintain or build supplies when War came. My sister had been going to go to friends in France, preparatory to going up to Edinburgh University, but her visit was cancelled. American friends offered to have us all to stay for the duration of the War, but when my father asked Jean if she would take Ian and me to safety' she said, 'No', her place was in England. So the family was not broken up. How totally different all our lives would have been, had we gone.

W.W. was made Deputy Chairman-Elect of both the York Board and the General Board in 1940. B.S.R. wrote to say how very happy he was, knowing that W.W. would keep the 'J.R.' tradition alive. W.W. was to succeed a Director who was soon to retire; but this promotion was greatly delayed as Rowntrees were asked to lend W.W. to the Ministry of Food as the Adviser, later to become the Director, for Cocoa, Chocolate and Sugar Confectionery. The only stipulation was that Rowntrees were not allowed to *raise* his salary while he worked for the Government (apparently to prevent bribery); we all had to go to live on the North Welsh Coast near Colwyn Bay, leaving behind our lovely new house and garden, to share another family's house: Tan-yr-allt Hall, Llanddulas, Near Abergele. Before he left for North Wales, W.W. had helped to arrange for Rowntrees to make a range of non-food products using their skilled workers (no longer needed as there were large reductions in confectionery activities) and so saving them from redundancy. He also joined the Local Defence Volunteers (forerunner of the Home Guard), and every Friday night he patrolled on an isolated country road in North Yorkshire with one companion, from 9.30 p.m.-6.30 a.m., his rifle at the ready.

In the Summer of 1940, the threat of invasion was very real. Soldiers from the nearby camp parked their vehicles under our hedge and slept rough or kept guard. Sometimes William and Nancie were woken before dawn by the revving of engines as the Army

Chapter 13. Changes in the 1930's

moved off: on manoeuvres, or for real? They could not tell, and it was not easy to go back to sleep again. My father, who, as you will by now have gathered, always looked ahead, feared that at least the coastal margin of the British Isles could become a battle ground. He arranged for the three of us to stay with our Aunt Dorothy near Chipping Campden (where he and Nancie had gone in 1919), as far from the sea as possible. My aunt offered us as unskilled 'agricultural labourers' to cousins in Evesham and district who had large-scale market gardening concerns. As soon as we were free from school and University we went by train from York, taking our bicycles. Until the middle of August we worked on the land in Gloucestershire and Worcestershire, rising early to cycle to the place appointed for that day, where we picked peas, or did whatever other work needed to be done. (see photo p.131.). I remember the marvellous feeling on receiving my first wage-packet at the end of the week. I also remember vividly the day we worked at Upton-on-Wold, above Moreton-in-Marsh. We found fossilised shells in the dry red soil, relics of a time when the sea covered that part of Britain. We also felt the reverberations of the land under us during the day-light bombing of Bristol, over fifty miles away. It was while we were at Aunt Dorothy's in Summer 1940 that Ian and I cycled over to Sherrif's Lench to visit Cousin Mollie Bomford (née Fowler), whose tenth birthday is described in Chap.4. There I met her youngest son - for half-an-hour in a harvest field - and found him again last year, which introduced me to many members of the Fowler and Bomford family, and so has helped with the writing of this book.

Knowing he was going to work in Colwyn Bay in the Autumn, my father had booked a holiday for us on a farm in Anglesey near a very modest holiday bungalow used by some of the Rowntree family. From there he reconnoitred for accommodation for us when he would move to the Ministry of Food. We three travelled by train from Chipping Campden to the nearest station on the Holyhead line, to be met by our parents. The farmhouse where we stayed for our holiday was over nine hundred years old. If you heard a plane fly over and looked up the wide chimney in the kitchen you could see it pass overhead against the blue sky. We were less than five minutes from a secluded private cove, where strangers were charged to use it, which gave it the name of 'Sixpenny Beach'. My father and I, being the only ones keen on such a cold pursuit, used to run over the rabbit-warren of sandhills to bathe before breakfast. (photo p.134.).

From the farmhouse, we three young ones cycled one day to the ferry which crossed the Menai Straits to Conway; cycled from there to the Llanberis Pass; climbed Snowdon (the highest mountain in Wales); and retraced our steps back to Anglesey. (The following Summer we made a similar excursion, by train and by bike, from Llanddulas to the top of Snowdon. On each occasion the summit of the mountain stood out clear and sunlit, morning and evening; but each time we reached the top, to eat our sandwiches and enjoy the view, the noon mists came down and enveloped us, shutting out the sun and the expected prospect.)

Nearly twenty years later I arranged to rent a cottage by the sea within a few miles of our farmhouse and we took our three children to enjoy the same delights of sand and sea and the warm hospitality of the lovely Welsh family who had welcomed us in 1940. (See photo p.134.). Since then our eldest has taken her children to the same cottage by the sea for their summer holidays. My parents returned for at least one more holiday (1941) to the tranquillity of this secluded farm, where there was no phone, and the Ministry of Food could be left behind. Sometimes we helped on the farm with the harvest (see photo p.134.); one year we risked our lives climbing over the cliffs to harvest gulls eggs to be 'put down' in water-glass for the winter to help alleviate chronic shortages.

The biggest change William and Nancie had to face throughout their married life was the outbreak of War in 1939 which led to their move to Colwyn Bay: just when they had settled into their new home, hoping to stay there for the rest of their lives. Now they had to rent it out. Tenants can be very cruel, often unwittingly. Beds and carpets were ruined, and the garden and Nancie's special plants and bulbs destroyed by too-intrusive dogs. The wife of the last tenant, who was a personal colleague in a superior position, was so busy with Civic affairs that she left others to run the house. A treasured tea-service was smashed, piece by piece; a new Chinese carpet was never turned from under the heavy piano, so that the bright blue border was eaten by moth. These were minor domestic

Chapter 13. Changes in the 1930's

tragedies when discovered later; now the important thing was that they must be together wherever they had to go. There was, of course, no question of Nancie remaining alone behind, even for a day.

Anglesey: 1. William bathing before breakfast. 2 'Sixpenny Beach' was magical (1940) 3. Hilary hay-raking 4. Our holiday cottage (1958): John and the car are resting 5. Our children with Mr and Mrs Williams 6. Elizabeth, Alison and William on the 'Sixpenny Beach' (1959) (All these photos, exc. 3, taken by HMF)

134

Chapter 14

William and Nancie In Wales (1940-1944) and Home Again (1944-1949)

After the Summer holidays of 1940, Ian and I returned to school; Jean went back to Edinburgh University; and my parents moved from their new house in Strensall to their new home at Tan-yr-allt Hall, Llanddulas, between Abergele and Colwyn Bay. My father had agreed to go to the Ministry of Food, on loan from Rowntrees, as I explained in the last chapter. Tan-yr-allt Hall is a large house, half-way up a hill with a superb view across the bay towards Rhyl and beyond, to Liverpool. It had been used originally as a quarry-manager's house. Just over the high garden wall was a huge quarry, from which the stone was lowered to a small jetty on the shore below, and taken away by sea. At stated times (three-hour intervals) during the day, a bell was rung to warn us to take cover, and a great blast went off. We did take cover, and just as well. One day a huge piece of quarry stone, bigger than a man's head, thumped down just outside the window.

From the house, we watched the attacks on Liverpool by the German bombers who apparently flew first to the lights of Dublin and then turned east through the black-out to the docks of Liverpool. One December night, when I had newly-arrived that evening for the first time in Llanddulas, having left boarding school for good, a German bomber lost its way. Our house was in a commanding position; dining-room, breakfast-room and sitting-room had large French windows facing the view out over the sea, fortunately with old-fashioned wooden shutters on the inside. When the bomber released an H.E. (high explosive) bomb and a landmine over our village, all the plate-glass in our windows shattered, but the wooden shutters held firm. The blast blew the locks on the rear doors of the house and, dramatically, lifted the doors of the double garage from their rollers and deposited them to lean drunkenly against the wall. The landmine fell into the village pond, blew out the windows of the Vicarage and shot mud all over the furniture inside. So far as I know, no-one was hurt.

The husband of the family with whom we shared the house, who in turn rented it from the quarry-owners, was retired. With the help of "Happy" Williams, the gardener, and some from my mother and me when I was there, he kept the large kitchen garden in order. We used to pick very good loganberries which he grew inside wire cages; and fruit and vegetables which helped with the war-time diet. The surrounding countryside was beautiful; we explored it on foot and by bicycle. If you let yourself out of the door in the top wall of the kitchen garden you were already part-way up what the locals called 'The Mountain': the hill above and behind the house. From the top of the hill, the view was even more magnificent than from the verandah outside the French windows. Once (only) from the top of the 'mountain', we saw not only the blasted and broken buildings of Liverpool (by then a common sight), but the peaks of the Lake District floating apparently well above the ground. Unforgettable.

The Ministry of Food was billeted all around Colwyn Bay (and in the next town, Rhos-on-Sea) in large hotels, small hotels and boarding-houses. W.W. was able to have his much-prized and skilful secretary to come from Rowntrees to assist him. One Summer, for two months, I worked in the Ministry of Food in BINDAL, the Bacon and Ham Division. My job was to "chase 3/2's": to hurry on certain special forms from one Department to another. I worked in Penrhos College (school for girls) which the Government had commandeered. Each night duplicates of particularly important documents were strapped into a large parcel inside a waterproof cover and taken elsewhere by a member of staff to cover the possibility of the College building being bombed in the night. Once, this unwieldy object was given to me to transport to a safe house and to be returned in the morning. The only trouble was that I reached work by bicycle (from five miles along the coast) and on this particular morning it was raining. In the centre of the town my bicycle wheel caught in a tram-line, I skidded, and the weight of the parcel on one handle-bar shot me across the road to land at the feet of a policeman,

Chapter 14. William and Nancie In Wales and Home Again

who picked me up.

I also enjoyed some of the social side of the Ministry of Food organisation, playing my flute in its orchestra and singing in its choir. I attended concerts by famous orchestras - e.g. the London Symphony Orchestra who came from London, following their evacuated audiences. The Board of Trade and other Government Departments (Inland Revenue, the Board (sic) of Education, etc) were all housed along the coast. I went to concerts, by bike, alone, in the Pier Pavilions at Llandudno and Rhyl, each about ten miles distant from our house, hurrying back before dark in the long Summer evenings. My father much regretted that he was always too busy to come with me.

My father was much burdened with work and worry; my mother had to adjust to new contacts, and new living and shopping patterns under War conditions in a somewhat alien land. The diabetes inherited from her father, which had already troubled her in earlier years, had returned for good just before War started. She was allowed extra portions of meat and cheese (but, of course, no sugar), but even so it was difficult to get enough of the right food for her, and she was painfully thin. We used to pour each day's milk into a large mixing bowl, and when it had settled we skimmed off the cream with a spoon into a little jug for my mother as she was so undernourished. My sister and I tried not to cast covetous eyes at the cream. Correct diet was essential as Nancie was not yet on insulin. My father would not allow this because if she had been on insulin and the supplies had suddenly been cut off, it would probably have killed her. (This actually happened many years later to the mother of a particular friend of ours when the Turks invaded Cyprus in 1974. She lived only five days). During anxious months, when my father knew of measures being taken by the Government to locate and stock-pile food against possible invasion and enemy action, our car in the garage went to sleep each evening with its boot loaded with emergency rations. Just in case we had to flee in the night.

But we were together, unlike so many during the War. Our splendid Yorkshire cook-general, Linda, went with us to Wales. During some extra months I had at home between School and University she taught me to bake bread and make wonderfully light pastry. She was very homesick, especially when her mother was ill, but she was a great source of help and comfort to us. My mother relied on her in her illness; our housemaid from Strensall had been directed to war-work before we left York. (This now sounds so old-fashioned to have resident domestic help, but this is the way it was in the 1930's).

My father worked very hard indeed, too hard, as did other heads of Departments 'borrowed from Industry'. One-third of these specially-recruited private citizens, several brought back from retirement, died or became totally incapacitated as time went on, through sheer pressure of work. W.W. made himself ill with overwork in 1942. I was told that Government staff at the Ministry of Food was made up of brilliant first-class Civil servants at the top, specially seconded for the work; and those whom other Departments were most willing to spare. This did not make it easy for the top administrators to handle and organise the huge volume of work efficiently. W.W. reckoned he worked a twelve-hour day for six-and-a-half days a week at the Ministry of Food. He had at first to handle everything himself from drafting answers to Parliamentary questions to answering a letter from a ten-year-old about the supply of sweets. His difficulty there was that he was precluded from giving any full or free answer. For twelve months he had to answer questions about consumer rationing of confectionery by saying that the matter was having "full consideration" when he had already decided how it was to be done. When sweet rationing came, it was announced not by W.W., nor by Lord Woolton, the Minister of Food, but by Winston Churchill himself.

W.W. had endless meetings in Colwyn Bay, Chester and London. Here is a paragraph he wrote about a typical 'day':

"Then I had an endless series of Ministry and industry meetings in Colwyn Bay, Chester (which became the industry headquarters) and London. Dashing off to Chester without lunch, leaving my car at the Colwyn Bay station (sometimes in the snow) with distributor-arm removed, with a sandwich in my bag; and then, after a day of meetings, on to London, changing, often late at night, at Crewe. Getting into London at 11.35 p.m.

Chapter 14. William and Nancie In Wales and Home Again

(if up to time) and into the safest hotel I could find in the centre of London during bombing; paying what I must for this with a 24 hour Ministry expense allowance (for bed and food) of £1.3s.6d., and often sleeping, with others, on own mattresses in the bedroom corridor because the unprotected glass windows of the bedrooms so often were broken by bomb-blast. I see in one such typical morning in London I met the Public Relations Division of the Ministry; attended a conference with the Medical Section of the Ministry of Supply to decide the border between medicinal lines coated with sugar or chocolate and confectionery lines containing certain medicaments; and then visited the Ministry of Labour to endeavour to agree a further contribution of labour from the industry to the Services and to munitions. My industry by then had already given up almost fifty percent of its total labour with a reduction of only twenty-five percent of its own production, whilst itself making a wide range of certain types of 'munitions'. After twenty minutes for a snatched one-course lunch, I met the industry representatives to seek their views on my proposals. Then a hurried hand-written record of what had been discussed during the day, and to the late train to Colwyn Bay. I remember my first meeting with Lord Morris of Borth-y-Gest was spent standing with him one night in the corridor all the way from Euston to Crewe. On arrival at Colwyn Bay I might have to remove the snow from my parked car and get the engine to start; and so home. It was not so surprising that I saw the great necessity of "rationalising" this situation; and that under such strain and with so small a staff I had a breakdown later."

There are, I understand, official and unofficial histories of the Ministry of Food. W.W. wrote a formal and business-like history of his own work at the Ministry in war time in his book, *"Enterprise First"*, published in 1946. (Chapter VII). He therefore concentrated in his Autobiography on the personal aspects of his time there and I shall do the same here, and briefly. Some readers may remember much about what went on there. Less may be known about the two separate bodies which W.W. proposed and saw created: The Cocoa and Chocolate (War-Time) Association, and the Sugar Confectionery (War-Time) Association, launched in May, 1941. All his work was carried out in close and friendly relationship with these two War-Time Associations and I well remember him speaking with admiration and affection of many of the members who served on them. A range of other food industries under the Ministry followed the same pattern of War-Time Associations.

Price Control was introduced, but with a flexible approach. W.W. records that "in the sixth year of War, 95% of total production of chocolate and confectionery together was being sold at consumer prices not exceeding 2s.8d. per lb. In August 1944, standard plain chocolate was being sold at or below the price ruling in August 1914; standard brands of cocoa cost less than in 1939".

W.W. realised that without rationing of confectionery, the same people with sufficient time were able to chase the restricted amounts, while munition and other workers were kept by long factory hours from getting a fair share; children and invalids also. The "Personal Points" Scheme, allowing everyone an equal share, was approved by Winston Churchill and introduced in Spring 1942. Churchill had vetoed the Scheme in November 1941, but a few months later, he announced that children must have their sweets. It was many years after the war before sweet rationing ended. W.W. worked himself to a standstill in July 1942 and was forced to rest. As a result, his superiors, who had been appealed to for extra help and had done nothing, sat up and took notice. He was transferred to a larger and more imposing office. Eric Mackintosh from Mackintosh Ltd. was appointed Deputy Director, and several other able men from Rowntrees, Cadburys and elsewhere were brought in to help. Rather amusingly, one outcome of this was a query by an Establishment Officer about why there had been *four* people in London from W.W.'s Division as well as himself in one week. Each had been doing some of the work which W.W. for two years had covered *single-handed*.

Rowntrees were finding it difficult to manage without W.W. because of retirements (already belated) and ill-health; they asked him to return by September 1944. His Civil Servant co-partner said he could not let him leave, so a part-time arrangement was agreed, with difficulty. It was recognised both that Nancie, far from well, had made a "valuable and self-sacrificing contribution" and that William, by agreeing to remain

Chapter 14. William and Nancie In Wales and Home Again

(1) Tan-yr-allt Hall
(2) W.W. working on his knee outside the dining-room window (which smashed when the bomb dropped), his black (government) bag beside him. The bag was his constant companion for nearly 5 years; he was very sad when not allowed to keep it. (3) Nancie and William: June 14th, 1943
(4) Our complete family at Tan-yr-allt (1943 or 44)
(5) Hilary and Nancie: June 14th, 1943. Nancie used her binoculars constantly for bird-watching
(6) "Mon Abri": Hilary with stirrup pump, Jean with hurricane lamp, William in his gas mask. After VE Day. I don't think the shelter was ever used except for storing garden tools (7) Victory celebrations (May, 1945)

Chapter 14. William and Nancie In Wales and Home Again

unpromoted and on his pre-war salary, had foregone thousands of pounds. Living in a rented house, he had nevertheless been paying tax on the small sum received for the necessary renting out of his own house. (This was let at a low rate because the first arrangement was with the son of his old friend, Ernest Benn the Publisher, who was stationed at Strensall Camp. As it happened, the Benns found a smaller house they preferred and handed on the offer of our house at a low rent to another family at the Camp who left the running of the house and the minding of their children to a girl of sixteen. Nancie was horrified at the state of the house when these people moved out, and she and I visited it before the next tenants came).

I had joined my exiled parents in Wales in December, 1940, on the night the bombs were dropped near the house. For a couple of months, I attended Colwyn Bay Secondary School to prepare for some exams. Luckily there was a through, if erratic, bus service, although a little snow frightened the buses off the road. Sometimes the only way to get home was to walk several miles carrying a case, small but heavy with books. On one of these lonely snowy walks a police car stopped and gave me a lift saying to me that if they could not still get about, who could?

My parents did a very little war-time entertaining, such as inviting out W.W.'s treasured Secretary from York and other members of the staff at the Ministry of Food, especially those who had left their families at home. Tan-yr-allt Hall (see photo opp.) and its gardens were very pleasant to visit with the view across the bay to Rhyl which we used to say rivalled the Bay of Naples. Small Welsh daffodils cascaded down under the trees where the driveway climbed to the house. My father's sisters and their husbands and other relatives came to stay (by train) several times during the four years we were there; but on June 14th, 1943 on the actual day of their Silver Wedding I was the only member of the family at home. (see photos opp.). A little cardboard label, addressed in careful capitals to Mrs. William Wallace at our Llanddulas address from H.J. Small (her cousin), Fruit Grower, Blackminster, Evesham, was among the treasures kept. On the back of the label my mother wrote: 'Much luv from Me'. I paid little attention to it at first; but it occurs to me that it was probably attached to a box of fruit ordered by Nancie to be sent to her in Wales so that she could give it to her Bill on their Silver Wedding Anniversary. On *all* their Wedding Anniversaries throughout the years he gave her flowers. I remember especially while we were in New Earswick, she was given huge bunches of sweet peas, probably from Mr. Johnson in Poplar Grove, as he grew them for sale. This Mr Johnson was, I think, also the lamplighter in the early days of New Earswick, going round on his bicycle with a ladder and a long pole, putting on and turning off the gas lights. He was the village gardener as well.

Petrol of course was tightly-rationed. W.W. got just enough to drive into his office and back, or to Colwyn Bay station (often returning there long after public transport had ceased for the night; anyway ours was a two-hourly bus service at best). I went a good distance by bike; my brother and I cycled right round Wales one Summer to visit an ex-student friend of mine, stationed in the R.A.F. at St. David's, Pembrokeshire. Once my father saved up enough petrol to drive us to Criccieth to visit Megan Lloyd George and her sister and family in the house where they had stayed in 1927. He used to pick up in his car anyone waiting for a bus or wanting to go to Colwyn Bay, and was known locally as "the man who gives lifts". Fortunately W.W. had bought his first *new* car, a Wolseley, in January 1939, so it stood him in good stead all through the War and beyond. (See p.141).

While my parents soldiered on in North Wales I had left them in October 1941 to go to Scotland to University, to St. Andrews to take a degree in languages, especially English, in the shortened time of two years demanded by War-Time regulations; had I said I hoped to teach, I would have been allowed more years to study for an Honours degree and a further year of Teacher Training. By then the War would have been over and the restrictions lifted. In the event, much later, I taught for twenty years. In 1943 I went on to Edinburgh University (with the Ministry of Labour's blessing) to take a two-year post-graduate Course in Social Studies for which only one year was allowed. I returned to Tan-yr-allt in the vacations: sixteen hours' travelling with six changes in war-time trains. Sometimes in the summer I remained in the North to do Land Army work, S.C.M. (Student Christian Movement) Conferences, trips round Scotland by bike and Youth

Chapter 14. William and Nancie In Wales and Home Again

Hostel accommodation, or to stay with the family who had adopted me in St. Andrews. My parents travelled to my graduation in St. Andrews in July 1943, as they had to my sister's graduation in Edinburgh in 1942. Jean had gained her Bachelor of Commerce degree and spent another year taking the Social Studies Diploma. After that she went to work as a Personnel Officer in a large Munitions factory in Chester, from which she was able to get home to Tan-yr-allt each week-end. With our Quaker background we did not apply to join the Forces but were subject to controlled employment. On their visit to St. Andrews my parents met for the first time the lovely family of the Forresters with whom they were later to be connected and share their first grandchildren: the family with whom I had fallen in love as well as with their eldest son.

HOME AGAIN

William and Nancie returned to their home in Strensall in September, 1944, and set about restoring both home and garden as best they could after the ravages of a series of tenants; and acute war-time shortages. The garden was used more productively for vegetables and fruit and Nancie started to keep those hens. I had just finished the practical work connected with my Social Studies (in Dundee, because London was considered too dangerous) and had applied for a post as an Organiser of Youth Clubs in North Yorkshire, based on the North Riding County town of Northallerton. I had seen by chance an advertisement for the post in 'The Scotsman' while working in Dundee. The copy of the newspaper, forgotten or mislaid for a week or two, had turned up under a cushion in the University settlement where we were based, just in time for me to apply before the closing date. It was the only job for which I applied. I went to Yorkshire from Dundee for interview and was appointed. Obviously the job was meant for me. As well as being stimulating and worth-while it satisfied the war-time regulations as suitable work following my training. It also meant that when I was free at week-ends I could go home to Strensall. I went home for one week at the end of my time in Dundee, had six driving lessons in six days in York, and began work in Northallerton on November 1st, driving the pre-war Morris attached to the job, all over North Yorkshire. Driving tests had been suspended. I learnt as I went, in spite of the black-out, and the absence of sign-posts, removed in order to confuse the Germans should they invade. (cf. Cook's Alley Chap.2)

W.W. continued to spend part of each week at the Ministry, back at Colwyn Bay or in London, until some time after his official retiral date of 30th June, 1945. He had already taken over the Deputy Chairmanship at Rowntrees with special responsibility for all Associated Companies, Home and Overseas. The year after the War ended, the Chairman of the Company who had succeeded B.S.R. was seriously ill and unavailable for eight months, so that W.W. was Acting-Chairman during that time, on top of his current work.

Just after the War, W.W. was invited to join the Control Commission in Germany under the Head of the Economic Division to help with the provision of food, clothing and housing for the civilian population. He was also recommended to apply for the post of first Principal of the new Administrative College in Henley; in 1949 he was asked to become Trade Adviser to the Ministry of Food; and in 1952, Harold Macmillan as the new Minister of Housing asked him to become Chairman of the Regional Housing Board in the North. Each of these jobs presented a challenge but he was committed to his work at Rowntrees, both in the factory and with Joseph Rowntree Trusts, about which I'll write later. Also, without doubt he cared very deeply about his wife and their home, and he liked nothing better than to return to both at the end of each day whenever possible. Nancie had gone to the London Clinic under Dr. Lawrence, the Diabetic Specialist, for a week in September 1945 to begin insulin injections which kept her alive for another thirty-two-and-a-half years. William wanted to provide peace and quiet in a well-ordered house and to save her stress. Their home life was very quiet, apart from the family and occasional visits from relatives or friends. They were both teetotallers and did not throw parties. The evening meal, exactly on time for Nancie's diet, was the simplest possible: fish or scrambled egg or salad, followed by Wensleydale cheese. William liked to finish his meal with brown bread and an apple. This was always so, nothing to do with rationing. Before the evening meal in Summer after his return from work he would sit in the small side loggia in the

Chapter 14. William and Nancie In Wales and Home Again

westering sun, reading the newspaper.

Towards the end of his time at the Ministry of Food in 1945 and before he returned full-time to Rowntrees, W.W. wrote another book, *"Enterprise First"* about the relationship of the State to Industry, with particular reference to private enterprise (published 1946). In it he recommended a Ministry of Industry; and urged the Government to adopt a new approach to the problems of monopoly, including the establishment of a Tribunal to examine how far restrictions on competition were consistent with public interest. He was told this led to the setting up of the Monopoly Commission in 1948 and the Restrictive Trade Practices Act in 1954. It also led to W.W.'s appointment later as a Lay Judge. He sent a copy to his 'Partner', the Duke of Windsor, and had a personal letter of thanks remembering when their paths had crossed before.

I was released from my work in North Yorkshire in time to go to Cambridge at the beginning of the University Session in October, 1945, to read for a degree in Moral Science. Jean also arranged to begin research in Cambridge at the same time. Ian was working for a degree in Applied Science (Agriculture) at Durham University from which he graduated in 1947 a few days after he was twenty. So William and Nancie were much on their own during term-time. Formerly whenever they were at Strensall they had welcomed home on Sundays a car-load of their children with their friends to a dinner of roast beef and Yorkshire puddings and a tea of Linda's special chocolate cake. My mother used to take me round the garden in those days to look at special plants and flowers and to pick for me bunches of pinks, I remember especially, and other delights to take back for my study at school. Later in the Summer she would cut her borders of lavender and dry the stalks in the sun, which filled the house with their perfume.

William and Nancie were not to be quiet for long. Just before Christmas 1946, I brought home my special friend from St. Andrews who was reading Medicine at Oxford. In the New Year we became engaged. My mother organised the wedding, arranging the guest and present lists. Once my Finals at Cambridge were over in Summer 1947 I came back home to make my "trousseau" from pieces of parachute and gifts of uncouponed material. I made a dressing-gown for my fiancé from an elaborate Vogue pattern, in red silk-rayon parachute material, and was busy and happy until leaving in September to begin work in Oxford. My parents got much amusement from my various activities. My husband and I were married on the first available day after the University term in Oxford ended in December, 1947. A very well-known confectionery and cake firm gave us our three-tier wedding cake. As the ingredients were strictly rationed, I reckoned that the Queen, who was married three weeks before we were, may have been the only other bride to receive an elaborate wedding-cake as a gift at that time.

'We Have Come Through'. Home Again! Notice how thin Nancie is.
The faithful Wolseley car

Chapter 15

Spreading Their Wings (1949-1963)

Canada called in 1949, and William took Nancie with him on a tour as Overseas Director. As well as extensive visits to the Rowntree factory in Toronto, and to Sales outlets across the continent, they also went to Vancouver Island to stay with Nancie's brothers who had emigrated over forty-six years before. Nancie had last seen Avery and his wife Vera (through whom Nancie and William first met) in 1919; but Fred had remained in Canada since he first went there in 1903. As Ted had died earlier in 1949, and as their visit had been postponed for a year on account of the Rowntree Chairman's illness, Nancie never saw Ted again. Avery had had to abandon in 1937 the farmstead and its outbuildings which he had built, and the tennis court, terraces and plantations which he had laid out, when farming on the prairies collapsed and nobody wanted to buy their farm. Avery and Vera had put what they could in their Ford car, left their Homestead forever and driven to Vancouver. They bought a little house in the woods at Royal Oak, Vancouver Island, not far from where Ted and Fred were in business as store-keepers, and lived there happily for many years. (See photos opp.) Avery and Vera, according to Uncle Jack, "grew tulips and other nice things" on the land they bought with their house. Avery had a disability pension from the War which helped. Jack refers to Avery as "an inventive craftsman" (which of the Hancoxes were not?), with a rather poetic outlook on life, a terrific worker of somewhat bulldog pertinacity. Avery also carved; and had made a music Cabinet with the Monogram "J.H." on the door to the design of their sister Mary. It was a present (? Wedding) to Uncle Jack, and as my mother bought it from Jack's son Avery when Jack died, I am lucky enough to have it now.

Many years before, the 'Evesham Journal' published an account (date unknown but apparently during the early years when Ted, Fred and Avery were homesteading in Saskatchewan) based on a letter sent from there by a friend of Ted's who had just been staying with them. There had been a most destructive prairie fire, and the friend wrote that he "had a sight of a lifetime... but I never want to see another large prairie fire covering thousands of acres". The grass, he wrote, "is very fine and dry and brittle and very thick and of course easily burns". The wind blew, "very much like the sea winds, very rough". He and Ted were out for a stroll when they suddenly saw one mass of fire, five or six feet high, tearing down on them, and they heard the shrieks of horses being burnt. The horses gallop until they fall exhausted, but oxen apparently lie down and get roasted. Antelopes and wolves raced by; every now and then they heard human shrieks and yells, followed by a tremendous tongue of flame shooting up forty feet high and knew another homestead had succumbed to the fire.

Ted and Charlie Pace (his friend) got all the cattle and horses safely into a ring, hitched bronchos to the ploughs and ripped up the ground to make a fire-break, starting fires on the outer side of the ring to burn to meet the huge blaze. He says they had bags of snow to beat down the fire. They fought the fire, together with Avery, from ten a.m. until five p.m. as hard as they were able. The fire reached a big straw pile and they thought everything was lost, but they still kept on, throwing snow and water round the pile until at last they had contained it. Ted had to stay up all night to keep throwing water on small places which still burnt. Avery went to see a married neighbour with three children who fought the fire until their hay, barn and house were burnt and they had to leap into a wagon and pull out behind the fire. Charlie reckoned that if they had been sound asleep when the fire started they would none of them have stood a chance. Ten thousand acres or more were burnt; no-one had ever seen anything like it before in that part of the prairie.

It made a dramatic column in the local paper for the Evesham people.

Three of Nancie's five brothers died within fifteen months in the 1950's: Jack at Great Alne, on July 2nd, 1953, aged eighty; Will in Coventry, on February 28th, 1954, aged seventy-five; and Avery in Vancouver Island on October 28th, 1954, aged seventy. When Avery died, the 'Evesham Journal' printed an Obituary; and Fred wrote to Nancie - in

Chapter 15. Spreading Their Wings

(1) Avery's house on Vancouver Island
(2) Ted's house kept on by Fred (1953)
(3) Visit from the Rockefellers

Chapter 15. Spreading Their Wings

handwriting curiously like her own - on the day that Avery died in the Veterans' Hospital, Victoria, British Columbia. Fred had been staying at the Red Cross Lodge there, provided for patients' relatives, for the last ten days. Avery had had an operation and seemed to be improving, his chances of recovery fluctuating day by day; but then he slipped into a coma and "gradually faded away", wrote Fred. The pattern of Will's going was similar; he had an operation, appeared to be recovering, but rather suddenly died. My parents were coming to visit me and my family in Oxford, after their visit to Buckingham Palace for an Investiture, (see below) when I got the phone message that Will had died. I kept the news until after they and my sister had had their exciting day, but then I had to tell them. Fred lived on until February 2nd, 1960, exactly eleven years to the day after Ted died. Vera survived, living I think with her sister, Gypsy, for some years more.

The meeting of Nancie and her brothers in Vancouver after thirty and forty-six years respectively caused quite a stir locally. They were photographed in the street and interviewed by the Press. (see opp.) W.W. was greeted as "Plain Mr. York in person". Everyone was very helpful. They returned via New York and a homeward voyage on the Queen Mary, just in time to become grandparents for the first time. Our first child, Elizabeth Anne, as you may remember, was born on the real birthday of Nancie's father: November 9th. We called her Elizabeth Anne, thinking we had chosen family names (of Nancie's mother, and the Elizabeths and Annes which came from the Roxburgh forebears of my husband's father). While writing this book it has occurred to me that I may have chosen these names in response to an echo in my mind of my mother's grandmother, Elizabeth Ann Hawkes, although I did not realise this at the time. Her name had been mentioned quite often, when I was a child.

In 1950, U.S.A. came to Rowntrees in the form of John D. Rockefeller III, descendant of the world-famous American multi-millionaire philanthropist. Nancie's first cousin, William Nash of Cleveland, Ohio, son of her mother's sister Winifred (née Fowler), married a niece of Rockefeller I, so the visitors were cousins (see chap.3) (see photo p.143). The following year, W.W. attended the First International Conference of Western Industrialists as one of a dozen representatives of British Industry. This took him to New York, Baltimore, Annapolis, Washington (plus visit to the Pentagon), Minneapolis (General Mills), Chicago (Stock Yards), and back to Washington, where they were entertained by the British Ambassador, Sir Oliver Franks and his wife. Lady Franks was the daughter of an outstanding Quaker, a friend of W.W.'s who had asked him to gather all possible news about Lady Franks and the grandchildren, so he was placed between her and Sir Oliver at the official lunch in order to do so.

W.W. reckoned this visit to the U.S.A. was his first real respite since 1939, twelve years before. It did not last. The Chairman of Rowntrees was again taken seriously ill. W.W. had to return with all speed to take over. The following month (January 1952), he was appointed Chairman of the Company. He also took over the Chairmanship of the York Committee and found time to take a continuing interest in Overseas and Home Associated Companies and, of course, in industrial relations. In 1951 W.W. had been elected President of the Cocoa, Chocolate, and Confectionery Alliance, inaugurated in York in December 1901, on the initiative of B.S.R. The issues in January 1952 when the Jubilee dinner was held centred round delicate questions of de-control. Just when the industry was expecting total de-rationing of sugar and other necessary commodities, there was an actual cut in sugar supplies which upset the anxiously-waiting manufacturers. Soon, however, extra purchases of Cuban sugar allowed the de-controls to go ahead.

Canada called again in August 1953, because of urgent problems. Nancie was again able to go too and once more they stayed a few days with Avery and Vera in their small wooden house in the woods. There, unfortunately, W.W. developed gall-bladder trouble and was in such pain that the doctor wanted to operate; but W.W. chose to haul himself back, via important business talks in Toronto. On his return, the operation was performed by his old school-friend, the Professor of Surgery in Newcastle. By then he had jaundice and his gall-bladder had just about disintegrated.

The next excitement was a visit to Buckingham Palace on March 2nd, 1954 when W.W. was invested with the C.B.E. (Commander of the British Empire) by Queen Elizabeth, the Queen Mother, deputising for her daughter who was in Australia. W.W. had been asked,

Chapter 15. Spreading Their Wings

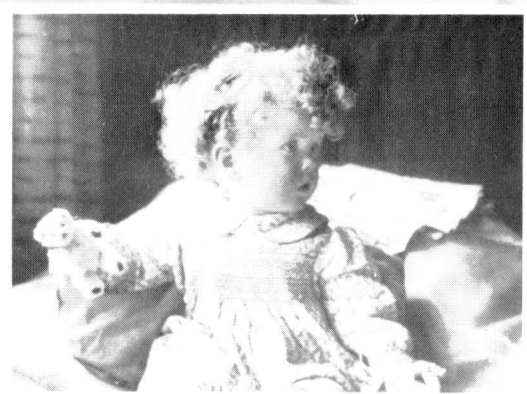

(1) The Meeting in Victoria (1949): Avery, Nancie, William and Fred
(2) The First Grandchild: Elizabeth Anne (1951)
(3) Princess Alexandra with William and Nancie (1956)

Chapter 15. Spreading Their Wings

because he was convalescent, whether he would rather wait for a later date; but he chose to go as arranged, feeling a special affinity with the Scottish Queen, and conscious that she had been his Queen for much longer than had her daughter. Later, the Queen and the Duke of Edinburgh visited York. William and Nancie were presented to her and of course found her charming. W.W. also met the Duke of Edinburgh on other occasions to do with industry and enjoyed his quick replies and sense of humour. One of these meetings was at the Duke of Edinburgh Study Conference on the Human Problems of Industrial Communities within the Commonwealth, in Oxford in July, 1956. That same month, Princess Alexandra (then aged nineteen) visited York. W.W. sat beside her at luncheon in the Mansion House and later took her round the Rowntree factory on a tour which she asked to be extended as she particularly wished to see more Departments, especially the one where the Smarties were made. W.W. was impressed by her knowledge of business affairs and her questions on export trade, as well as being charmed by her personally. (See photo p.145.).

In the Autumn of 1956, William and Nancie arranged to go for their first visit to Australia, where he needed to discuss major questions of policy. They went to Melbourne by sea, via the Panama Canal and up the Pacific Coast of the United States. William swam before breakfast most mornings in the ship's pool; he also, during the voyage, wrote most of the first draft of his next book, *"Prescription for Partnership"*. He could never just sit and do almost nothing, even in a deck-chair on a cruise liner! Visiting Hollywood from the ship, they were given lunch and shown round by the author Nigel Balchin, who had once worked in both Rowntrees and the Ministry of Food, under W.W.. At Vancouver, Fred flew across from the Island to see them once more.

The ship called at Honolulu and Fiji. Everywhere they were met with overwhelming kindness: restaurant owners and taxi-drivers among others trying to save them dollars as these were still limited; pleased to welcome and help them because they were British. The same was true on the Australian Continent, especially when their road journey of over six hundred miles had to pass through terrifying floods. W.W. had two weeks of useful talks at the Rowntree factory in Melbourne while Nancie was entertained by the Chairman's wife and others; and taken to see the Kangaroos and Koala bears. They also visited the Rowntree agents in Adelaide and Perth. As they returned to Britain by sea they could not pass through the Suez Canal as planned as it was not possible in 1956. They returned by the direct Cape route, and were entertained by the Mayor of Capetown in the Mayor's Parlour.

W.W. retired from Rowntrees on December 31st, 1957, when he was sixty-six and a half years old: still active, still deeply interested in industrial relations and the future of industry; and preparing to take up his appointment as a Lay Judge in the Restrictive Practices Court based on the model he had devised in his book, *"Enterprise First"*. The published statistics over the ten-year period ending with 1957 show that the average net profits available for the parent Company in Rowntrees had an increase of some 85% during his six years as Chairman. He got no "golden handshake". His initial salary in 1919 (£400) had risen in 1940 to £2,500 where it had to stay until he returned to York in 1944 as his firm was forbidden to raise it. He got no expense allowance from his firm while in Colwyn Bay, and the Ministry of Food expense allowance barely covered the tax he had to pay because his own house was let furnished. He served his four and more years at the Ministry of Food at a cost to himself of several thousand pounds - and this when the costs of his children's education were at their peak, with boarding-school fees for courses they had begun before the War, and University degree courses. (No grants in those days; parents paid). He always bought and used his own car, without a chauffeur, who were more common, then. No wonder their tastes in food, clothes, holidays and entertainment were very modest or they could not have managed. He had other calls on his resources. He kept very quiet about it, but all through the times in the 1920's and 1930's when some members of his family found the going hard, he helped them financially. His mother and Aunt Meggie lived in a single-storey house, similar to the one in which he had been born in Sunderland, just along the road from Chris and her family. Help was sometimes needed there. When they could no longer manage on their own, Chris took them into her home, where my Granny Wallace died in January, 1933. Her estate was valued at £158. 3s. 10d.. Aunt Meggie stayed on with Chris, who looked after

Chapter 15. Spreading Their Wings

her tenderly until she died in 1937.

While he was still Chairman of Rowntrees W.W. continued his membership of the Central Works Council, his Chairmanship of the Pension Fund, the meetings with the Profit-Sharing Committee, etc. He also enjoyed, for many years after he left, being President of the Rowntree Players and presenting one of them each year with the "William Wallace" Cup for the best acting or producing of the year. Occasionally, if he was not able to go, Nancie presented it on his behalf. When he retired from this Presidency, he and Nancie were made the first Honorary Life Members of the Rowntree Company Amateur Dramatic Society, which gave them much pleasure.

The Rowntree Board arranged to have made an illuminated Minute on parchment and bound in leather (Minute No. 4052; November 12th, 1957). It traces the whole history of W.W.'s time at Rowntrees detailing all he did. The Minute contains twenty-one paragraphs. I will quote only the last two, as he did in his Autobiography:

'William Wallace has (as the foregoing history makes clear) made great practical contributions to this Company over a long number of years and, in this Minute, his colleagues on the Board gladly and freely pay tribute to this. Beyond this, however, his colleagues want to acknowledge the man - a man of integrity, a man of kindliness, a true democrat who really believed - and worked on the belief - that "there is that of God in every man."

'The Board will miss his presence, his friendliness, his quiet thought for others; and fellow workers (and he would regard them as such) of all ranks recognise freely that he has been to them a true friend'.

"This Minute makes abundantly clear", added W.W., "the warm friendship I had enjoyed for almost forty years. It can therefore illustrate exceptionally well how one can feel, by retirement, the sudden, almost guillotine effect of the termination of such a relationship."

Leaving the Company made an enormous hole in W.W.'s life as it does for all of us in similar circumstances though he was moving to new and exciting challenges. Three small courtesies by those he left behind warmed his heart: George Dickinson, a fellow Director, invited him annually to a little Christmas Tea Party which he ran for colleagues and retired colleagues concerned with Associated Companies; a later Chairman, Donald Barron, invited him to the pre-Christmas lunch which W.W. thinks he first started; and his immediate successor, Lloyd Owen, refused to take back his master-key for the Works. So he still had his happy continuing contacts.

He retired from Rowntrees, himself beyond normal retirement age, into what was arguably still more strenuous and taxing work because it meant leaving home and Nancie each Sunday afternoon for London, not to return until late the following Friday; taxing because it was a new world which demanded application of his skills in new ways. As a Lay Judge (with equivalent standing to that of a High Court Judge) in the new Restrictive Practices Court, he had to sit with others in Court listening to hours, indeed days and weeks, of evidence. After the Court rose, there were discussions and then the reading and studying of the daily transcripts, usually till midnight. Back in Court next day there were discussions with the others until a decision was reached when a Report needed to be drafted. This sometimes kept him at work until late into the night. When one case was concluded, another followed. He enjoyed the stimulus and the company of the other members of the Court: he had great admiration for Lord Justice Devlin, his first President of the Court. He was glad to use his knowledge and experience of industry, law and economics for the benefit of the Court. He missed Nancie badly and hated leaving her on Sunday afternoons. He considered moving house to London so that he could go home each night, but decided it was better for her to stay where she was and not be uprooted. She was not alone as a most faithful housekeeper, supported by others, looked after her. But her social life would be restricted as she did not drive and I do not think I ever remember her calling a taxi.

W.W. was in favour of enterprise as can be seen from the title of his book which helped to launch the idea of the Restrictive Practices Courts; but he defined it as free enterprise and not "private exploitation dressed up as enterprise" nor "restrictions masquerading as

Chapter 15. Spreading Their Wings

*(1) William and Nancie attended the Special Service in Westminster Abbey
on October 1st, 1958 to inaugurate the Restrictive Practices Court
(2) Windrush in the snow - after addition of Garden Room and Greenhouse (1962)*

Chapter 15. Spreading Their Wings

competition". He encourages the idea that monopolies should be enquired into by a tribunal based on a Court. The Restrictive Trade Practices Act required the registration of certain collective agreements between the persons or companies carrying on businesses in the production or supply of goods under which certain restrictions are accepted - e.g. with regard to prices to be charged. The aim was to safeguard the public from "unreasonable" restrictive practices set up by a group who had continued to have a monopoly in a commodity, and so were in a position to eliminate competition, and charge whatever price they chose.

As a member of such a Court, W.W. had to surrender all direct association with Industry: with Rowntrees, his membership of the Grand Council of the Federation of British Industries (as it was then), Chairmanship of the Industrial Co-Partnership Association etc.. He hesitated to accept; but was reminded that he had "set out the blueprint for this Court" and so he had a moral obligation to help establish it. Still, he hesitated. Then, as he and Nancie were driving one day over the Yorkshire Moors, she said, "How proud your Father would have been if he knew you had been offered this job. What would his reaction have been if he knew you had turned down the opportunity to sit on a Bench in the High Court?" So that settled it. W.W. wrote, "the high moorland road gradually turned into a clear narrow, one-way track; so I said, 'Very well; so be it. I will accept that I must take this road'."

The first case before the Court in which W.W. sat was the Cotton Yarn Spinners, where the hearings lasted for about six weeks. After he had "heard" it, W.W. immediately thought that there was a need for a fundamental rationalisation of the Lancashire cotton industry which was in fact soon carried out. One of his most interesting cases was the Scottish Bakers in Edinburgh in June, 1959. It was the first in Scotland, and there was said to be some strong feeling against two "English Judges" being brought in to hear the case. However, Lord Cameron introduced his two Lay Judges from England as William Gordon Campbell and William Wallace; there was no further protest.

Pressure on the Court was intense, especially for W.W., as illness and other calls drained off the other Lay members until sometimes he was the only whole-time Lay member left. Also, every case needed an understanding of economics which few of the others could provide. In spite of this, he was asked towards the end of his three-year term of office whether he would wish to continue in a part-time capacity? The offer came in an unexpected letter, bleak and formal. W.W. regretted that those in charge did not offer the courtesy of an informal chat about the matter as he would have done in industry. His expenses of travel and staying in London (including taxi-fares with bags full of Court papers) had all come out of his own pocket without the right to deduct for tax purposes; this meant little or no financial gain from his salary (which he had foregone anyway for the first nine months as the Court did not commence until October of the year in which he was appointed on January 1st). This did not weigh with him. But deserting the friends and causes dear to him in industry mattered a good deal. He was not prepared to forego the right to speak out as he had always done before in exchange for a part-time appointment to the Court when he might or might not be called to serve. He left at the end of his three-year full-time appointment by December 31st, 1960.

The Counsel before W.W. in the last case was a Mr. Thomas Roche. Curiously, fifty-three years before, when W.W.'s father had taken him to London as a sixteen-year-old, he had been introduced to Mr. Roche's father in the Admiralty Court, where Mr. Adair Roche regularly appeared for Mr. James Wallace in shipping cases. A long time had passed; here were the two sons, after a life-time of experience, meeting in another Court of Law. Mr. Roche, in 1960, expressed his regret that W.W. was leaving and his thanks for his patience, expertise and lucidity of expression, as did the other members of the Court.

On his return to York, at his second retirement, W.W. pursued again his other interests, foremost of which in 1961 was help in promoting York University. A memorandum stating York's case for a University had been lodged with the University Grants Committee (U.G.C.) in February 1947. Dr. John Bowes Morrell (J.B.M.) (formerly Vice-Chairman of Rowntrees) had been pursuing the idea for many years, and had mentioned it in his inaugural address as first Chairman of the York Civic Trust in 1946.

Chapter 15. Spreading Their Wings

The grandchildren 1. Granpa with Bill and Liz 2. Granpa with Ali
3. Nancie, Ian's daughter, her Granny's namesake: in the Wallace tartan
4. William John, Ian's son 5. Picnicking in the Cotswolds
6. Ali, aged 3, with 'Rosebud' in the blue pram with the red hood, made by us for Liz's 3rd Christmas 7. Liz and Bill on the garden wall 8. Bill: painting 9. Ali: all ready for school 10. The Ruby Wedding: Jill, William, Ian, Nancie, John and Hilary (taken by Jean)

Chapter 15. Spreading Their Wings

The U.G.C. turned down the idea, but said York could prepare the ground if they wished. J.B.M. invited W.W. in 1951 to become a member of the Academic Committee who were working towards a University. He stressed that as Chairman of the Joseph Rowntree Village Trust (J.R.V.T.) W.W. could make a special contribution. The York Institute of Architectural Study was founded.

In 1956 the Academic Trust became a limited company: The York Academic Trust. J.B.M. had in 1955 arranged for the Rowntree Social Service Trust to buy Heslington Hall and its gardens of seventeen acres as the future centre (he hoped) of York University. The Academic Trust applied again to the U.G.C. in 1959. W.W. set about freeing money to assist the scheme. Under the original terms of the J.R.V.T., W.W. as Chairman was not allowed to vote money for a University, so he applied for a Private Act of Parliament to give the Trust these powers. He was staying with all of us and my parents-in-law on holiday in Aviemore, Inverness-shire in June 1959, when he took the overnight train to London; appeared before the Private Bills Committee of the House of Lords for twenty minutes; had his application granted; and returned that same night to re-join us in Speyside. The former J.R.V.T. was thus able to covenant £100,000 over ten years; J.B.M. offered a similar amount from his Family Trust; the Rowntree Social Service Trust offered £150,000, over a similar period; and the Rowntree Company added another £100,000.

10th October, 1963 saw the grant of the Royal Charter for York University. Social Science would have a central place, very fitting in the home town of B.S.R.. The Institute of Social and Economic Research was established and was aided again by the successor to the J.R.V.T. (now called the Joseph Rowntree Memorial Trust since the Act of Parliament to free its scope beyond the Village). J.B.M. was elected a Pro-Chancellor of York University on the eve of his ninetieth birthday, on which day he made a wise and witty speech of thirty-five minutes at a luncheon in his honour. Eight days later, after finishing dictating his last letter of thanks for birthday messages, he sat back in his chair and quietly died. W.W. felt the loss deeply. J.B.M. had been a wise friend to his colleagues and to the City of York.

During the years this Chapter covers, much had happened on the personal front. Ian was married in February 1954 and went to live in Suffolk, where he is still. B.S.R. was a welcomed and loved guest at the wedding as he had been at ours, seven years previously. Our son, William Wallace (Forrester) was born in August, 1952; and our second daughter, Alison McColl, in June, 1956. Ian and his wife had a son, William John Galbraith, in April, 1957; and a daughter, Nancie Margaret, on February 29th, 1960. These four, added to our first daughter, Elizabeth Anne, whom you have already met, were the full complement of their grandchildren in whom they had much pleasure and delight. Granny knitted for them as she had done for all of us, and took very many charming photographs. (See opp. & p.145.) Granpa played games with them, took us for drives, and kept them well-stocked with Smarties.

In June, 1958, they celebrated their Ruby Wedding with a family dinner-party at a favourite hotel out in the country, near York: a very happy occasion. (See opp.) W.W. put an announcement in 'The Times', five years later, for their forty-fifth anniversary. William and Nancie went on holiday, touring in Norway (while Jean was living there) and in France with Jean, and sometimes with Cousin Doris Davis. They began to go regularly to Moretonhampstead, Devon, twice a year, at each end of the northern Summer to extend it, sometimes taking Jean or Ian as they were unmarried. Here they enjoyed an eighteen-hole Golf course, although in the later years Nancie no longer played. While we lived in Nottinghamshire they always came to see us as they drove down and back again. They had almost ceased to go to Scotland as they used to do; but when we moved to Edinburgh in 1963 they were tempted back a few times, in connection with Forrester Weddings and other occasions. In 1963 they began again their lively Sundays with girls from The Mount School as our Liz (as she came to be called) became a boarder there and so she was able to carry on the tradition of bringing friends to eat roast beef and Yorkshire pudding. Ian's son was at Bootham later so he in turn went out to Windrush on Sundays. We also stayed there frequently, partly to see our children at school; and Jean went to live in York from the early 1960's so at no time were they without happy family visits.

Chapter 15. Spreading Their Wings

During this period - in the same month that Nancie's brother Avery died - (October 1954), they also lost William's friend and mentor, B.S.R.. W.W. spoke and wrote about him fully after his death. In a speech to Rowntree employees, he reminded them what a great man B.S.R. had been: made a Companion of Honour in recognition of this. He was a man who loved his fellow men... in dedication to their service as individual fellow creatures. He sought truth, beauty and goodness, like the Ancient Greeks. He also had a faith; and believed that this faith should show itself in works. This is what W.W. said about him just after he died:

"I believe that the key to the man was to be found in his religion. He was a very human man; he could fail to achieve the standards he set himself. But he took all his problems, and his decisions, into the silent worship of the Quaker meeting; or to the silent prayer of his own home. If there were errors, or unfairness, or lack of faith, it was there they became apparent: and he came back, in that case, and freely confessed his error or his weakness; and found strength to renew the struggle for the causes which he believed were those of his Master. There lay the source of his hidden strength".

W.W. received a letter from B.S.R., the morning after he died - probably the last thing he ever wrote, in which he disclaimed, with his usual modesty, W.W.'s statement that future social historians would regard him as having made perhaps the most outstanding contribution in this field in the first half of the twentieth Century. "This letter fluttered down like the last leaf from his tree of life", wrote W.W., who left a brief account of B.S.R.'s last few days: "The circumstances of his death were sad - perhaps rather tragic - but in a way a fitting climax. His wife had died and he was living in a wing of Disraeli's old house at Hughenden owned by the National Trust, into which he had moved from North Dean when that happened. On 5th October 1954 he had a hard day's work in London, continuing on into the evening. He would not have his friends phone his chauffeur to meet him "after hours". When he arrived at his station there was pouring rain and no taxis available. Frail as he was, in his eighty-fourth year, he set out to walk the two or three miles of country road to Hughenden. At one point he fell exhausted by the roadside, but he struggled up and finally arrived. He was looking forward to a happy occasion, a Jubilee Social gathering three days later at the Folk Hall in the Rowntree Trust village of New Earswick to celebrate its Fiftieth Jubilee. He wanted to get home that night to clear up some work the next day and collect his papers and then come up to York to stay with me. So, still with his great spirit, he walked alone, and two days later he died of resulting exhaustion. So, as Chairman of the Village Trust, I could only report his passing, and turn our Jubilee Meeting into a sad meeting of remembrance; but also pride.

My warm affection for my old friend, B.S.R., must be obvious. I treasure in particular two things. One night, sitting in his armchair in his study, he said to me suddenly, "W.W., we have done some very interesting things together?" The other is that when he died his family, with warm imagination, gave me that armchair, in which I now sit."

As well as the ones I have already mentioned, William and Nancie had a number of other 'royal' occasions, most of these while W.W. was Chairman of Rowntrees. They had seats to watch the Queen's Coronation on June 2nd, 1953, and attended a Dinner that night as guests of the President of the Federation of British Industries (as it was then). In July, 1954, W.W. was put next to the Princess Royal at a tea reception in the Assembly Rooms in York; he tried various subjects of conversation, mentioning the Queen Mother and the Duke of Windsor, both of whom he'd met, but made no headway. Then someone who knew our family asked after me and the children, and W.W. got out his photos. At that, the Princess Royal relaxed and discussed the delights of grandchildren, as she enjoyed her own.

Later that year, the Duke of Gloucester attended a Reception in the Mansion House, York, as President of the National Association of Boys' Clubs. W.W. scribbled on his invitation card afterwards, "Duke amused at my Prince of Wales story". A year later, W.W. attended a Luncheon at the York Assembly Rooms to welcome the Duke of Edinburgh on a visit to the City; and in 1957, both William and Nancie were presented to the Queen and the Duke when they came to York to see the Mystery Plays "if the weather is clement". There is an Alternative Programme set out in the booklet provided, in case it rained; I rather think it did. Finally, there was their last visit to a Royal Garden Party at Buckingham Palace, in July, 1962.

Chapter 15. Spreading Their Wings

(1) On holiday in Norway (c. 1962)
(2) Nancie beside the lilies she planted below the dining-room window (early 1970's)

Chapter 16

Folding Their Wings (1963 -)

William continued to ponder on all he had learnt from his long experience, and used it to advise as and where he could. He never ceased to pursue his goal of improving industrial relations and bettering the lot of the employees. It was his Holy Grail.

The Pain of the New Idea was the chief concept he recognised when he looked back over his fifty years' involvement with social economics. He saw the vast improvement in living conditions which had taken place; he saw the similarity in problems and their remedies over that period; he saw above all how slow we, as a nation, had been to bring about change and introduce innovation so that by comparison with other nations we had lost ground. This last observation is not true of the best in British industry; W.W. was himself in a company that forged ahead, and broke new ground. It is unfortunately true of too many, especially of our corporate life and in our own Government policies - e.g. housing and unemployment - that those who take the decisions are too much under the influence of politics and the Treasury to take imaginative action.

W.W. knew from his own experience the value of a joint co-operative 'Council' approach to a difficult economic situation; he recommended a similar approach to the industrial relations and economic problems of Britain as a whole. In 1927 he had suggested a "National Industrial Council" in a memorandum to Lloyd George; in further speeches and in a pamphlet, *"The Riddle of Unemployment"* (in 1930), he had pursued the idea. As soon as he ceased to be a Judge, in January 1961, he wrote a long letter to 'The Times' putting the case for a carefully constituted **Council of Industry** to do for British industry as a whole what an effective Works' Council had done in a variety of different large businesses. The then Editor of 'The Times' confirmed that this was the first suggestion of such a Council, later realised as the **National Economic Development Council** or **"Neddy"**. Unfortunately, in spite of this advance, it had not been enough. The lack of consistency in policy, and the curtailing of Neddy's powers, along with the failure to recognise sufficiently the need for conscious national united constructive planning has left us still in a parlous state.

Another of W.W.'s messages for industrial workers was: Strikes damage the nation and the community as a whole. Strikers are usually sincere and may have legitimate grievances, but they have not been helped to understand sufficiently the hurt they do to the community, including themselves and their families. A far wider education in economic fundamentals is needed for all sections of the community. Those who help to precipitate strikes are not without blame. This plea for us to recognise how slow we are to initiate and accept innovation was one of the main reasons why W.W. wrote his Autobiography (which took all his spare time from 1964-1968). In it he traces the history of our attempts to conquer unemployment and inflation during the middle fifty years of the twentieth century. He does not place responsibility for failures on any party or individual with the exception of the Governor of the Bank of England in the years up to 1944. Nineteenth-century thinking dominated the policies in the City and at the Bank of England; mistakes were made which missed chances and set us on the wrong course. W.W. cared passionately about the chances for the ordinary man to lead a satisfying and solvent life, at home and at work. He did all he could to achieve this. Looking back he could not fail to grieve at the chances missed by those in authority.

He believed implicity in the quality of our own population, in their technical skill and ability, in their character, tolerance, good humour and sense of justice. He re-iterated that we have, in general, 'the nicest chaps in the world'. The difficulty was to link every one together in a conscious constructive effort; and to find the right leadership in industry. Here, in his Autobiography, he quoted the one recorded speech of Sir William Wallace, when he gathered his Scots at Falkirk to face Edward I and his far larger army:

"I have brought you to the ring; dance if you can."

He wanted the leaders of industry to 'dance' in the same sense of giving their all.

Chapter 16. Folding Their Wings

W.W. continued to serve on a number of Trusts and Committees as well as the University's Academic Trust; the Joseph Rowntree Social Service Trust; the Institute of Social and Economic Research of York University; the Acton Society Trust; The National Birthday Trust. He was also a Vice-President of the British Society for International Health Education, and continued as a happy member of the Industrial Co-Partnership Association which was part of his life for over half a century.

When he was seventy-three he started to write his Autobiography, continuing for over four years between his other duties in York, London and elsewhere. He wrote his account by hand, referring to his background papers and correspondence, virtually all of which he had kept. He typed - and re-typed, after comments and criticisms of friends, especially his colleague from the Restrictive Practices Court, William Gordon Campbell, - every word of his book. I remember him at this time spending hour after hour tap-tapping at his machine, in the sunny window of the billiard room at the top of the house: the billiard table, where not even the ghosts of the billiard balls disturbed it any more, piled high with all his papers. The manuscript was too long for publication, and he simply hadn't the heart to cut it down. Every thought, every memory, every anecdote was part of him. I have used much of it as well as my own memories and other sources to write some of the chapters in Part III of this book. I hope that by summarising I have still given you the essence of the man and his ideals without including too much that is outside the reader's interest.

William and Nancie continued for many years to holiday at the Manor House Hotel at Moretonhampstead, twice a year for about three weeks each visit, to extend the summer. They welcomed the bluebells in Devon and then again in North Yorkshire, in Spring; they caught the warmth of the early Autumn in Strensall, and again in Devon. Each time they travelled they stayed two nights at Chipping Campden en route, able so to visit Nancie's sister Dorothy, several times a year. Nancie and Dorothy kept up their weekly correspondence until Dorothy's failing powers and Nancie's failing eyesight prevented this in the last two or three years of their lives, and others passed on the news. William and Nancie enjoyed family and friends who came to stay; they delighted in their garden and the greenhouse which William had built on (along with a large garden room) for Nancie's pleasure. To do this he had to have altered the stipulations governing what they were allowed to do on the building plot when they originally bought it.

In 1968, they celebrated their Golden Wedding (see (press) photo on cover) with a reception in the Merchant Taylors' Hall in York, followed by a family lunch. At that occasion were William's sisters and brother and their families; Nancie's nephew and cousins; their own children and grandchildren; and many friends. William, as the eldest in his family, had more surviving members of his own generation as their guests; Nancie, as the youngest, had none; her sister Dorothy, the only surviving one, could not travel. In his speech at the Golden Wedding, William said he had been asked to say what stood out for him most as he looked back. His reply was four-fold; in ascending order:

his **work**, because he had a "concern" for his fellows and wished to serve them; in this he had found great interest and happiness;

friends and their friendship in working together;

his **family**, their interests and achievements and true friendship;

but above all his **wife**.

At the end of his Autobiography, W.W. wrote that he had tried to follow the Quaker way of life, and to recognise that "there is that of God in every man"; he rated the three greatest virtues as courage, courtesy and compassion; and he quoted these lines of Kipling's:

> "And only the Master shall praise, and only the Master shall blame;
>
> "And no-one shall work for money, and no-one shall work for fame,
>
> "But each for the joy of working, and each in his separate star,
>
> "Shall draw the Thing as he sees it for the God of Things as They are".

Chapter 16. Folding Their Wings

This is the calibre of the man who was my father: an idealist, who believed in people; he remained true to his ideals, and to the people who put their trust in him; I knew him for over fifty years and I'm not aware of his having a shabby thought nor doing a shabby deed. There was love between him and his parents and his brother and sisters; and with his own wife and family. There were no divisions, family quarrels nor fallings out (which are not so uncommon). With my mother it was the same, as I have tried to show: all her family gave each other loving support, and kept in close touch in each generation. Differences there must have been, but these were reconciled. Commitment and loyalty carried them over the difficult times; love found a way. No marriage in either of their families ended in separation or divorce. Nor, as it happens, did any of the widowed re-marry (except Owen Hancox).

Nancie continued to play her part for several years after the Golden Wedding, although she had to have a cataract operation, and her sight deteriorated further. She controlled her diabetes well and was in hospital only once because of it, after 1945. She still went into York, by bus, to shop. She wrote to each of us without fail every Wednesday. Thursday mornings were never the same for me after she could no longer see to write. She tended her greenhouse and her collection of cacti; and played bridge with her friends. W.W. remained remarkably fit until he was well over eighty, more like the physique of a man twenty years younger, until one day when he stepped down from a stool after reaching up to fix something. This seemed to jolt him, and he had pain which moved up and down his body, and made him less flexible. He continued to do his utmost to help Nancie, carrying things for her, doing her sugar tests, pushing her round the garden in a special chair we got until this jolted him more, and she forbade it. He had finally to give up his car, a very great loss to him as he loved driving and had driven his own car for nearly fifty years. In Wales as I have said, he was known in the village as "the man who gave lifts". He played golf for as long as he was able, and went for daily walks until the last few weeks, down the nearby country roads and round the outside edge of the Golf course, on his doctor's advice. He read 'The Times' and 'The Guardian' until one o'clock in the morning, marking articles of interest to himself and his family, which he sent on to us.

Nancie became bed-ridden, early in 1976. Jean, helped by our marvellous housekeeper and her daughter, tended her with the utmost love and care. I went to see them whenever I could, especially in the last few years, but with a very taxing, full-time job and a house and family to care for, this was never easy. A week-end, once a month from Edinburgh, and the inside of every fourth week from Oxford, during much of 1975, when I was not teaching, was the most I could manage, and this I did gladly. About ten years ago, I had the one remaining blurred copy of my father's Autobiography typed out. I did some minor editing, and I tried to get it published, though it was rather too long and too late. But I did manage to send copies of the first six chapters, all about his childhood and growing up, to his surviving brother and sisters, which they read with great joy. The following paragraph which I have taken from my Introduction to this edition of "I was Concerned" tells of my visits during his last summer:

'On my last visit to Windrush while my father was still at home, in August 1976, so that Jean could have a holiday, we had golden days together. The weather was beautiful and both my daughters visited, so that Granpa said he seemed to have "three Hilarys". He and I went out together in my Mini, and we went walks together. On one of these, he asked me very particularly to "see about his book". "I'm relying on you", he said. I think of all his material possessions, he cared most - perhaps only - for his "book". After that, I did not see him for eight weeks - the longest gap in years - as we had deaths in the family in Edinburgh, and I was in hospital for an operation. I went next to York only a few days before his death when he was already in a Nursing Home, and beyond discussing anything.'

This fortnight in August was a last little Indian Summer. I took him to his favourite camera shop in York where he had not been for years. With the housekeeper's help, we got him to his optician for the new reading glasses, though they were ready too late. I was so glad to have been able to be with him, and to retain now in my mind bright pictures of our last days together. I finished my Introduction to his book by saying:

Chapter 16. Folding Their Wings

'This is the personal record of a truly remarkable man; he was an idealist who was also practical; he thought of others before he thought of himself; he offered himself as one not good at religion, but he obeyed each one of the Commandments, positively; he was much-loved, and by me he will be always missed'. So also will my mother.

On Nancie's seventieth birthday, William wrote her a poem, which he quoted at the Golden Wedding:

> "Through the mid-day of life we have travelled,
> Fine comrade, where 'er the road wends,
> Her fragrance and charm in full flower
> Have blessed husband and children and friends.
>
> Now the autumn of life is upon us,
> Though with warmth in the westering air,
> The smile of a girl still she carries,
> Her voice still as soft as her hair.
>
> I thank the kind Lord for the treasure
> Of her beauty and sweetness and charm.
> I ask the good Lord in his kindness
> To keep my sweet treasure from harm.
>
> I ask the good Lord in his justice
> That whatever the future may bring
> Our spirits may ride on together,
> Then the stars in their courses will sing!"

Nancie was not one for making speeches; and she did not write poems or her Autobiography. But her story was part of his, and she inspired the poems. Without her he would not have been the man he was, nor done the things he did. His poem shows the sort of person *she* was. He finished his Autobiography with this old Gaelic Blessing:

> "May the roads rise with you,
> And the winds be always at your back:
> And may the Lord hold you in the hollow of His hand."

William died on October 21st, 1976. Nancie lingered on, although she did not wish to, until she joined him, still utterly uncomplaining, on March 8th, 1978: sixty years and one week after she had accepted his proposal of marriage.

Their ashes lie in the Quaker Burial ground in York, each under a very small, flat stone, with their details carved on the top:

WILLIAM WALLACE DIED 21ST OF 10TH Mo: 1976 AGED 85 YEARS	NANCIE E WALLACE DIED 8TH OF 3RD Mo: 1978 AGED 87 YEARS

Index of Main Family Members Mentioned in Text

Avery	Catharine m. Owen Hancox 55, 75, 77
	(Uncle) Joe 75, 77
Bebb	Family Tree 29
	Charles 26, 63, 70
	Rev. Douglas 19, 20, 23
	Jeremiah I 26
	Jeremiah II 22-30, 63, 68, 70, 75
	Lillian (m. Emil Perkin) xii, 26
	Louisa (m. Jeremiah II) **See Hancox**
	Minnie xii, 19, 26, 28
Bomford	Harriet (m. H. Bomford) **See Hancox**
	Herbert (m. Harriet) 23, 30, 55
	J.H. (Jack) 23, 32, 46
Bostock	Isabel (née Perkin) 26, 28
Butcher	family 23, 35
Cooke	Charlotte (née Harris) 20
	Edmund, s. of Henry 20
	Harriett (m. James Hancox) **See Hancox**
	Henry (m. Charlotte) 20, 22, 29
Ford	Elizabeth (née Hadland) 35, 37
	William 35, 37
FOWLER	Anne (née Hancox) (b. 1849) 35, 44-5, 52-3, 55, 57, 61, 63, 66, 68-9, 78, 97, 101, 115
	Bessie (b. 1837) 32, 45
	Elizabeth Ann (née Hawkes) (m. 1836) 44, 48, 51 (See also Hawkes)
	Henry (b. 1803) 35, 44-5, 55, 70
	Henry (b. 1843) 45
	Harry/Henry (b. 1870) 45-6, 52, 66
	Jane (m. Small) 45-6, 50-1
	Mary (Mollie) (m. J.H. Bomford) 32, 46, 48-52
	Mary (Polly) (née Hughes) 45, 48-52
	Sarah 45, 51
	Susan 45, 51
	Winifred (m. John Nash) 45
Gardner	Elizabeth m. Joseph Hancox 13
Hadland	Elizabeth (m. Ford) 35, 37
Hancoks	John (m. 1676) 11
	Lydia (b. 1676) 11
HANCOX	Family Tree 10
	Anne, m. of Nancie **See Fowler**
	Avery (b. 1884) 57, 66, 77, 97-8, 142, 144, 152
	Avery, s. of J.J.H. 23, 55, 64, 142
	Catharine (née Avery) 55, 74
	Charles Owen (b. 1871) 32, 55, 57
	Dorothy (b. 1888) 30, 32, 52-3, 59, 61, 66, 68-9, 74, 101, 155
	Edmund Owen (b. 1840) x, xii, 13-15, 20, 23-4, 26-32, 40, Ch.5, 73
	Elizabeth (née Gardner) 13-14
	Florence (d. of Alfred) 22, 70, 99
	Fred (b. 1882) 57, 64, 66, 142, 144, 146
	George (b. 1800) 9, 12, 18
	Harriett (née Cooke) 20-3, 26-32, 82
	Family Tree of Harriett 29
	Harriet (b. 1837 m. Bomford) 20, 24, 30-2, 55
	Helen (b. 1869 m. Davis) 55, 63
	Henry (s. of Will) 7, 30, 63, 155
	Jack (J.J.H.) (b. 1872) 23, 32, 44, 52-64, 66, 74, 78-9, 142, 177
	James (b. 1804) x, xii, 14-15, Ch.2, 42, 55, 82
	(James) Alfred (b. 1830) 19, 20, 22-3, 32
	John (b. 1747) 7-9
	John (b. 1792) 14, 17, 18

HANCOX (cont.)	Joseph (b. 1753) **3, 9, 11, 13, 14**
	Joseph's siblings and children **12**
	Joseph's children (details) **15-18**
	Joseph Avery (b. 1874) **55**
	Louisa (b. 1832 m. Bebb) **20, 23-30, 61, 63, 68, 70, 75, 99**
	Mary (b. 1868 m. Hartley Smith) **55, 63, 74, 78**
	NANCIE throughout
	Ted (b. 1880) **57, 64-6, 77, 142**
	Thomas (b. 1723) **6-7**
	Thomas (b. 1751) **9**
	Will (b. 1878) **22-3, 57, 64, 97, 142**
Harris	family **20, 29**
	Susannah (b. 1733) **20, 22-3**
HAWKES	Family Tree **41**
	Elizabeth (née Hadland) **39**
	Elizabeth Ann (m. Fowler) **35, 37, 39, 40, 42-4 (now see Fowler)**
	Thomas (b. 1777) **37, 39, 40, 44**
Perkin	Lillian **(See Bebb)**
Small	Jane **(See Fowler)**
	John **52, 64**
Stephens	Kate (m. J.J.H.) **64, 75, 77**
WALLACE	Alice (m. of William) **78, 83, 93, 99, 108, 115, 146, 156**
	Charles **78, 82, 89-90, 92, 97, 110, 115, 155-6**
	Chris **78, 82, 89-90, 93, 108, 110, 115-6, 146, 155-6**
	Dorothy **78, 82, 89-90, 108, 115-6, 155-6**
	James (f. of William) **Ch.7, 92, 149, 156**
	Jean **102, Ch.11, 122, Ch.13, 135, 140-1, 151, 155-6**
	Hilary **Ch.11, 122, Ch.13 & 14, 151-2, 155-6**
	Ian **110, 112, 120, 135, 141, 151, 155**
	WILLIAM throughout

ACKNOWLEDGEMENTS

Grateful acknowledgement is made to all the Staff who have helped me in the Record Offices; and for permission to reproduce documents in their care: the Trustees & Guardians of the Shakespeare Birthplace Trust, Stratford-on-Avon (James Hancox's Indenture, and the photo of Stratford-on-Avon Grammar School); the City of Bristol R.O. (photo of St. George School); Gloucestershire R.O. (Map of Buckland, 1779: D2001); Hereford and Worcester R.O. (John Hancox's Will); Oxfordshire County R.O.; Warwick County R.O.; Wiltshire R.O. (Map 4); the Public Record Office; also the Trustees of the National Library of Scotland (Maps 1,2 and 3); The Evesham Journal (reproductions of photographs on pp 48 and 76); Mrs Rendal Ridges (photos of New Earswick taken from slides which belonged to her late husband); the Headmasters of Prince Henry's High School, Evesham (Mr A.G. Stafford) and St. George School, Bristol (Mr Morgan, O.B.E.); Roger Angerson (Society of Friends, Bristol); to Elsa Noak (reproduction of a page from 'Meditation on Marriage'); to the Vicar of the Parishes of Tysoe, with Oxhill and Whatcote (drawing of Whatcote Church); and to all those members of the family, past and present, who have taken an interest, recorded information in books and even on scraps of paper, and have cherished the heritage of our family. What I have done is for them; I hand on to those who follow.

Select Bibliography

Ackworth School: Elfrida Vipont (Lutterworth Press 1959)
Ackworth School (1779-1929): published by Sessions (no author given)
Ackworth School Bicentenary Exhibition 'Then & Now' (1979)
Ackworth School: Mentor & Amander: By a late teacher (1814)

Corn Milling: Martin Watts (Shire)
The History of Corn Milling: Bennett & Elton (1973)
The Mills of Medieval England: Richard Holt (Blackwell 1988)
Watermills: Peter Wenham (Hale 1989)

Gloucestershire: The Georgian Jubilee Number (1944) Private publication
Buckland (Gloucestershire) Parish Registers: A E Oldaker (1947)
100 Years' History of Bristol Friends' 1st Day (Boys) School 1810-1910
History of Mangotfield and Downend (Gloucestershire): Rev. A Emlyn Jones (1899)

Warminster: The Way We Were: Danny Howell (1988)
History of Non-Conformity in Warminster: HMG (1853)
Victoria County History of Wiltshire (for Warminster)

Warwickshire: Victoria County History
Warwickshire Villages: Lyndon F Cave (Hale) (1976)
General view of the Agriculture of Warwickshire: John Wedge (1794)
General view of the Agriculture of Warwickshire: Adam Murray (1814)
Joseph Ashby of Tysoe (1859-1919): M K Ashby (Merlin Press 1974)
100 Years of Poor Law Administration in a Warwickshire Village: (Tysoe 1727-1827): Arthur Wilfred Ashby (1912) (In Oxford Studies in Social and Legal History: Vinogradoff Vol. III)
The Parish Registers of Tysoe: Denis B Woodfield (1976)
New Towns of the Middle Ages in England, Wales and Gascony: Maurice Beresford (1967)
The Lay Subsidy Roll for Warwickshire of 6 Edward III (1332)
A History of the English Agricultural Labourer: W Hasbach (1966)
The Village Labourer 1760-1832: J L & Barbara Hammond (1920)
The State of the Poor: Sir Fdk. Morton Eden (Routledge 1928)
A History of England Under the Hanoverians: Sir Charles Grant Robertson (1911)
Economic History of England: H O Meredith (1910)
A History of Ettington (publ. Warwickshire Village History Society 1934)
The Driftway: Penelope Lively

Non-Conformity in **Worcester**: Rev. William Urwick (1897)
Place-Names of Worcester: Mawer & Stenton (1927)
Portrait of Worcestershire: Peter J Neville Havins (Hale 1974)
The Book of Evesham: Benjamin Cox (1977)
The Revelation of the Monk of Evesham (Glasgow 1904)
The Manufacturing Industries of Worcestershire: William D Curzon (late 19th Century)

Meditation on Marriage: translated by Elsa Noak (publd. by Sessions)
Phillimore's Lists of Marriage Registers
Wallace William: I was Concerned (private publication)
York: One Man's Vision (the story of New Earswick) (George Allen & Unwin) (1954)
New Earswick: A Pictorial History: Joe Murphy
Record Offices: How to find them: Gibson & Peskett. (Federation of Family History Societies).

<u>Publications</u> by W.W. during his working life
Business Forecasting and Its Practical Application (1927)
Enterprise First (1946)
Prescription for Partnership (1959)
Associated with:
We Can Conquer Unemployment (1929)
The Agricultural Dilemma (1935)
British Agriculture (1938)